PANAMA CITY & THE PANAMA CANAL

WILLIAM FRIAR

Contents

PANAMA CITY &
THE PANAMA CANAL

PANAMA CITY

Panama City surprises newcomers. It is by far the most cosmopolitan city in Central America, which becomes obvious as soon as one sees its densely packed towers. But its vibrant modernity really shouldn't be surprising, given the capital's status as an international banking center and its location next to the Pacific entrance of the Panama Canal, the crossroads of the world. Panama City has been important to world commerce since its founding nearly 500 years ago.

It's also an international city. The shops of Indian and Chinese merchants have been city institutions for generations. Any given day might find Colombian émigrés having a drink in a British pub, Japanese businesspeople making a deal in an Argentine steak house, and North American retirees looking for their place in the tropical sun.

The city's rich diversity can be seen in its houses of worship: Along with its Roman Catholic churches are synagogues, mosques, one of the world's seven Baha'i Houses of Worship, the Greek Orthodox Metropolitanate of Central America, a prominent Hindu temple, and gathering houses for every conceivable Protestant congregation.

The one faith that draws all these people together is business. Deals are being made everywhere at all times, from kids hawking cell-phone accessories at congested intersections to developers determined to build on every square centimeter of open space. Life is

© WILLIAM FRIAR

HIGHLIGHTS

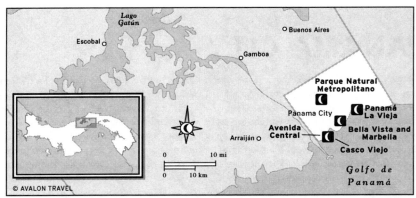

© AVALON TRAVEL

LOOK FOR **◖** TO FIND RECOMMENDED SIGHTS, ACTIVITIES, DINING, AND LODGING.

◖ Panamá La Vieja: Founded nearly 500 years ago, this original Panama City was the first Spanish city on the Pacific coast of the Americas. Its stone ruins transport you back to the time of gold-hungry conquistadors and pillaging buccaneers (page 16).

◖ Casco Viejo: This charming colonial neighborhood is the cornerstone of modern Panama City. An ambitious renovation project has brought restaurants, theaters, and clubs to its historic buildings, sidewalk cafés to its quaint plazas, and new life to its crumbling churches (page 17).

◖ Avenida Central: The walking street that extends from Plaza Cinco de Mayo to Parque Santa Ana is one of the most vibrant parts of town, a bustling commercial center that draws a cross section of Panamanian society (page 26).

◖ Parque Natural Metropolitano: More than a city park, this 265-hectare tropical forest within the city limits offers a glimpse of Panama's flora and fauna (page 32).

◖ Bella Vista and Marbella: Panama City's most dynamic nightlife lies along Calle Uruguay, where trendy new restaurants and clubs open and close constantly (page 37).

fast-paced compared with the rest of Panama, and the city's residents are comparatively assertive, street-savvy, and no-nonsense. Panama City is to, say, the Azuero Peninsula as New York City is to rural Nebraska. Everyone on the road is in a great hurry, and skyscrapers pop up overnight.

Still, by the standards of many other countries' capitals, Panama City is a mellow, fun-loving place. Any excuse for a party will do, and big celebrations, especially Carnaval, shut down the whole city.

Those who come to Panama solely for its natural treasures will be tempted to blast right through the capital on their way to the country's forests, mountains, islands, and beaches. But it'd be a shame not to spend some time in Panama City. Hundreds of years of history live on in its streets, and its more modern attractions are especially appealing after roughing it in the wilderness for a while. Besides, it has its very own tropical forest. Even city streets aren't far removed from nature; an entire book has been written on the birds of Panama City.

Sights

ORIENTATION

Panama City is a growing metropolis of 813,000 people, or more than 1.2 million if you include the greater metropolitan area. Streets and public transportation have not kept pace with the city's growth, and the roads are usually busy and during morning and evening rush hours can become absolutely jammed. In recent years the city has grown east toward Tocumen International Airport, and with its absorption of the former U.S. Canal Zone, urban sprawl has been creeping north and west as well.

Panamanians typically drop the "city" when referring to the capital and just call it "Panama." As with the country, the accent is on the last syllable—Panamá (pah-nah-MA)—when speaking Spanish. Formally, it's La Ciudad de Panamá.

The city is bounded by the Bahía de Panamá (Panama Bay) and the Pacific Ocean to the south and the Panama Canal to the west. The terrain is fairly flat—the United States dug the canal nearby because the Continental Divide is particularly low-lying here—though a few isolated hills, most notably Cerro Ancón, jut up near the canal's Pacific entrance.

The section of the city of most interest to visitors runs along the coast from Casco Viejo, the cornerstone of modern Panama City, east to the ruins of Panamá La Vieja, eight kilometers away. Most of the cosmopolitan parts of the capital lie between these two landmarks.

An exception to this rule is **Costa del Este,** a new city within (or, more accurately, on the outskirts of) Panama City. It's a rapidly growing mini-metropolis of upscale homes and condos whose skyline is beginning to rival downtown's in its concentration of skyscrapers. It's a new frontier for privileged Panamanians escaping the city's congestion and noise and for international jet-setters adding to their portfolio of

vacation homes. But it doesn't yet hold enough interest to the average visitor to justify making the long trip from the city center.

Getting one's bearings can be tricky in Panama City, given its confusing mass of winding streets and its topsy-turvy geography (some never get used to seeing the Pacific Ocean lying to the south, for instance).

The city is organized into a series of loosely defined neighborhoods. The only ones most travelers will be concerned with are **Punta Pacífica, Punta Paitilla, Marbella, Bella Vista, El Cangrejo, Calidonia/La Exposición, Santa Ana,** and **San Felipe/Casco Viejo.** There are also a few places of note a bit farther east, in **Obarrio** and **San Francisco.**

Vía España, a busy commercial street, has long been the heart of modern Panama City. In recent years, though, the action has spread just north to El Cangrejo and south to Bella Vista and Marbella. Most of Panama's upscale hotels, restaurants, and shops are in these areas.

An area of about three square blocks between Bella Vista and Marbella, centered on **Calle Uruguay,** is a booming nightlife destination of restaurants and clubs, as is, to a lesser degree, the main strip through Marbella, **Calle 53.** The Calle Uruguay nightlife area is being eroded by the building boom, with clubs and restaurants being knocked down to put up yet another skyscraper, but there's still enough going on here to justify a visit.

An older commercial center is found along **Avenida Central** in the Calidonia and Santa Ana districts. Bordering it is the district of **San Felipe,** which contains the historic neighborhood of **Casco Viejo,** tucked away on a small peninsula.

Avenida de los Mártires, formerly known as **Fourth of July Avenue,** used to mark the boundary between Panama City and the former Canal Zone.

A major artery is the **Cinta Costera** (Coastal

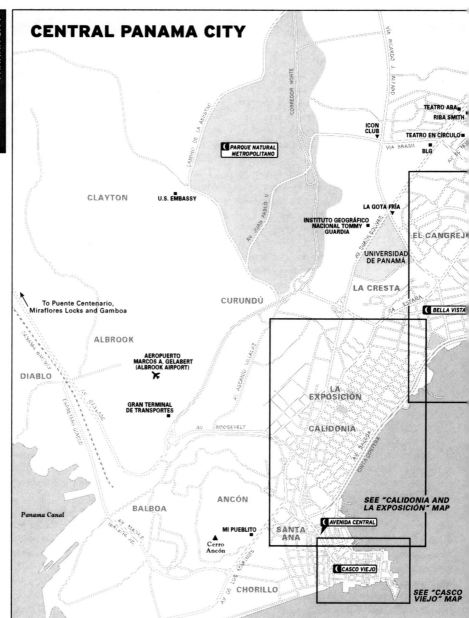

CENTRAL PANAMA CITY

TEATRO ABA
RIBA SMITH
ICON CLUB
TEATRO EN CÍRCULO
VIA BRASIL
BLG

PARQUE NATURAL METROPOLITANO

CLAYTON

U.S. EMBASSY

LA GOTA FRÍA

INSTITUTO GEOGRÁFICO NACIONAL TOMMY GUARDIA

EL CANGREJ

UNIVERSIDAD DE PANAMÁ

LA CRESTA

CURUNDÚ

BELLA VISTA

To Puente Centenario, Miraflores Locks and Gamboa

ALBROOK

AEROPUERTO MARCOS A. GELABERT (ALBROOK AIRPORT)

DIABLO

LA EXPOSICIÓN

GRAN TERMINAL DE TRANSPORTES

CALIDONIA

AV. ROOSEVELT

ANCÓN

SEE "CALIDONIA AND LA EXPOSICIÓN" MAP

Panama Canal

BALBOA

MI PUEBLITO

Cerro Ancón

SANTA ANA

AVENIDA CENTRAL

CASCO VIEJO

CHORILLO

SEE "CASCO VIEJO" MAP

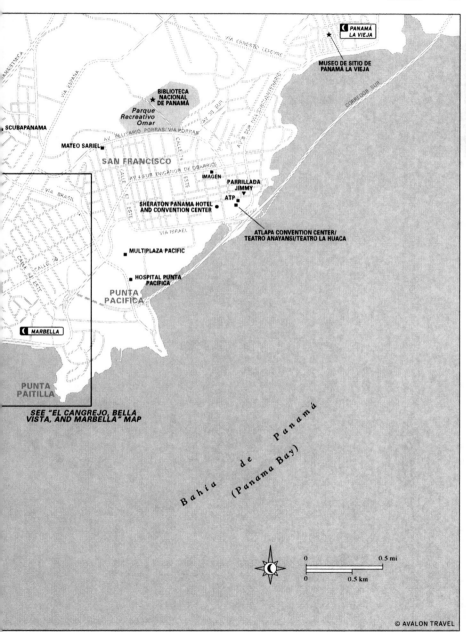

PANAMÁ
LA VIEJA

MUSEO DE SITIO DE
PANAMÁ LA VIEJA

BIBLIOTECA
NACIONAL
DE PANAMÁ

Parque
Recreativo
Omar

SCUBAPANAMA

MATEO SARIEL

SAN FRANCISCO

IMAGEN

PARRILLADA
JIMMY

ATP

SHERATON PANAMA HOTEL
AND CONVENTION CENTER

ATLAPA CONVENTION CENTER/
TEATRO ANAYANSI/TEATRO LA HUACA

MULTIPLAZA PACIFIC

HOSPITAL PUNTA
PACIFICA

PUNTA
PACIFICA

MARBELLA

PUNTA
PAITILLA

*SEE "EL CANGREJO, BELLA
VISTA, AND MARBELLA" MAP*

Bahía de Panamá
(Panama Bay)

0   0.5 mi

0   0.5 km

© AVALON TRAVEL

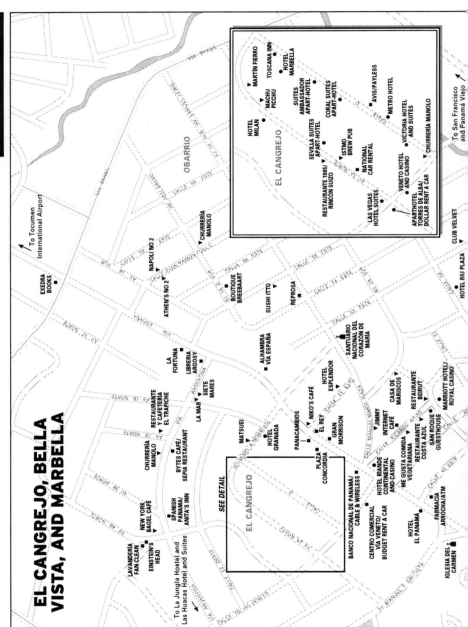

EL CANGREJO, BELLA VISTA, AND MARBELLA
To La Jungla Hostel and Las Huacas Hotel and Suites
To Tocumen International Airport
To San Francisco and Panamá Viejo
SEE DETAIL
EL CANGREJO
OBARRIO
LAVANDERÍA FAN-CLEAN
EINSTEIN'S HEAD
NEW YORK BAGEL CAFÉ
SPANISH PANAMA/ ANITA'S INN
CHURRERÍA MANOLO
BYTES CAFÉ/ SEPIA RESTAURANT
RESTAURANTE Y CAFETERÍA EL TRAPICHE
LA MAR
SIETE MARES
LIBRERÍA ARGOSY
LA FORTUNA
EXEDRA BOOKS
ATHEN'S NO 2
NAPOLI NO 2
CHURRERÍA MANOLO
BOUTIQUE BREEBAART
SUSHI ITTO
REPROSA
ALHAMBRA VÍA ESPAÑA
MATSUEI
HOTEL GRANADA
PANACAMBIOS
PLAZA CONCORDIA
NIKO'S CAFÉ
EL REY
GRAN MORRISON
HOTEL ESPLENDOR
SANTUARIO NACIONAL DEL CORAZÓN DE MARÍA
BANCO NACIONAL DE PANAMÁ/ CABLE & WIRELESS
CENTRO COMERCIAL VÍA VENETO/ BUDGET RENT A CAR
HOTEL RIANDE CONTINENTAL AND CASINO
JIMMY
INTERNET CAFÉ
CASA DE MARISCOS
RESTAURANTE BEIRUT
ME GUSTA COMIDA VEGETARIANA
RESTAURANTE COSTA AZUL
SAN ROQUE GUESTHOUSE
MARRIOTT HOTEL/ ROYAL CASINO
HOTEL EL PANAMÁ
FARMACIA ARROCHA/ATM
IGLESIA DEL CARMEN
CLUB VELVET
HOTEL RIU PLAZA
HOTEL MILAN
MACHU PICCHU
MARTÍN FIERRO
TOSCANA INN
HOTEL MARBELLA
SUITES AMBASSADOR APART-HOTEL
CORAL SUITES APART-HOTEL
AVIS/PAYLESS
METRO HOTEL
SEVILLA SUITES APART-HOTEL
ISTMO BREW PUB
NATIONAL CAR RENTAL
VICTORIA HOTEL AND SUITES
CHURRERÍA MANOLO
RESTAURANTE 1985/ RINCÓN SUIZO
VENETO HOTEL AND CASINO
LAS VEGAS HOTEL SUITES
APARTHOTEL TORRES DE ALBA/ DOLLAR RENT A CAR
VÍA BRASIL
VÍA ESPAÑA
VÍA ARGENTINA
VÍA VENETO
AV SAMUEL LEWIS
AV APEL BRAVO
AV 1A SUR
AV 1A NORTE
AV 2A NORTE
AV 2A SUR
AV 3A SUR
AV 3B NORTE
AV 4B NORTE
AV 2B NORTE
AV 1B NORTE
AV MANUEL E BATISTA
CALLE MANUEL MARÍA ICAZA
CALLE RICARDO ARIAS
CALLE EUSEBIO A MORALES
CALLE JUAN RAMÓN POLLI
CALLE D
CALLE 60
CALLE 58 ESTE
CALLE 56 ESTE
CALLE 55 ESTE
CALLE 54 ESTE
CALLE 53 ESTE
CALLE 51 ESTE
CALLE 49 ESTE
CALLE 51
CALLE 55
CALLE 53 OESTE

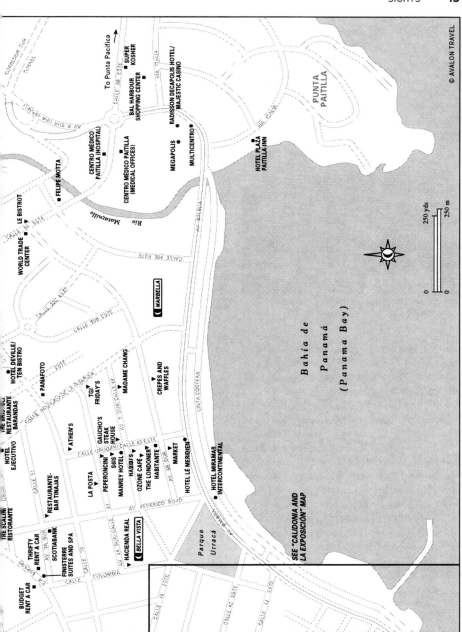

PANAMA CITY

© AVALON TRAVEL

To Punta Pacifica

SUPER KOSHER ■

BAL HARBOUR SHOPPING CENTER ■

RADISSON DECAPOLIS HOTEL/ MAJESTIC CASINO ■

CENTRO MÉDICO PAITILLA (HOSPITAL) ■

CENTRO MÉDICO PAITILLA (MEDICAL OFFICES) ■

MEGAPOLIS ■

MULTICENTRO ■

PUNTA PAITILLA

HOTEL PLAZA PAITILLA INN ●

FELIPE MOTTA ■

LE BISTROT ▼

WORLD TRADE CENTER ■

Río Matasnillo

VÍA ITALIA

VÍA ITALIA

AV. B SUR (VÍA ISRAEL)

CALLE 58 ESTE

CALLE 55 ESTE

CALLE 54 ESTE

CALLE 53 ESTE

CALLE 50A ESTE

CALLE 52A ESTE

AV. BALBOA

CALLE 58A ESTE

■ MARBELLA

HOTEL DEVILLE/ TEN BISTRO ■

PANAFOTO ■

MADAME CHANG ▼

CREPES AND WAFFLES ▼

TGI FRIDAY'S ▼

ATHEN'S ▼

GAUCHO'S STEAK HOUSE ▼

RESTAURANTE BARANDAS ▼

THE SCALINI RISTORANTE ▼

HOTEL EJECUTIVO ●

RESTAURANTE-BAR TINAJAS ▼

LA POSTA ▼

PEPERONCINI ▼

S60S ▼

MANREY HOTEL ●

HABIBI'S ▼

OZONE CAFÉ ▼

THE LONDONER ▼

HABITANTE ▼

MARKET ●

HOTEL LE MERIDIEN ●

HOTEL MIRAMAR INTERCONTINENTAL ●

■ BELLA VISTA

HACIENDA REAL ▼

THRIFTY RENT A CAR ■

SCOTIABANK ●

FINISTERRE SUITES AND SPA ●

BUDGET RENT A CAR ■

Parque Urracá

CALLE RICARDO ARIAS

CALLE URUGUAY

CALLE 49 ESTE

CALLE 47 ESTE

CALLE AQUILINO DE LA GUARDIA

AV. FEDERICO BOYD

AV. 5B SUR

AV. 4A SUR

AV. 3A SUR

AV. EUSEBIO A. MORALES

CALLE 51

CALLE 50

CALLE 49

AV. BALBOA

CINTA COSTERA

CALLE 38 ESTE

CALLE 41 ESTE

CALLE 43 ESTE

CALLE 44 ESTE

CALLE 45 ESTE

CALLE COLOMBIA

Bahía de Panamá (Panama Bay)

SEE "CALIDONIA AND LA EXPOSICIÓN" MAP

0   250 yds

0   250 m

© WILLIAM FRIAR

the cathedral tower of the original Panama City, sacked by Henry Morgan in 1671

Belt), a multilane highway built on landfill at the edge of Panama Bay. It runs roughly parallel to **Avenida Balboa,** which extends from Casco Viejo to the posh condo towers of Punta Paitilla and Punta Pacífica. The bustling commercial street of **Calle 50** runs between and parallel to Vía España and Avenida Balboa.

North of all of these is the **Transístmica (Avenida Simón Bolívar),** which cuts across the city and then heads north across the isthmus. However, those planning to drive toward the Caribbean are much better off taking the toll road, **Corredor Norte,** which extends across the isthmus and ends close to the city of Colón. Another toll road, **Corredor Sur,** leads from Tocumen International Airport to Panama City, where it meets Avenida Balboa. A project to extend the Corredor Norte to meet the Corredor Sur, near the international airport, may finally be completed by the time you read this.

◖ PANAMÁ LA VIEJA

Known in English as Old Panama, these extensive ruins (8:30 A.M.–6:30 P.M. Tues.–Sun., US$4 adults, US$2 students) are all that's left of the original Panama City. The ruins are on the eastern outskirts of the modern-day city, an easy drive east along Vía Cincuentenario. The Corredor Sur arcs right by it, making for an especially impressive sight at night, when the ruins are illuminated. The site is commonly known as Panamá Viejo, though that's not its proper name.

The city was founded on August 15, 1519, by the notorious conquistador Pedro Arias de Ávila, better known as Pedrarias, and burned down during a battle with the equally notorious Welsh pirate Henry Morgan in 1671. After that disaster, the Spanish moved Panama City to a more defensible site a few kilometers southwest, in the area now known as Casco Viejo.

Since most of Panamá La Vieja was made of wood, only the partial remains of a relatively few stone buildings were left standing. Two of the best-preserved structures are near the main entrance. The first is the **cathedral tower,** which is largely intact. It's one of Panama's national symbols and was built between 1619 and 1626. The cathedral was known officially as La Catedral de Nuestra Señora de la Asunción, a name that was later transferred to its replacement in Casco Viejo. The other well-preserved structure, a bit farther in, is the Casa Alarcón, also known as the **Casa del Obispo** (Bishop's House). Built in the 1640s, it was a three-story building with a wooden top floor. It's the largest and most intact house on the site, but it's still just fragments of walls. There are other ruins worth exploring, but try not to wander too far—the more distant structures border a neighborhood plagued by crime and gangs.

For that same reason, visitors should come only during regular opening hours, even though parts of the site can be explored anytime. It's also the only time visitors can climb to the top of the cathedral tower.

A restoration project is buttressing the crumbling, rough-hewn stone walls with red bricks completely out of keeping with the original architecture. There are signs in English and Spanish that explain the history of some of the ruins.

There are lots of souvenir kiosks in the buildings next to the ruins that sell devil masks, *molas* (handcrafted blouses), Ngöbe-Buglé necklaces, and various other trinkets. There's a cafeteria inside as well. An ATP information booth is on the premises, but you'll have a better chance turning up lost pieces of eight than finding anyone actually working there.

Museo de Sitio de Panamá La Vieja

During the restoration archaeologists found Spanish pots, plates, and utensils dating from the 16th and 17th centuries, as well as a much older cemetery with bones dating from 50 B.C. These and other relics are kept in the Museo de Sitio de Panamá La Vieja (tel. 226-9815 or 224-6031, www.panamaviejo.org, 9 A.M.–5 P.M. Tues.–Sun., US$3 adults, US$0.50 students), about a kilometer before the ruins themselves. It's one of Panama's best museums, a modern, two-story place with attractively presented displays. If you stop here first, be sure to buy a ticket that includes entry to the ruins; it's cheaper than buying them separately.

Start on the top floor and work your way down. Displays include indigenous artifacts from the hundreds of years before the Spanish conquest, when the site was a fishing village. One of the more haunting exhibits is the skeleton of a woman believed to have died at about age 40; she was apparently an important figure, whose grave also included the skulls of nine males. Other displays include items from the early Spanish colonial days, such as shards of cooking pots, coins, lead musket balls, trinkets, and so on. There's also a model of the city as it looked before Morgan's incendiary visit. The ground floor has details on the restoration of the site. There is limited information in English; there are no English-speaking guides.

◖ CASCO VIEJO

Casco Viejo has always had a romantic look, but for decades the romance has been of the tropical-decadence, paint-peeling-from-the-walls variety. Since the 1990s, though, it's been undergoing a tasteful and large-scale restoration that's giving the old buildings new luster and has turned the area into one of the city's most fashionable destinations for a night out. Elegant bars, restaurants, and sidewalk cafés have opened. Hotels and hostels are arriving. Little tourist shops are popping up. Amazingly, this is being done with careful attention to keeping the old charm of the place alive. Unfortunately, the renovation is squeezing out the poorer residents who've lived here for ages.

The "Old Part," also known as Casco Antiguo or the San Felipe district, was the second site of Panama City, and it continued to be the heart of the city during the first decades of the 20th century. UNESCO declared it a World Heritage Site in 1997. It's a city within the city—940 buildings, 747 of which are houses—and one from a different age. It's a great place for a walking tour. You can wander down narrow brick streets, sip an espresso at an outdoor café, visit old churches, and gaze up at wrought-iron balconies spilling over with bright tropical plants. Its buildings feature an unusual blend of architectural styles, most notably rows of ornate Spanish and French colonial houses but also a smattering of art deco and neoclassical buildings.

In some respects Sunday is a good day for exploring Casco Viejo. For one thing, it's the likeliest time to find the churches open and in use. However, though more bars and restaurants are now staying open on Sunday, most aren't, and even some of the museums are closed. Several places are also closed on Monday. Getting a look inside historic buildings and museums is easiest during the week, especially since some are in government offices open only during normal business hours. Churches open and close rather erratically.

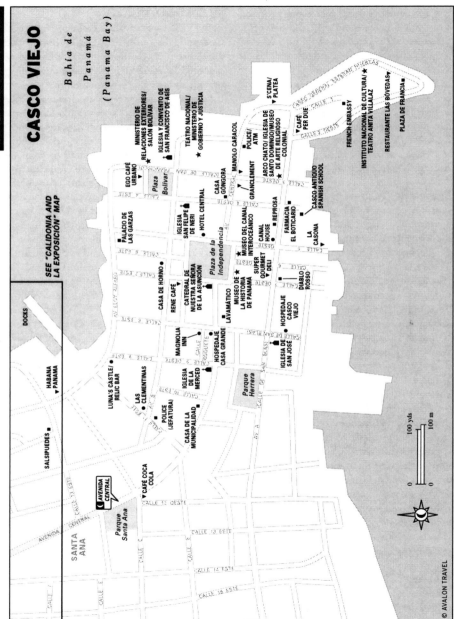

CASCO VIEJO

Bahía de Panamá (Panama Bay)

SEE "CALIDONIA AND LA EXPOSICIÓN" MAP

DOCKS

HABANA ▼ PANAMA

SALSIPUEDES ■

SANTA ANA

Parque Santa Ana

AVENIDA CENTRAL

▼ CAFÉ COCA COLA

LUNA'S CASTLE/ ● RELIC BAR

LAS ● CLEMENTINAS

POLICE (JEFATURA) ■

CASA DE LA MUNICIPALIDAD ■

IGLESIA DE LA MERCED ●

MAGNOLIA INN ●

HOSPEDAJE ● CASA GRANDE

CASA DE HORNO ●

RENE CAFÉ ●

CATEDRAL DE NUESTRA SEÑORA DE LA ASUNCIÓN ★

Plaza de la Independencia

LAVAMATICO ●

MUSEO DE ★ LA HISTORIA DE PANAMÁ

SUPER GOURMET DELI ●

HOSPEDAJE ● CASCO VIEJO

IGLESIA DE SAN JOSÉ ★

Parque Herrera

DIABLO ● ROSSO

LA CASONA ●

FARMACIA ● EL BOTICARIO

REPROSA ●

CASA GÓNGORA ■

MANOLO CARACOL ●

EGO CAFÉ URBANO ●

Plaza Bolívar

PALACIO DE LAS GARZAS ■

IGLESIA SAN FELIPE DE NERI ■

HOTEL CENTRAL ●

MINISTERIO DE RELACIONES EXTERIORES/ SALON BOLÍVAR

IGLESIA Y CONVENTO DE ★ SAN FRANCISCO DE ASÍS

TEATRO NACIONAL/ MINISTERIO DE ★ GOBIERNO Y JUSTICIA

MUSEO DEL CANAL INTEROCEÁNICO ■

CANAL HOUSE ●

GRANCLEMENT ●

ARCO CHATO/ IGLESIA DE SANTO DOMINGO/MUSEO ★ DE ARTE RELIGIOSO COLONIAL

POLICE/ ■ ATM

CASCO ANTIGUO ■ SPANISH SCHOOL

S'CENA/ ▼ PLATEA

▼ CAFÉ PER DUE

FRENCH EMBASSY ■

INSTITUTO NACIONAL DE CULTURA/ ★ TEATRO ANITA VILLALAZ

RESTAURANTE LAS BÓVEDAS ▼

PLAZA DE FRANCIA ■

100 yds

100 m

0

0

© AVALON TRAVEL

Safety Considerations

Even with the makeover, Casco Viejo is not the safest part of Panama City. Ironically, the area's renaissance seems to be driving crime: With more tourists and affluent residents in Casco Viejo, there's more appeal for criminals.

There's no reason to be overly concerned, but use common sense and try not to stand out. If you're pale and gringo, try to look as though you're a resident foreigner. Don't wander around at night, and be cautious when venturing beyond the major hubs of activity (Plaza Bolívar, Plaza de la Independencia, and Plaza de Francia). Look at the map of Casco Viejo and mentally draw a line from Luna's Castle to Parque Herrera: At night, do not venture west of this area on foot. Also avoid the block of Calle 4 between Avenida Central and Avenida B at night. Parque Herrera is still on the edge of a sketchy area.

The neighborhood is well patrolled by the *policía de turismo* (tourism police), who cruise around on bicycles and are easy to spot in their short-pants uniforms. They've been trained specifically to serve tourists, and they're doing an impressive job. It's not unusual for them to greet foreign tourists with a handshake and a smile and offer them an insider's tour of the area or help with whatever they need. Don't hesitate to ask them for help or directions. Their station is next to Manolo Caracol and across the street from the Ministerio de Gobierno y Justicia (Avenida Central between Calle 2 Oeste and Calle 3 Este, tel. 211-2410 or 211-1929). It's open 24 hours, and the officers will safely guide you to your destination night or day.

There's a heavy police presence around the presidential palace, but those police are stern and no-nonsense. Their job is to protect the president, not help tourists.

Plaza de la Independencia

In the center of Casco Viejo is the Plaza de la Independencia, where Panama declared its independence from Colombia in 1903. This area was the center of Panama City until the early 20th century. The buildings represent a real riot of architectural styles, from neo-Renaissance to art deco. Construction began on the cathedral, the **Catedral de Nuestra Señora de la Asunción,** in 1688, but it took more than 100 years to complete. Some of the stones used come from the ruins of Panamá La Vieja. It has an attractive marble altar and a few well-crafted stained-glass windows, though otherwise the interior is rather plain. The towers are inlaid with mother-of-pearl from the Perlas Islands. The bones of a saint, Santo Aurelio, are contained in a reliquary hidden behind a painting of Jesus near the front of the church, on the left as one faces the altar.

© JIM GUY

Panama City's cathedral, on Plaza de la Independencia, is a good place to start touring Casco Viejo.

Museo del Canal Interoceánico

The Museo del Canal Interoceánico (Avenida

Central between Calle 5 Oeste and Calle 6 Oeste, tel. 211-1995 or 211-1649, www.museodelcanal.com, 9 A.M.–5 P.M. Tues.–Sun, US$2 adults, US$0.75 students) is dedicated to the history of the Panama Canal. The museum is housed in what started life as the Grand Hotel in 1874, then became the headquarters of the French canal-building effort, and later spent the early part of the 20th century as the capital's central post office. It's worth a visit, but be prepared for some frustration if you don't speak Spanish. Everything is Spanish only, which is significant since the exhibits often consist more of text than anything else. However, an audio guide in English, Spanish, and French is available. The displays tell the story of both the French and American efforts to build the canal, and throw in a little bit of pre-Columbian and Spanish colonial history at the beginning. There's some anti-American propaganda, and most of what's written about the canal from the 1960s on should be taken with a big chunk of salt. There's a good coin collection upstairs, as well as a few Panamanian and Canal Zone stamps. There's also a copy of the 1977 Torrijos-Carter Treaties that turned the canal over to Panama. You can tour the whole place in about an hour.

Museo de la Historia de Panamá

The Museo de la Historia de Panamá (Avenida Central between Calle 7 Oeste and Calle 8 Oeste, tel. 228-6231, 8 A.M.–4 P.M. Mon.–Fri., US$1 general admission, US$0.25 children) is a small museum containing artifacts from Panama's history from the colonial period to the modern era. It's in the Palacio Municipal, a neoclassical building from 1910 that is now home to government offices. At first glance it seems like just another one of Panama's woefully underfunded museums housing a few obscure bits of bric-a-brac. But anyone with some knowledge of Panama's history—which is essential, since the Spanish-only displays are

poorly explained—will find some of the displays fascinating.

Among these are a crudely stitched Panama flag, said to have been made by María Ossa de Amador in 1903. She was the wife of Manuel Amador Guerrero, a leader of the revolutionaries who conspired with the Americans to wrest independence from Colombia. The flag was hastily designed by the Amadors' son, and the women in the family sewed several of them for the rebels; the sewing machine they used is included in the display. If the revolution had failed, this quaint sewing circle might have meant death by hanging for all of them. Instead, Manuel Amador became the first president of Panama.

On a desk by the far wall is the handwritten draft of a telegram the revolutionaries sent to the superintendent of the Panama Railroad in Colón, pleading with him not to allow Colombian troops from the steamship *Cartagena* to cross the isthmus and put down the revolution. This was one of the tensest moments in the birth of Panama. In the end, they didn't cross over, and the revolution was nearly bloodless. The telegram is dated November 3, 1903, the day Panama became independent, and those who sent it are now considered Panama's founding fathers.

Other displays include a stirrup found on the storied Camino de Cruces, a plan for the fortifications built at Portobelo in 1597, 17th-century maps of the "new" Panama City at Casco Viejo (note the walls that originally ringed the city, now all but gone), and the sword of Victoriano Lorenzo, a revered hero of the War of a Thousand Days.

Western Fringes of Casco Viejo

The church with the crumbling brown facade and whitewashed sides near the corner of Avenida Central and Calle 9 Oeste is **Iglesia de la Merced,** which was built in the 17th century from rubble salvaged from the ruins of

Panamá La Vieja. It's worth a quick stop for a look at its wooden altars and pretty tile floor. The neoclassical building next to it, the **Casa de la Municipalidad,** is a former mansion now used by the city government.

The little park, **Parque Herrera,** was dedicated in 1976. The statue of the man on horseback is General Tomás Herrera, an early hero of Panama's complex independence movements. Some of the historic buildings ringing the park are undergoing major renovation, with at least three hotels planned for the area.

Church of the Golden Altar

The massive golden altar *(altar de oro)* is a prime tourist attraction at **Iglesia de San José** (Avenida A between Calle 8 and Calle 9, 7 A.M.–noon and 2–8 P.M. Mon.–Sat., 5 A.M.–noon and 5–8 P.M. Sun.). Legend has it that the altar was saved from the rapacious Welsh pirate Henry Morgan during the sacking of the original

© WILLIAM FRIAR

Church of the Golden Altar, Panama City

Panama City when a quick-thinking priest ordered it painted black, hiding its true value.

The Flat Arch

The original **Iglesia de Santo Domingo** (Avenida A and Calle 3 Oeste) was built in the 17th century, but it burned twice and was not rebuilt after the fire of 1756. It remains famous for one thing that survived, seemingly miraculously: the nearly flat arch (Arco Chato). Since it was built without a keystone and had almost no curve to it, it should have been a very precarious structure, yet it remained intact even as everything around it fell into ruins. One of the reasons a transoceanic canal was built in Panama was that engineers concluded from the intact arch that Panama was not subject to the kinds of devastating earthquakes that afflict its Central American neighbors.

On the evening of November 7, 2003, just four days after Panama celebrated its first centennial as a country, the arch finally collapsed into rubble. It has since been rebuilt, but its main appeal, its gravity-defying properties through the centuries, can never be restored. The church itself is undergoing a slow restoration.

Plaza de Francia

The Plaza de Francia (French Plaza) has seen a great deal of history and was among the first parts of Casco Viejo to be renovated, back in 1982.

The obelisk and the marble plaques along the wall commemorate the failed French effort to build a sea-level canal in Panama. The area housed a fort until the beginning of the 20th century, and the *bóvedas* (vaults) in the seawall were used through the years as storehouses, barracks, offices, and jails. You'll still hear gruesome stories about dungeons in the seawall, where prisoners were left at low tide to drown when the tide rose. Whether this actually happened is still a subject of lively debate among amateur historians. True or not, what you will find there now is one of Panama's more colorful restaurants, Restaurante Las Bóvedas. Also in the plaza are the French Embassy, the headquarters of the **Instituto Nacional de Cultura** (INAC, the National Institute of Culture) in what had been Panama's supreme court building, and a small theater, **Teatro Anita Villalaz.** Tourists are not allowed into the grand old building that houses INAC, but it's worth peeking into from the top of the steps or the lobby, if you can get that far. Note the colorful, if not particularly accomplished, mural depicting idealized versions of Panama's history. (The building was used as a set for the 2008 James Bond film *Quantum of Solace,* as were the ruins of the old Union Club.) Next to the restaurant is an **art gallery** (tel. 211-4034, 9:30 A.M.–5:30 P.M. Tues.–Sat.) run by INAC that displays works by Panamanian and other Latin American artists.

Walk up the staircase that leads to the top of the vaults. This is part of the old seawall that protected the city from the Pacific Ocean's dramatic tides. There's a good view of the Panama City skyline, the Bridge of the Americas, and the Bay of Panama, and the breeze is great on a hot day. The walkway, **Paseo General Esteban Huertas,** is shaded in part by a bougainvillea-covered trellis and is a popular spot with smooching lovers. Along the walkway leading down to Avenida Central, notice the building on the waterfront to the right. For years this has been a ruin, though there have long been plans to turn it into a hotel. This was once the officers' club of the Panamanian Defense Forces; it was largely destroyed during the 1989 U.S. invasion. Before that, it was the home of the Union Club, a hangout for Panama's oligarchy that's now on Punta Paitilla.

Casa Góngora

Built in 1756, the stone house of Casa Góngora (corner of Avenida Central and Calle 4, tel. 212-0338, 8 A.M.–4 P.M. Mon.–Fri., free) is the oldest house in Casco Viejo and one of the oldest in Panama. It was originally the home of a Spanish pearl merchant. It then became a church and has now been turned into a small, bare-bones museum. It's had a rough history—it has been through three fires and the current wooden roof is new. A 20th-century restoration attempt was botched, causing more damage. There isn't much here, but the staff can give free tours (in Spanish) and there have been noises about making it more of a real museum in the future. There's an interesting, comprehensive book on the history of the house and neighborhood (again, in Spanish) that visitors are welcome to thumb through, containing rare maps, photos, and illustrations. Ask for it at the office. The museum hosts jazz and folkloric concerts and other cultural events in the tiny main hall on some Friday and Saturday nights, and occasionally hosts art shows.

Iglesia San Felipe de Neri (corner of Avenida B and Calle 4) dates from 1688 and, though it has also been damaged by fires, is one of the oldest standing structures from the Spanish colonial days. It was renovated in 2003, but is seemingly never open to the public.

The National Theater

The intimate Teatro Nacional (National Theater, between Calle 2 and Calle 3 on Avenida B, 9:30 A.M.–5:30 P.M. Mon.–Fri.) holds classical concerts and other posh events. It was built in 1908 on the site of an 18th-century monastery. It's housed in the same building as the **Ministerio de Gobierno y Justicia** (Ministry of Government and Justice), which has its entrance on Avenida Central.

Inaugurated on October 1, 1908, the neo-baroque theater is worth a brief visit between concerts to get a glimpse of its old-world elegance. The public can explore it during the week but not on weekends. The first performance here was a production of the opera *Aida,* and for about 20 years the theater was a glamorous destination for the city's elite. Note the bust of the ballerina Margot Fonteyn in the lobby; she married a Panamanian politician in 1955 and lived out the last part of her life in Panama.

The ceiling is covered with faded but still colorful frescoes of cavorting naked ladies, painted by Roberto Lewis, a well-known Panamanian artist. Leaks in the roof destroyed about a quarter of these frescoes, and the roof partially collapsed. The roof was restored and the theater reopened in 2004. Be sure to walk upstairs to take a look at the opulent reception rooms.

Plaza Bolívar

Plaza Bolívar (on Avenida B between Calle 3 and Calle 4) has been undergoing a charming restoration. It's especially pleasant to hang out on the plaza in the evening, when tables are set up under the stars. It's a good rest stop for a drink or a bite. A good café to check out is Restaurante Casablanca.

The plaza was named for Simón Bolívar, a legendary figure who is considered the father of Latin America's independence from Spain. In 1826 Bolívar called a congress here to discuss forming a union of Latin American states. Bolívar himself did not attend and the congress didn't succeed, but the park and the statue of Bolívar commemorate the effort.

The congress itself was held in a small, two-story building that has been preserved as a museum, now known as the **Salón Bolívar** (Plaza Bolívar, tel. 228-9594, 9 A.M.–4 P.M. Tues.–Sat., 1–5 P.M. Sun., US$1 adults, US$0.25 students). While the museum is designed attractively, there's not much in it. The room upstairs contains the text of the protocols of different congresses called during the independence movement. There's also a replica of Bolívar's jewel-encrusted sword, a gift from Venezuela (the original is now back in Venezuela). The actual room where the congress took place is on the ground floor.

The little museum is entirely enclosed by glass to protect it and is actually in the courtyard of another building, the massive **Palacio Bolívar,** which was built on the site of a Franciscan convent that dates from the 18th century. The building that houses the Salón Bolívar was originally the *sala capitula* (chapter house) of that convent, and is the only part of it that is still intact. The *palacio* dates from the 1920s and was a school for many years. Now it's home to the Ministerio de Relaciones Exteriores (Foreign Ministry). During regular business hours (about 8 A.M.–3 P.M. Mon.–Fri., 9 A.M.–1 P.M. Sat.), it's possible, and well worthwhile, to explore the huge inner courtyard, which has been outfitted with a clear roof that's out of keeping with the architecture, but protects it from the elements. The courtyard is open to the surf in the back, where part of the original foundation can be seen. Be sure to notice the beautiful tilework and the posh chandelier at the entrance.

Next door but still on the plaza is a church and former monastery, **Iglesia y Convento de San Francisco de Asís.** The church dates from the early days of Casco Viejo, but was burned during two 18th-century fires, then restored in 1761 and again in 1998. It's an attractive confection on the outside, particularly its soaring tower, which is partly open-sided. It resembles a gothic wedding cake. It is not currently open to the public.

The Presidential Palace

The presidential palace, **El Palacio de las Garzas** (Palace of the Herons), is on the left at Calle 5 Este, overlooking Panama Bay. It's an attractive place that houses the presidential office and residence. Visitors are not permitted, and the palace and the neighboring streets are surrounded by guards. Everyone walking past the front of the palace must now go through a metal detector; they're set up at either end of the street. Guards may ask for your passport, but more likely they will just wave you through after the cursory search. Be polite and deferential—they should let you walk by the palace. As

© JIM GUY

The presidential palace, El Palacio de las Garzas, is named for the herons wandering its courtyard.

you pass, sneak a peek at the courtyard through the palace's front door, visible from the street, and try to spot the herons around the fountain.

Vicinity of Casco Viejo

A pedestrian path with great views links Casco Viejo to the city markets, running through the dockyard area known as known as the **Terraplén.** This is one of the more colorful and lively parts of the city. The path is part of the Cinta Costera along the Bay of Panama. Pedestrians, cyclists, and runners can enjoy great views of the bay, skyline, and fishing fleet while exploring the waterfront area. Four wide, busy lanes of the Cinta Costera separate the path from the densely packed and rather squalid streets of the Santa Ana and Santa Fé districts, making the path appealing even to the more safety-conscious.

For hundreds of years, small fishing boats have off-loaded their cargo around the Terraplén. These days fish is sold through the relatively clean, modern fish market, the two-story **Mercado de Mariscos** (5 A.M.–5 P.M. daily), on the waterfront just off the Cinta Costera on the way to Casco Viejo, right before the Mercado Público. This is an eternally popular place to sample ceviche made from an amazing array of seafood, sold at stalls around the market. There's usually a line at Ceviches #2 (4:30 A.M.–5 P.M. daily), though whether it's because the ceviche is truly better or because it's simply closer to the entrance and open later than the other stalls is something I'll leave to true ceviche connoisseurs. The large jars of pickled fish don't make for an appetizing scene, but rest assured that ceviche is "cooked" in a pretty intense bath of onions, limes, and chili peppers. Prices for a Styrofoam cup of fishy goodness range from US$1.25 for corvina up to US$3.50 for *langostinos.* You shouldn't leave Panama without at least trying some ceviche, whether here or somewhere a bit fancier.

Other stands, some with seating areas, are next to the main market building closer to the dock, but they tend to be smellier than the market. Those with sensitive noses will want to visit the area early in the morning, before the sun ripens the atmosphere.

Meat and produce are sold at the nearby **Mercado Público** (public market) on Avenida B, just off Avenida Eloy Alfaro near the Chinese gate of the Barrio Chino. The market is plenty colorful and worth a visit. It's gated and has a guard at the entrance.

The meat section, though cleaner, is still not fully air-conditioned, and the humid, cloying stench of blood in the Panama heat may convert some to vegetarianism. The *abarrotería* (grocer's section) is less overwhelming and more interesting. Shelves are stacked with all kinds of homemade *chichas* (fruit juices), hot sauce, and honey, as well as spices, freshly ground coconut, duck eggs, and so on. The produce section is surprisingly small.

Panama City's Mercado de Mariscos (fish market) is just outside Casco Viejo.

There's a **food hall** (4 A.M.–3 or 4 P.M. daily) in the middle of the market. The perimeter is ringed with *fondas* (basic restaurants) each marked with the proprietor's name. A heaping plateful costs a buck or two.

Lottery vendors set up their boards along the walls by the entrance, and across the gated parking lot is a line of shops selling goods similar to and no doubt intended to replace those on the Terraplén. These include hammocks, army-surplus and Wellington boots, machetes, camping gear, and souvenirs such as Ecuadorian-style Panama hats. Each store keeps different hours, but most are open 8 A.M.–4 P.M. Monday–Saturday, and some are open Sunday mornings.

The market is staffed with friendly, uniformed attendants who can explain what's going on, especially if you speak a bit of Spanish. There's a Banco Nacional de Panamá ATM near the entrance.

Up Calle 13 is the crowded shopping area of

Salsipuedes (a contraction of "get out if you can"). The area is crammed with little stalls selling clothes, lottery tickets, and bric-a-brac. Just north of this street is a small **Chinatown,** called Barrio Chino in Spanish. Most of the Chinese character of the place has been lost through the years; the ornate archway over the street is one of the few remaining points of interest.

Practicalities

There is one ATM in Casco Viejo, next to the tourism police station on Avenida Central near Calle 2. It's best to come to Casco Viejo with sufficient cash.

Farmacia El Boticario (Avenida A and Calle 4 Oeste, tel. 202-6981, 8:30 A.M.–7 P.M. Mon.–Fri., 9 A.M.–6 P.M. Sat.) is Casco Viejo's only pharmacy.

Getting Around

A good way to explore the area is to come with a knowledgeable guide or taxi driver who can drop you in different areas to explore on foot.

© WILLIAM FRIAR

You'll probably save time this way, as the streets are confusing and it's easy to get lost. Do major exploring only during the daytime; those who come at night should taxi in and out to specific destinations. Restaurant and bar owners can call a cab for the trip back.

Even locals get lost here. Watch out for narrow one-way streets and blind intersections. Street parking is hard to find in the day and on weekend nights. There's a paid lot with an attendant on the side of the Teatro Nacional that faces Panama Bay. It's open 24 hours a day.

◖ AVENIDA CENTRAL

The west end of Avenida Central, from Plaza Cinco de Mayo to Parque Santa Ana, is a busy walking street lined with shops. Except for the handicraft stalls on Plaza Cinco de Mayo, the shops won't interest foreign visitors much, as they deal mainly in cheap clothes and jewelry, electronics, and photo-development services.

People-watching on Avenida Central is always fun.

© WILLIAM FRIAR

But the people-watching on the street is fun. The area provides a real sense of daily life in an older, humbler section of Panama City. The walk along Avenida Central goes through the heart of the Santa Ana district to the outskirts of San Felipe/Casco Viejo.

To take a walking tour, start at the highly congested **Plaza Cinco de Mayo.** Note the massive building. It was inaugurated in 1912 as the terminus of the Panama Railroad and had an on-again, off-again life as Panama's anthropology museum until the museum was finally moved to the Curundu area. To the east is the rather unattractive Palacio Legislativo, which houses the Asamblea Legislativa (Panama's national legislature). A new home for the Asamblea is being built next to the current one.

Now head down Central. The area is a photographer's dream. On a typical stroll one can spot Guna women going about their business in traditional clothing, juice vendors squeezing tropical fruit or crushing sugarcane in hand-cranked presses (try some!), and hawkers luring customers into stores by clapping their hands. The crumbling old buildings reflect a real mishmash of architectural styles, including neoclassical, neo-baroque, and art deco. Some are quite striking. When you come to the major intersection, note the art deco building on the corner, the one housing the **Banco Nacional de Panamá.** Also check out the facade of the old building right next to it on the walking street. Its tiles are covered with pretty murals depicting the history of Panama from the conquest to the building of the Panama Canal.

Be sure to walk all the way to **Parque Santa Ana.** The twice weekly lottery drawings were held here for many years, and it's like a place from another, very Spanish era. It's very pleasant to get here before 8 A.M., when it's still cool under the ancient shade trees, and eavesdrop on the old men sitting around reading newspapers or arguing politics while getting a spectacularly vigorous shoeshine.

Slip into the maze of side streets if you want to do some more exploring. A good spot is the major intersection with Calle I; head uphill to Calle Estudiante, where you'll find Pizzeria Napoli and the **Instituto Nacional.** The latter was built in 1911 and has a rather heroic, neoclassical yellow facade. Students here are known for frequent participation in demonstrations, most notably the Flag Riots of 1964, which had as its main battleground the nearby Avenida de los Mártires (Martyrs' Avenue, which until the riots was called Fourth of July Avenue).

MUSEUMS

You'd never get a sense of the rich history of Panama if all you had to go on were the museums of its capital city. They are neglected and underfunded, and what few exhibits they contain are generally poorly presented and contain almost no explanation of their significance.

Panama has paid more attention to its cultural treasures in recent years. The city's anthropology museum, Museo Antropológico Reina Torres de Araúz, has a new home. The modern art museum, Museo de Arte Contemporáneo, once an art gallery more than anything else, has emerged as a respectable repository of Panama's better-known and emerging contemporary artists. And one day the ambitious new Museum of Biodiversity, designed by Frank O. Gehry, may actually be completed. The latest estimate is that it will finally open in the first half of 2013.

El Museo Antropológico Reina Torres de Araúz

Panama's anthropology museum (Avenida Juan Pablo II and Calle Curundu, tel. 501-4731, 9 a.m.–4 p.m. Tues.–Sun., US$2,50 adults, US$1 students) has a troubled history, including a dramatic robbery in 2003 and funding shortages that forced it into a moribund existence for years. As of 2006, the Museo Antropológico Reina Torres de Araúz (sometimes known by

the acronym MARTA) is a cement monolith from the exposed-duct school of modern design. The museum's permanent collection is comprised of 15,000 pieces.

Most intriguing are the pieces from the **Barriles culture,** believed to be Panama's earliest major civilization. The figures on display came from a ceremonial center that dates from around 60 b.c. and consist of about a dozen and a half carvings of stone figures and fragments.

The museum's **gold collection** includes figures of animals, armor plates, ceramics, jewelry, breastplates, a crown, and other items made by ancient indigenous peoples and recovered from archaeological sites around the country. Most of these items are *huacas,* ceremonial treasures buried with prominent indigenous people. The oldest item, a copper and gold nose ring found on Cerro Juan Díaz on the Azuero Peninsula, dates from 180 b.c.

El Museo de Arte Contemporáneo

The Contemporary Art Museum (Avenida San Blas, in Ancón, next to the old Ancón Elementary School, tel. 262-3380 or 262-8012, www.macpanama.org, 9 a.m.–5 p.m. Tues.–Sun., US$5 adult, US$3 students, US$2 children) is one of Panama's best and best-maintained museums. It more resembles an art gallery than a museum (many of the pieces are for sale). But it does present a reasonable cross section of Panama's best-known and emerging modern artists as well as some work from other parts of Latin America. It sometimes presents film series.

El Museo de Ciencias Naturales

Panama City's Natural Sciences Museum (Avenida Cuba and Calle 29 Este, tel. 225-0645, 9 a.m.–3:30 p.m. Tues.–Sat., US$1 adults, US$0.25 students) is a modest place consisting of four rooms mainly containing some stuffed and mounted animals and geological specimens. It's worth a quick visit, at least if you're in the neighborhood, to get a

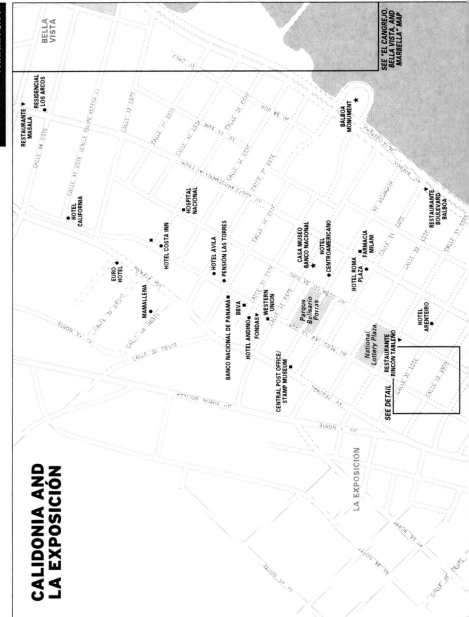

CALIDONIA AND LA EXPOSICIÓN

SEE "EL CANGREJO, BELLA VISTA, AND MARBELLA" MAP

RESTAURANTE MASALÁ

RESIDENCIAL LOS ARCOS

BELLA VISTA

BALBOA MONUMENT

HOTEL CALIFORNIA

HOSPITAL NACIONAL

RESTAURANTE BOULEVARD BALBOA

HOTEL COSTA INN

HOTEL AVILA

PENSIÓN LAS TORRES

CASA MUSEO BANCO NACIONAL

HOTEL CENTROAMERICANO

HOTEL ROMA PLAZA

FARMACIA MILANI

EURO HOTEL

MAMALLENA

BANCO NACIONAL DE PANAMÁ

BBVA

WESTERN UNION

HOTEL ANDINO

FONDASY

Parque Belisario Porras

HOTEL ARENTEIRO

CENTRAL POST OFFICE/ STAMP MUSEUM

National Lottery Plaza

RESTAURANTE RINCÓN TABLEÑO

SEE DETAIL

LA EXPOSICIÓN

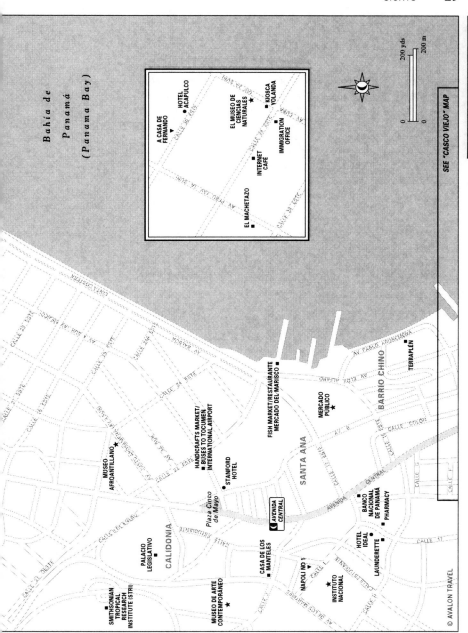

Bahia de Panamá (Panama Bay)

SEE "CASCO VIEJO" MAP

200 yds
200 m

A CASA DE FERNANDO
HOTEL ACAPULCO
EL MUSEO DE CIENCIAS NATURALES
KIOSCA YOLANDA
INTERNET CAFÉ
IMMIGRATION OFFICE
EL MACHETAZO

FISH MARKET/RESTAURANTE MERCADO DEL MARISCO
TERRAPLÉN
AV. PABLO AROSEMENA
BARRIO CHINO
AV. ELOY ALFARO
MERCADO PÚBLICO
CALLE COLON
CALLE G
HANDICRAFTS MARKET/ BUSES TO TOCUMEN INTERNATIONAL AIRPORT
CALLE F
STANFORD HOTEL
MUSEO AFROANTILLANO
SANTA ANA
AVENIDA CENTRAL
AVENIDA
BANCO NACIONAL DE PANAMÁ
PHARMACY
Plaza Cinco de Mayo
AVENIDA CENTRAL
HOTEL IDEAL
CALLE 17
PALACIO LEGISLATIVO
CALIDONIA
CASA DE LOS MANTELES
NAPOLI NO 1
LAUNDERETTE
SMITHSONIAN TROPICAL RESEARCH INSTITUTE (STRI)
MUSEO DE ARTE CONTEMPORANEO
INSTITUTO NACIONAL
AV. DE LOS MARTIRES

© AVALON TRAVEL

close-up look at some of Panama's more inter-esting animals, including a jaguar, harpy eagle, howler and spider monkeys, and a huge iguana. It's also fun to get a close look at the amazing hanging nest of an oropendola (a common bird in Panama). But the most interesting display is probably a handful of fossilized bones of a 50,000-year-old sloth *(Eremotherium rusconi)*, estimated to have been four meters long. The remains were found on the Azuero Peninsula in 1991. Only the geology and paleontology room is air-conditioned, ensuring that the rocks stay nice and cool while the snake exhibit, for in-stance, is hot and humid.

Museo Afroantillano

The Afro-Antillean Museum (Calle 24 Este off Avenida Justo Arosemena/Avenida 3 Sur, tel. 262-5348, 262-1668, or 501-4130, 8:30 A.M.–3:30 P.M. Tues.–Sat., US$1 adults, US$0.25 children) pre-serves the memory of the thousands of West Indian workers, mostly from Barbados, who supplied the bulk of the labor for the building of the Panama Canal. These workers, who had the most danger-ous and grueling jobs during canal construction, are often little more than a footnote in accounts of the building of the canal. Their descendants today make up a significant part of the population of the country.

The museum is tiny and worth a quick visit. However, be aware that its location is on a dicey street. If you do come, take a taxi and have the driver wait outside the entrance for you; you can see everything the museum has to offer in about a half hour.

The museum is installed in an old wooden house stocked with canal construction-era fur-nishings and photos meant to give a sense of what life might have been like for these work-ers, though it is certainly much more comfort-able than the shacks many of the workers had to make do with in those days.

Casa Museo Banco Nacional

This elegant little house (Calle 34 Este and Avenida Cuba, tel. 225-0640, 8 A.M.–12:30 P.M. and 1:30–4:30 P.M. Mon.–Fri., free), the former residence of a doctor, dates from 1925 and is now owned by the Banco Nacional de Panamá. It has rotating exhibits of arts and crafts for sale, though those I've seen have been quite poor. It does have a tiny but in-teresting collection of Panamanian commemo-rative coins, including a silver 20 balboa piece about the size of a fist, a small gold 100 balboa piece, and a tiny 2.5 centavo piece. Other coins date from 1904, some of the earliest days of the republic. It's worth visiting just to see how the well-heeled lived in early-20th-century Panama City. The house is lovely, with marble stair-cases, ornate wrought-iron fixtures, and several types of tile floors.

Mi Pueblito

Also known as Los Pueblitos, Mi Pueblito (off the westbound side of Avenida de los Mártires near the base of Cerro Ancón, 9 A.M.–9 P.M. Tues.–Sun., US$1), literally, "my little town," is a charming, if idealized, re-creation of a typi-cal Panamanian town on the Azuero Peninsula, Panama's heartland. The architecture is Spanish colonial, which is especially notable in the red-tile roofs and whitewashed walls, the mission-style church, and the central plaza and fountain. The builders have included lots of small, loving touches, from the lesson plan on the blackboard of the schoolhouse to the telegraph office that looks as though the operator has just left for a siesta. There's even a rustic outhouse behind the buildings. Nearby is a small *pollera* (traditional embroidered dress) museum.

The Mi Pueblito complex has been expanded to recognize the traditional dwellings of some of the other peoples of Panama. These are di-rectly across the street from the Spanish co-lonial village. The first site honors the West Indian immigrants who provided most of the labor force for the building of the Panama Canal. The brightly painted two-story wooden buildings are an extremely fanciful take on what the laborers' accommodations were really like. A walk through a little forest takes you to more accurate re-creations of the way three indigenous peoples—the Guna, Emberá-Wounaan, and Ngöbe-Buglé—lived, and in many cases still do.

CHURCHES AND SHRINES

Panama City's cathedral and most of its historically significant Catholic churches are in Casco Viejo. A couple of other prominent churches are scattered around modern Panama City.

Despite being an overwhelmingly Catholic country, Panama has a live-and-let-live attitude toward the many minority faiths brought by immigrants from around the world or still practiced by its indigenous peoples. The Baha'i House of Worship and Hindu Temple are especially prominent and draw curious visitors.

Santuario Nacional del Corazón de María

The National Sanctuary (on Calle Manuel María Icaza near Calle 53 Este, tel. 263-9833) was dedicated on August 22, 1949. It's a relatively simple church with pretty stained-glass windows and a modern interior, but atmosphere is provided by a riot of peacocks. Other domesticated birds wander around a fountain near the crypts. The crypts themselves are a bit creepy but worth a look; they're out the side entrance to the right as one faces the altar. Masses are held several times daily. The church's facade is attractive at night, when it's illuminated and provides a striking contrast to the glittery modern buildings that surround it. It's not worth making a special trip for, but given its central location it might be convenient to pop in briefly.

Iglesia del Carmen

The Iglesia del Carmen (at Vía España and Avenida Federico Boyd, across the street from the Hotel El Panamá, tel. 223-0360) is the most conspicuous church in modern Panama City. A cream-colored, neogothic confection with tall twin towers, built in 1947, it's a Panamanian landmark and worth a quick peek for those in the neighborhood.

Baha'i House of Worship

Panama's Baha'i House of Worship (tel. 231-1191, 9 A.M.–6 P.M. daily, free), the only one in Latin America and one of only seven in the world, is an impressive structure that resembles an egg, with huge, open arched entrances that let the breezes blow through but keep the rain out. The temple interior is entirely unadorned. It has an unusual panoramic view of the city, the Pacific Ocean, and the surrounding countryside.

The temple is northeast of Panama City, near Las Cumbres. To get there, head east and then north on the Transístmica (Avenida Simón Bolívar) from downtown Panama City. After about 15 kilometers there's a big intersection with Tumba Muerto (Avenida Ricardo J. Alfaro). Continue north on the Transístmica. About four kilometers past the intersection there should be a Bacardi rum factory on the left. Turn left here and head uphill for 1.5 kilometers to the temple.

Hindu Temple

The Hindu Temple (7:30 A.M.–noon and 4–8 P.M. daily, free) is less impressive than the Baha'i House of Worship, but easier to get to. It's a rather modern, spartan place that looks more imposing from a distance than it does close up. The most interesting thing about it, at least when worshippers are around, is the sense it gives you of how extensive and well-established Panama's South Asian community is.

The temple is off Tumba Muerto (Avenida Ricardo J. Alfaro). Head east a couple of kilometers past Calle de la Amistad (Friendship Highway) and make a left turn. Visitors must sign in at the gate. The temple is a short drive uphill.

PARKS

Other than Parque Natural Metropolitano, Panama City isn't blessed with much in the way of impressive or well-tended open spaces. Even little plazas are hard to find outside of Casco Viejo and the walking section of Avenida Central—they're one bit of the city's Spanish heritage that, sadly, is slipping away.

The Cinta Costera and Avenida Balboa

Panama City's newest and grandest avenue also offers some of its most dramatic views. Built on landfill, the Cinta Costera (coastal belt) sweeps along the edge of Panama Bay from Casco Viejo to ritzy Punta Paitilla and Punta Pacífica. It offers good views of the modern skyline of Panama City, Panama Bay, and the old seawall, churches, and historic buildings of Casco Viejo. The original concept for the promenade called for huge expanses of parkland and lovely facilities to attract families and tourists down to the sea edge.

The reality is far more pedestrian and far less pedestrian-friendly. While there are some playing fields and such, most of the common spaces are simply large fields of grass that turn brown in the dry season. Getting to these spaces isn't that easy, either. The few pedestrian overpasses are spaced widely apart.

These caveats aside, it's still a pleasant place for a morning or evening stroll or jog. Try to time your visit to coincide with high tide, when the view is nicer and the smell less potent. (Panama City has always dumped its untreated sewage into the bay, though an extensive and massively expensive new sewage treatment system is finally in the works after years of delay.) The Cinta Costera has recently been extended from the seafood market to the outskirts of Casco Viejo, a particularly scenic and colorful stretch of waterfront. The pedestrian path is wide and pleasant here.

The Cinta Costera runs parallel to Avenida Balboa, which for decades was the city's bayside promenade, lined with high-rises that hugged the edge of the sea. But with the advent of the Cinta Costera, Avenida Balboa is no longer on the waterfront, to the consternation, no doubt, of those who own property along it. About midway along Avenida Balboa is a little park that contains an enormous statue of Balboa "discovering" the Pacific, though these days he's so far from the water he looks like he's trying to hail a cab.

Parque Belisario Porras

Though it's not worth a special trip, those staying in Calidonia who need a little open space can visit Parque Belisario Porras, between Calle 33 Este and Calle 34 Este and Avenida Perú and Avenida Cuba. It's an austere, formal plaza with a monument to Porras, thrice president of Panama and one of its founding fathers, looking rather dapper and jaunty. The plaza is surrounded by attractive old buildings, housing various government offices and the Spanish embassy. A line of kiosks serves greasy fast food to office workers on Avenida Perú near Calle 35, next to the Ministerio de Economía y Finanzas.

Parque Urracá

This is just a small city park off Avenida Balboa and Avenida Federico Boyd, but it's often filled with people, and it's fun to wander from here north and west through the hilly backstreets of Bella Vista. This is the edge of the *area bancaria* (banking area), so-called because of its many banks, often built into old houses. They're fast disappearing thanks to the construction boom, but it's still possible to walk down tree-lined streets and see beautiful Spanish colonial mansions with red-tiled roofs and stone walls.

◖ Parque Natural Metropolitano

Amazingly enough, you don't even have to leave the limits of Panama City to find a tropical forest. This 232-hectare park (entrance on Avenida Juan Pablo II in the Curundu district, www.parquemetropolitano.org, tel. 232-6713 or 232-5516, trails open 5 A.M.–6 P.M. daily, free, donations encouraged) is just minutes from downtown, and it's a lovely little place with a surprising amount of wildlife given its location and size.

Most of the park is dry lowland Pacific forest, now rare in Central America because of deforestation, and it's home to about 45 species of mammals, 36 of reptiles, and 14 of amphibians. These include such colorful creatures as two- and three-toed sloths, *monos tití* (Geoffroy's tamarin), and boa constrictors. As usual, however, don't be surprised if you see only birds during a hike. The park has recorded 227 bird species.

Having an urban center this close to a nature park has its drawbacks: A highway, Corredor Norte, cuts right through the park's eastern edge, and other busy streets run by its borders. You're never far from the roar of the road. Sadly, there have also been reports of occasional muggings. Don't wander on a trail alone.

There are about four kilometers of trails spread among three main loops. Not surprisingly, the most strenuous one, **La Cienaguita,** also offers the best chance of seeing animals. It takes about two hours to walk. It's an interpretive trail; the visitors center sells an informative booklet about it for US$2. The **Mono Tití Road** is a wide trail which ascends 150 meters to **Cerro Cedro** (Cedar's Hill), which offers views of Panama City. The easiest trail is **Los Momótides,** across an extremely busy road—be careful crossing the street. It's short and level, designed for people in a hurry or who have difficulty walking, and it is a nice little walk.

The **visitors center** (8 A.M.–4 P.M. Mon.–Fri., 8 A.M.–1 P.M. Sat.) offers a free brochure, but ask for the glossy color trail guide, which has a much-needed map. Guided tours in English and Spanish are sometimes available, but you have to arrange this at least a day or two in advance.

Cerro Azul

This hilly area about an hour east of Panama City has long been popular with more affluent city dwellers looking to escape the hot lowlands—the elevation reaches 950 meters, high enough to cool things off significantly. Attempts have been made to attract tourists to the area, but only serious birders are likely to find it of great interest. They come for the foothill species, including some that are otherwise found only in the Darién. There are some stretches of elfin forest, but getting to the less-developed areas requires four-wheel drive with high clearance, and some places can only be approached on foot. Birders should go with a knowledgeable naturalist guide. Other than that, this is mostly an area of suburban homes and little else.

To get to Cerro Azul, take the Corredor Sur toll road toward the international airport. When the road ends at the Riande Aeropuerto Hotel and Resort, turn left onto the Interamerican Highway. Make another left at the Super Xtra supermarket and follow the Cerro Azul signs. Casa de Campo is about a 20-minute drive up the hill. Turn left at Urbanización Las Nubes and follow the signs. To get to Cerro Azul by public transportation, take any bus going to 24 de Diciembre. Get off at the Super Xtra supermarket and transfer to a Cerro Azul bus.

There is one nice place to stay on Cerro Azul. **Hostal Casa de Campo Country Inn and Spa** (39 Avenida Los Cumulos, Panama City tel. 226-0274, Cerro Azul tel. 297-0067, cell 6677-8993, infor@panamacasadecampo. com, www.panamacasadecampo.com, starts at US$77 s/d) is a large, upscale country home that's been turned into a pleasant, well-maintained inn with lots of character and extensive grounds. All rooms are different, and some are considerably nicer than others. Despite the name, this is not a hostel. There's a small swimming pool, a full-service spa, and good views of the surrounding forested hills and Lago Alajuela. The inn offers a variety of spa,

STRIP CLUBS, BROTHELS, AND BATHHOUSES

Prostitution is legal and regulated by the Panamanian government, but it's hardly free from exploitation. And AIDS and other sexually transmitted diseases are serious risks for those who engage in casual or commercial sex.

Consider the following: An estimated 20,000 people in Panama are living with HIV, and epidemiologists believe the true number could be twice that. Given the country's small population, that gives Panama one of the highest rates in Central America. More people die of AIDS in Panama than in any other Central American country; it is the country's seventh leading cause of death. And the rate of HIV infection is on the rise.

The prevalence of HIV/AIDS is especially high in Panama City and other metropolitan areas, but the United Nations' AIDS agency reports a high concentration of cases among poor indigenous peoples as well, especially the Guna.

While Panama has made some progress with its HIV/AIDS programs, much more needs to be done. The UN estimates that fewer than half the prostitutes in Panama have been reached by an AIDS-prevention program. It also has found that more than 10 percent of men who have sex with men are now HIV-positive. Many of these men also have sex with women. And there are plenty of other sexually transmitted diseases out there.

Panama has several "gentlemen's clubs" or "nightclubs" with strip shows and the like. These usually have fancy names with words such as "elite" or "palace" in them. Those interested will have no trouble finding advertisements in tourist-oriented publications.

Panama City has had gay bathhouses in the past, including one that was quite upscale. However, that one recently closed down and I'm not aware of any that have taken its place. Again, those who are determined will likely find any new ones, most likely through contacts at gay bars or the Internet.

The area around the public market in San Felipe and the backstreets near Avenida Central have lots of rough and seedy bars, including some bars catering to a gay clientele and places that are more or less brothels. This area can be quite dangerous, though, and one of the toughest Panamanians I know thinks it's a dumb move for a gringo to barhop around here—there's an excellent chance of getting mugged on the way home. You've been warned.

tour, and outdoor adventure packages, including bird-watching trips. Meals are available for an extra charge. The inn can arrange round-trip transportation from Panama City, about an hour away. The staff speak English, Spanish, and Italian.

Entertainment and Events

NIGHTLIFE

Panama City has experienced a nightlife boom in recent years, concentrated in a handful of streets and neighborhoods around the city.

The most popular area is a densely packed grid of restaurants, clubs, cafés, and bars bounded by the **Bella Vista** district to the west and **Marbella** to the east. The center of this area is **Calle Uruguay.** Businesses come and go overnight, but there's always someplace worth visiting. If the long-awaited Buddha Bar franchise ever opens an outlet in Panama, it will instantly be the hottest nightspot in the city. It's allegedly going up on Vía Brasil, but the estimate of when or if it might actually arrive keeps getting pushed back.

Calle 53 Este, the main street through the upscale business district of Marbella, draws young singles and couples to its music clubs. The renovation of **Casco Viejo** has made it an ideal place for clubs, sidewalk cafés, and bars, at least on the weekends. The most popular entertainment area in Panama City is not actually in the city proper, but along the Calzada de Amador (Amador Causeway) in the old Canal Zone.

Clubs have traditionally opened very late in Panama City. Typically they didn't really get going until midnight or later, and the partying often lasted all night. However, in late 2011 a new law, commonly known as the *ley zanahoria* (carrot law), came into effect that prohibits the sale of alcohol between 3 A.M. and 9 A.M. Thursday–Saturday and between 2 A.M. and 9 A.M. Sunday–Wednesday. Enforcement of the controversial law has been uneven, and it remains to be seen whether it will stick.

Cover charges at prominent clubs on a big night can be US$10–20, though there are all kinds of promotions to offset this. Many clubs don't charge a cover during the week or early in the evening, usually before 11 P.M. Women can get in free and/or get free drinks at least once a week, and some clubs have all-you-can-drink open bar specials before 11 P.M. Less-trendy spots typically have cover charges of US$5 or less.

Oddly, in a country where kids learn to dance to salsa and merengue as soon as they can walk, and where partying is virtually a civil right, it's not unusual to see little or no dancing at a Panama City club these days. Even if the place is packed and the music deafening, most people may just be talking, flirting, and drinking.

Don't ask a taxi driver to take you to a good nightclub unless what you're looking for is a strip club or brothel. What gringos call "nightclubs" or "clubs" are usually still known as "discos" or *discotecas* in Panama.

Clubs and bars come and go fast in Panama City, and what's popular one week can be dead or out of business the next, so it's best to aim for a neighborhood rather than a specific bar or club. If you want a nice quiet bar, upscale hotels are a good option. The **Sparkles Bar,** on the fifth floor of the InterContinental Miramar, has a terrific view of the skyline and Panama Bay.

Internet entertainment listings in Panama are getting a bit better, but including addresses, hours, and phone numbers is still an alien concept, and entertainment-listings websites are constantly abandoned without warning. Try cocoas. net, www.dealante.com, or www.elcuara.com.

Casco Viejo

Something of a bohemian, international art scene has begun to bubble up from the underground, fueled by the arrival of young backpackers and, especially, European and South American expats. Most of the more mainstream action is concentrated around Plaza Bolívar, though nightspots pop up from time to time on the streets leading up to Plaza de Francia. The Parque Herrera area looks poised to take off in the next couple of years. Be careful in this area at night, particularly around Parque Herrera. It's best to come and go by taxi; ask the bar or club to call one for you.

Relic Bar (at Luna's Castle: Calle 9 Este and Avenida Eloy Alfaro, tel. 262-1540, www. relicbar.com, Mon.–Sat. nights) is a funky bar with an underground vibe. It's on the lowest level of the Luna's Castle hostel, so patrons must be buzzed in through the security gate. The bar opens onto a huge patio that looks up into the homes of residents of Casco Viejo, who no doubt find the shenanigans of the tourists below at least as interesting as the tourists do the *Rear Window* peek into locals' lives. The bar itself is cave-like and contains part of the old wall that used to ring Casco Viejo.

The bar's most prominent neighbor has stopped by at least once: Panama's president, Ricardo Martinelli, and assorted ministers showed up unexpectedly to an event at the bar a couple of years ago.

La Casona (end of Calle 5, off Avenida A, cell 6706-0528, http://cascoviejo.com, hours vary Wed.–Sat.) is a combination bar/cultural center/DJ club. It has inspired more affection and excitement since it opened in 2005 than

GAY AND LESBIAN BARS AND CLUBS

Panama City is still a place where gay bars have to keep a low profile, but you don't hear horror stories of police raids, gay bashings outside of clubs, and so on—not, at least, among the relatively affluent. It's more a matter of people wanting to be cautious and discreet. Gay bars and clubs are either in remote locations or hidden in plain sight—it's possible to walk right past one and not know anything's there at all.

Like other clubs, they come and go quickly. A mega-club on the outskirts of Panama City, known variously over the years as Boy Bar, Box, Glam, etc., has closed down. That leaves BLG as the longest-established of the prominent gay clubs, though a newer one, Lips Club, has the busiest events calendar. The Internet is the best source for current information, though websites are underfunded, often out of date, and go bust constantly. Start with www.farraurbana.com and www.gaypty.com. Facebook searches can often turn up current information (in Spanish), though usually written for those already familiar with the clubs and lacking in detail.

The three clubs listed here are the most prominent and popular spots that are most likely to still be around when you read this. They draw mostly a gay male clientele (the one lesbian bar closed many years ago), but lesbians and straight singles or couples are welcome. Lesbians seem particularly well-represented at Lips Club. Regardless of one's sexual orientation, visitors will likely find the vibe at these places friendlier, more low-key, more inclusive, and less macho than at many of the city's straight bars and clubs.

There are also so-called "camouflage" bars—ostensibly straight bars that draw closeted gays—and rough dives. Neither kind is included here, for reasons of privacy and safety.

BLG (Transístmica and Avenida Brasil, tel. 393-6298, www.blgpanama.net, 10 P.M.-late Wed.-Sun.), also known as Balagan's, is the most upscale gay bar in Panama. It moved a couple of years back from the Calle Uruguay area to a spot that's much less convenient for visitors, along the Transístmica near the Colpan Ford dealership. Even though it's relatively new, it's already had a renovation and a grand reopening in March 2012. Look for the "BLG" out front. The club draws men, women, and some straight couples. The music is mostly electronica. It has *transformista* (drag) shows, comedians, and other special events on some nights.

La Gota Fría/Lips Club (Avenida Manuel Espinosa Batista near the intersection of Avenida Simón Bolívar/Transístmica and Avenida Ricardo J. Alfaro/Tumba Muerto, no phone, 10 P.M.-late Wed. and Fri.-Sun., US$5-10 cover) has the most organized club schedule. It has a stage and frequently hosts *transformista* (drag) shows and other events. Foam parties are a popular shtick these days, which fit nicely with the car-wash motif. It hosts special shows throughout Carnaval. The club manages the neat trick of being in one of the most visible spots in the city but staying well hidden. It's on the 2nd floor of a building behind the Splash car wash, which is next to the large roundabout at the intersection of the Transístmica and Tumba Muerto. Everyone in the city knows this area, even if they don't know the club.

Icon Club (Tumba Muerto and Avenida Juan Pablo II, cell 6230-0378, www.iconclub-panama.com, 9 P.M.-3 A.M. Thurs.-Sun.), formerly called Oxen, is the massive warehouse club of choice these days. Like its predecessors, it can be bloody hard to find the first time. To get there from Tumba Muerto, first look for Plaza Edison, the distinctive cone-shaped office building. The cross street is Avenida Juan Pablo II; turn west onto it. The club is in the commercial complex on the right side of the road. The club hosts especially elaborate *transformista* (drag) shows from time to time. These can be entertaining even (or especially) when they're not particularly skilled.

any new place I can remember, having filled a major gap in the nightlife scene. People love its informal vibe—it's one of the few hot spots in Panama that doesn't have a dress code—as well as the mixture of people it attracts, from backpackers to the hipster art crowd to over-dressed yuppies. There's an art gallery, and La Casona occasionally hosts films, artists' talks, live concerts, and traveling exhibitions. This place keeps moving from one derelict building to another in Casco Viejo, keeping one step ahead of the wave of gentrification. Double-check its current location before venturing out.

Platea (near the intersection of Avenida Central and Avenida A, tel. 228-4011, www. scenayplatea.com, 8 P.M.–3 A.M. Wed.–Sat.) is a cozy cave of a bar on the ground floor of the same building that houses S'Cena, a Mediterranean restaurant, across from the ruins of the old Union Club. There's music every night, from live jazz, salsa, or world music to karaoke.

The bar at **Restaurante Las Bóvedas** (Plaza de Francia, tel. 228-8058 or 228-8068, 5:30 P.M.–late Mon.–Sat.) hosts live jazz Friday and Saturday after about 9:30 P.M.

The fairly new **Habana Panama** (Calle Eloy Alfaro and Calle 12 Este, tel. 212-0152, cell 6628-4189 or 5780-2183, www.habanapan-ama.com, usually Thurs.–Sat. nights) is an attempt to bring actual dancing back to Panama City clubs and to play something other than the same old *típico* and reggaeton. It's a Cuban music hall that quite accurately bills itself as *el bunker de la música cubana*. Bunker indeed: It's just down from the entrance to Casco Viejo, in an area that can be dangerous to wander around at night. Huge spotlights beam down onto the street from the entrance to the surprisingly upscale club. The proprietors are going for old Havana romance and old Havana sounds. The club manages to attract surprisingly big-name international acts, from salsa great Willie Colón to Los Van Van, one of the most venerable Cuban bands still playing.

◖ Bella Vista and Marbella

Most of the popular clubs and bars in this area are on or near Calle Uruguay, Panama City's major nightlife destination. Places fold and new ones pop up at lightning speed, so it's impossible to say what will be there when you visit. The best bet is just to stroll around late on a Thursday, Friday, or Saturday night and follow the crowds, particularly on Avenida 5B, Avenida 5 Sur/Calle 48, and Calle Uruguay itself, and see what looks appealing. Big venues tend to surface across the street from Crepes and Waffles (Avenida 5B between Calle Uruguay and Calle Aquilino de la Guardia) and next to the Panama City Hooters (Calle 49 and Calle Uruguay).

Street names are confusing around here. Calle Uruguay is also sometimes known as Calle 48 Este, and the cross streets have all kinds of names and are often called simply Calle 45, 46, 47, and so on, even though they are officially low-numbered avenues.

S6is (Calle Uruguay between Avenida 4A and 5A, tel. 264-5237, Tues.–Sun. nights until late), pronounced *seis* (the number six), is a DJ bar/cocktail lounge in an old house that projects the air of a party in a pleasant, minimalist apartment. It attracts a mid-twenty-something and older crowd.

T.G.I. Friday's (Avenida 4A Sur near Calle Aquilino de la Guardia/49 Este, tel. 269-4199) is a perennially popular destination for young singles on the prowl or just hanging with their friends. There's another one attached to the Country Inns and Suites on the Calzada de Amador (Amador Causeway).

As a Panama kid who now lives in London, there was no way I'd skip a Panama pub called **The Londoner** (Calle Uruguay between Avenida 5A Sur and Avenida 5B Sur, tel. 214-4883, 5 P.M.–late daily). Its owner is South African, it doesn't have beer on tap, and the Panamanian bartenders were puzzled by the concept of a gin and tonic, in any language.

On the other hand, they were gracious and eager to learn. That's service you rarely find in Panama. Bottled imports include Guinness, Newcastle Brown Ale, and Strongbow cider. The Londoner is a homey place with a pool table and a less gringo-heavy crowd than other expat magnets: It's a good place to encounter Brits and Commonwealth types. It's where to head to watch a soccer game on a big screen, rather than resort to a sports bar. The English pub grub (US$5–11.50) includes shepherd's pie, bangers and mash, and fish and chips.

El Cangrejo and Vicinity

Nightlife in El Cangrejo centers on the big hotels and casinos and a handful of venerable restaurants. It's popular with some Panamanians and resident expats, but many of its nightspots are overrated and/or overpriced.

A good place in the area is the **Istmo Brew Pub** (Avenida Eusebio A. Morales, tel. 265-5077, 4 P.M.–3 A.M. Mon.–Sat., 4 P.M.–12:30 A.M. Sun.). It's an open-air venue, right across the street from Wine Bar and Las Vegas Hotel Suites, with a friendly atmosphere, a pool table, and a big-screen TV showing whatever game happens to be on. This is the only place in Panama I know of that makes its own beer. It only makes three kinds, and on any given day only one may be in stock. The beer definitely tastes homemade rather than artisanal, and at nearly $5 a pint is steep for Panama, where a local bottle is easy to find for a tenth of that price. Still, the home brew is light and refreshing, and this is a comfortable spot to hang out and people-watch. They serve no domestic beers, only mass-market imported beers along the lines of Amstel Light, Corona, and Budweiser. As these cost nearly $4 a bottle, the pints are a far better value. There's a daily happy hour until 8 P.M. The pub also serves bar food.

CASINOS

Gambling is legal in Panama, and casinos are scattered throughout the city, primarily in the better hotels around Vía España. Centrally located ones include the **Royal Casino,** next to the Marriott (Calle 52 at Calle Ricardo Arias, tel. 210-9100); the **Majestic Casino** (tel. 215-5151) in the Multicentro Mall on Avenida Balboa; and the **Fiesta Casino** (tel. 208-7250) behind the Hotel El Panamá. The **Veneto Hotel and Casino** is the glitziest (Vía Veneto between Avenida 2 Norte/Eusebio A. Morales and Calle D, tel. 340-8888). The hotel itself is a 17-story, 300-room Vegas knockoff with decor that's an odd mix of the garish and the generic—more Atlantic City than Panama City.

CINEMAS

There are plenty of movie theaters in Panama City. Mostly these are multiplexes showing recent Hollywood spectacles and are generally in English with Spanish subtitles rather than dubbed. This is indicated in the listings: looks for "SUB" for subtitled films and "DOB" for dubbed films. The standard ticket prices are US$4–4.50 for adults, US$3.50 for students, US$3 for kids. Tickets are generally about half price on Tuesday or Wednesday.

The daily newspapers carry a list of current movies, locations, and show times. A good online list is at www.cine.com.pa/, or try the *La Prensa* newspaper's online listings: www.prensa.com.

The fancy Mexican-owned cinema chain **Cinépolis** (Multiplaza Pacific Mall, tel. 302-2463) has arrived in Panama, with its first beachheads in the upscale Multiplaza Pacific Mall and the newish Metro Mall (though the latter doesn't have VIP seats). It offers two kinds of movie experiences: the usual multiplex theater at usual multiplex prices, or Cinépolis VIP, which allows patrons to choose their (overstuffed, reclining) seat in advance. Moviegoers can order food and drink to be delivered to their seats. It's pretty posh. Tickets for this cost US$12.50, which strikes the average Panamanian as extortionate.

The **Diablo Rosso café/art gallery** (#11,

Avenida A and Calle 7, tel. 228-4833 or 228-4837, www.diablorosso.com) in Casco Viejo hosts an indie film night on Wednesday, a welcome addition to the movie scene for culture-starved residents.

CONCERTS AND THEATER

Panama City has an active theater scene, with regular productions featuring offerings by Panamanian playwrights as well as classic and contemporary plays from other countries. The easiest music performance to find on any given night is a *típico* combo, though salsa, Latin pop/rock, reggaeton, and other high-energy music forms are also popular. Most of these are local acts that perform in clubs, but with the opening of more modern, high-capacity venues such as the **Figali Convention Center** at the Panama Canal Village, the city is beginning to attract more big-name international pop acts.

Big concerts are sometimes held in the

© WILLIAM FRIAR

There are nearly 10,000 lottery vendors in Panama.

baseball stadium, **Estadio Nacional Rod Carew,** as well. Classical music and dance groups come through less often. Tickets for major concerts and other events are usually available through Blockbuster outlets or online at www.blockbusterpanama.com or through Ticket Plus outlets or online at hwww.ticket-plus.com.pa. Official ticket outlets are constantly in flux in Panama and may change by the time you arrive. Make sure you're buying from a legitimate source. Also, official online outlets restrict sales by region, so you probably won't be able to buy tickets for a hot show until you're actually in Panama.

Panama's elegant old **Teatro Nacional** (Avenida B between Calle 3 and Calle 4 in Casco Viejo, tel. 262-3525 or 262-3582) hosts visiting classical music ensembles and other arts events.

Teatro en Círculo (Avenida 6C Norte near Vía Brasil, tel. 261-5375), near Scubapanama, in a quiet residential area east of downtown, presents many of the city's highest-profile plays, from Spanish-language renditions of Shakespeare to well-received original productions by Panamanian playwrights. The small **Teatro Anita Villalaz** (Plaza de Francia in Casco Viejo, tel. 211-4017 or 211-2040) is another prominent playhouse. Performance groups often rent out the **Teatro ABA** (Avenida Simón Bolívar/Transístmica near Avenida de los Periodistas, tel. 260-6316) for their productions. It's near the Chinese restaurant Palacio Lung Fung and not far from Teatro en Círculo.

LOTTERY

The Lotería Nacional de Beneficencia, or national lottery, is a tenacious carryover from a time when Panamanians had fewer entertainment options. The first lottery was held in 1882, and the current system dates from 1919. It's still hugely popular.

Every Sunday and Wednesday at 1 P.M., a crowd gathers for the drawing, broadcast live throughout the country on TV and radio. Drawings are held in Plaza Víctor Julio Gutiérrez, which is covered by an open-sided shed that takes up an entire block between Avenida Perú and Avenida Cuba and Calle 31 and Calle 32. Anyone can drop by to watch.

The ritual is solemn and unwavering. First, the lottery balls are turned incessantly back and forth in a shiny steel cage by a designated official. This seems to last for hours. At last, the cage is stopped and a ball is extracted by a child dressed in his or her very best. The ball is twisted apart to reveal a number printed inside, which is held up for all to see, read aloud by the emcee, and then carefully recorded on a board behind the stage. Three sets of four numbers are chosen, corresponding to the first, second, and third prize. A ticket holder must have all four numbers in the correct order to win one of the three prizes, though there are small prizes (US$1–50) for getting some of the numbers right.

Going through this process 12 times turns the drawing into an event long enough to allow for all kinds of sideshows: beauty queens in *polleras,* folkloric dances, musical performances, visiting dignitaries, and so on.

All this for a first prize of US$2,000. Second prize is US$600 and third US$300. That's still a lot of money for the average hardworking Panamanian. And people often buy multiple tickets with the same numbers; theoretically, the maximum prize is US$570,000—if one bought 285 winning tickets.

There are also special drawings that pay more. *Gorditos del Zodíaco* (little fat ones of the Zodiac) are held on the last Friday of each month. First prize is US$4,000 (for a maximum of US$900,000 if one bought many, many winning tickets). A newer gimmick, the *sorteo de oro* (gold drawing), increases the payout if a winning ticket has certain letters printed on it. To purists, though, adding this alphabet soup to the mix ruins the charm of those three rows of numbers, which are posted diligently around the country on bus station chalkboards and other public spots twice a week, year in and year out.

Four-number tickets cost US$1. If that's too expensive, a two-number *chance* (CHON-seh) goes for US$0.25. These pay out if the numbers correspond to the last two numbers of any of the winning combinations. First prize for these is US$14, second prize is US$3, and third prize is US$2. The maximum for multiple tickets is US$280.

Tickets are sold by freelance vendors around the country. You can find vendors on any street with lots of foot traffic. A whole battalion has stalls set up on the Avenida Perú side of the lottery plaza, between Calle 31 and Calle 32. There are nearly 10,000 vendors in Panama.

Shopping

Panama has no shortage of shopping malls and commercial centers—at last count there were more than two dozen of various sizes. Many of these, however, look better stocked than they are, and the city is not the best place to look for the latest fashions. However, those in the market for cosmetics and perfumes can find better deals than they would in the United States at the nicer department stores, such as the **Stevens, Collins, Felix B. Maduro,** and **Dante**

chains. There are branches of these on Vía España, on Tumba Muerto (Avenida Ricardo J. Alfaro) in El Dorado, and in some of the malls.

One of the newer and glitzier malls is the upscale **Multiplaza Pacific,** in Punta Pacífica. The youth-oriented **Multicentro** is on the west end of Avenida Balboa near Punta Paitilla. There's a food court on the top floor that has a great view of the city and the bay. A particularly massive and constantly growing complex is the **Albrook**

BOUTIQUE BREEBAART: A DASH OF PARIS IN PANAMA

Helèné Breebaart with one of her creations

The small fashion house **Boutique Breebaart** (Calle Abel Bravo, Casa #5, Obarrio, tel. 264-5937, 9 A.M.-6 P.M. Mon.-Fri., open weekends by appointment) is housed in the home of its owner and designer, the warm and utterly charming Helèné Breebaart, an artist who first came to Panama as the local representative for Christian Dior perfumes. Try to chat with her, in any of her several languages, if she's around: She is a relentlessly creative and upbeat person, and she has some great stories of her years in Panama, ranging from life as a clothing designer during the military dictatorship to dressing Rosalynn Carter for a gala evening of former and current U.S. first ladies. This may not be easy, though, as Helèné is a human dynamo and very busy; she's never still for long.

The boutique offers unusual dresses, bathing suits, cushions, place settings, tablecloths, handbags, napkins, and other items. Recurring motifs include butterflies, hibiscuses, hummingbirds, pineapples, coral, and other tropical-Panama flora and fauna, usually appliquéd onto the dresses and other items. But most of all, her signature work is inspired by the colorful *molas* of the Gunas, who are the ones who actually stitch the clothing and other pieces she designs. Those staying in high-end hotels may recognize her work (or in some cases poorer-quality rip-offs) from the pillows and other furnishings in their rooms. Her collections appear from time to time in upscale department stores in the United States.

Much of the work is quite lovely and elegant; some is rather kitschy and works best on the beach. Each piece is handmade and can cost anywhere from US$10 to thousands of dollars. Tablecloths alone start at around US$300, or US$1,000 and up for custommade ones.

Women of considerable means who'd like a one-of-a-kind dress or jacket can meet with Helèné and brainstorm a colorful creation. Simple shifts start at about US$400. Producing the final article can take weeks and the boutique would like to do at least one fitting, but these can be created with extra material and shipped to the purchaser for final adjustments back home if time is short. Those on a more modest budget can pick up one of her butterfly, hibiscus, or hummingbird patches, starting at around US$10, and later pin or sew them onto an article of clothing, or even use them as drink coasters. The patches come in attractive wrapping and make nice little gifts.

A few items are on display, as are some jewelry, hats, and other accessories made by other designers. If you visit, peek in the back to see the dozen Guna sewers at work.

Mall, sometimes also called Los Pueblos II, next to the Gran Terminal de Transportes, the main bus terminal, which is near the domestic airport in Albrook. It's the favorite of many locals.

A newer ritzy shopping center is **Metro Mall,** about halfway between downtown and the international airport on Vía Tocumen, the old road (not the highway) to the airport. However, it's too far from town to be of much interest to visitors. Other upscale shopping destinations include the **Bal Harbour** mini-mall (mainly for food, especially kosher food) in the Punta Paitilla area, the designer-name shops along **Calle 53 in Marbella** (especially in the **World Trade Center**), and the tony jewelry stores and galleries on **Avenida 2 Sur/Samuel Lewis** in Obarrio. More bargain-oriented stores are on **Vía España** and in the malls and strip malls of the **El Dorado** neighborhood, though both places have higher-end shops as well.

ART GALLERIES

Panama's best high-end art gallery is **Imagen** (Calle 50 and Calle 77, tel. 226-8989, 9 A.M.–1 P.M. and 2–6 P.M. Mon.–Sat.). It's in a lovely old building, and the staff are gracious. It's small, but it's a good place to go just to get a sense of what's happening in the local art scene. **Habitante** (Calle Uruguay, tel. 264-6470, 9 A.M.–6 P.M. Mon.–Sat.), in the Calle Uruguay nightlife area, is also small, but less interesting, though it's certainly more central. **Mateo Sariel** (Vía Porras and Calle 66 Este, tel. 270-2404, 9 A.M.–6 P.M. Mon.–Fri.), though also well known, often feels more like a framing shop than an art gallery, though those willing to rummage around the piles of paintings sometimes unearth a find.

The hippest of the new art galleries sprouting up in Casco Viejo is the **Diablo Rosso café/art gallery** (#11, Avenida A and Calle 7, tel. 228-4833 or 228-4837, www.diablorosso.com, 11 A.M.–8:30 P.M., Tues.–Sat.). It frequently hosts after-hours art shows and events.

BOOKSTORES

Panama City is not a great town for readers, but the bookstore selections have gotten somewhat better in recent years. Don't expect bargains, though—shipping heavy books to Panama is expensive, and that's reflected in the prices. Both the Gran Morrison department store and the Farmacia Arrocha drugstore chains carry books and magazines. Offerings are hit-or-miss, though occasionally a rare find surfaces. The Gran Morrison on Vía España is particularly promising.

Librería Argosy (Vía Argentina near Vía España, tel. 223-5344, 10 A.M.–6 P.M. Mon.–Sat.), run by a friendly Greek émigré named Gerasimos (Gerry) Kanelopulos, has been a Panama City institution for more than three decades. It's a small, crowded place. Be sure to dig below the piles—a lot of books are buried under each other. The shop carries a substantial collection of works about Panama or written by Panamanian authors. Note Gerry's extensive collection of autographed photos: Pride of place belongs to Dame Margot Fonteyn, who spent her twilight years in Panama.

There are several outlets of **El Hombre de la Mancha** (www.hombredelamancha.com), a local bookstore/café chain, mostly in shopping malls. They typically have a small English-language book selection with a few best sellers and a lot of bulk discount books, as well as a reasonable selection of Spanish-language books by Panamanian authors. The branch near the Country Inns and Suites in El Dorado (Central Comercial Camino de Cruces, tel. 360-2063, 10 A.M.–10 P.M. Mon.–Sat., 11 A.M.–8 P.M. Sun.) has the best selection, at least in Spanish, but it's also the least conveniently located for most tourists. There are branches in the Multiplaza Pacific, Multicentro, Metro, Albrook shopping malls, and the domestic airport at Albrook.

Exedra Books (Vía España and Vía Brasil, tel. 264-4252, www.exedrabooks.com, noon–7 P.M. Mon.–Sat.) is modeled after U.S. chains such as Borders, minus the books. For such a large, attractive store, most of its offerings are odd and very limited. The English-language books in particular seem to consist of by-the-pound leftovers. It does have a decent selection of Spanish-language fiction, though, and it seems to be making a genuine effort to become a real bookstore. It also carries some used books at better prices. Upstairs there's an Internet café that actually has a café. It's also a ticket outlet for local concerts and other events. Literary talks, in Spanish, are given on Monday night at 7 P.M.

CRAFT SHOPS AND BOUTIQUES

The jewelry store **Reprosa** (Avenida 2 Sur/ Samuel Lewis and Calle 54 Este, tel. 271-0033, www.reprosa.com, 9 A.M.–6 P.M. daily) is a Panama institution. It's a great place to go for unique presents or souvenirs. There's a second Reprosa store (9 A.M.–5 P.M. daily) in Casco Viejo. Reprosa is most famous for its reproductions of gold and silver *huacas,* figures recovered from pre-Columbian graves. The figures are created by using molds made through the so-called "lost wax" process, which creates exact replicas, including the imperfections in the original. This process is virtually the same as that used to produce the ancient original pieces.

Prices at Reprosa are very reasonable—some pieces start at less than US$10, though the cost goes straight up from there depending on the purity of the gold or silver. Pieces include replicas of some of the finest and oldest *huacas* in the collection of Panama's anthropology museum. The store carries other jewelry as well, including replicas of pieces of eight and the pearl-encrusted brooches known as *mosquetas,* the latter traditionally worn with the *pollera*. Reprosa offers tours of its factory near Panamá La Vieja; email tours@reprosa.com for details.

Casa de los Manteles (Avenida de los Mártires near Calle J, tel. 262-0822, 9 A.M.–6 P.M. Mon.–Sat.), is known for its lovely embroidered tablecloths, napkins, and other linens. It also carries good-quality *guayabera* (the semiformal traditional Latin American shirt). The store has a parking lot behind the building.

There is a **handicrafts market** in Plaza Cinco de Mayo, behind the anthropology museum, that offers hats, *mola* blouses, hammocks, sandals, and the like. Hats are especially well represented. Most stalls open by 9 A.M. daily and stay open until sundown. If you have trouble finding this market, ask for the *artesanía* near Plaza Cinco de Mayo. Better handicrafts markets are in Balboa, in the old Canal Zone.

ELECTRONICS AND PHOTO SUPPLIES

Panafoto (Calle 50 and Calle 49A Este, tel. 263-3000, www.panafoto.com, 9 A.M.–7:30 P.M. Mon.–Sat., noon–6 P.M. Sun.) is a modern, glass-enclosed consumer electronics store and the first stop for camera buffs. There's an espresso bar upstairs.

TAILORED SUITS

La Fortuna (Vía España at Calle 55 Este near Vía Argentina, tel. 302-7890 or 263-6434, 9 A.M.–6 P.M. Mon.–Sat.) is Panama's best-known destination for tailored men's suits. It's been around since 1925 and has dressed ambassadors and presidents. A custom-made suit or tuxedo in high-quality imported fabric can be had for around US$500; knock US$100–200 off that estimate for less-expensive material. One of the nifty things about having a suit made here is that the tailors sew a panel inside the suit with the buyer's name and the statement that it was made *exclusivo* for him. If you don't care for any of their styles, you can bring in a photo of what you'd like and they'll create it for you. They carry a range of fabric from famous European and North American designers.

This is the tailor of choice for many high-ranking politicians, and it's said owner José Abadí was one of the inspirations for Le Carré's book *The Tailor of Panama*, about a tailor to powerful Panamanian officials who is forced by a British agent to spy on his customers.

Visitors should place an order at the start of their travels, as the process requires two fittings, and the shop normally needs at least 10 days to make a suit (more during peak seasons, such as before the independence holidays in November). Those pressed for time can sometimes have a suit made in 24 hours, but don't expect a perfect fit.

Sports and Recreation

Panama City is really not the best spot for either spectator or participant sports. Generally only the most expensive hotels have tennis courts, pools big enough to swim laps in, or decent gyms. Most sports clubs are upscale places open to members and their guests.

The best options for those interested in golf are Summit Golf, Hotel and Spa in the former Canal Zone or, for those going to the Pacific beaches, the course at the Coronado Hotel and Resort or the newer El Mantaraya Golf Club at the Royal Decameron Resort. They are well-maintained, championship courses with good facilities.

BASEBALL

Panama produces a disproportionate number of U.S. Major League baseball players for its size. *Fútbol* (soccer) is beginning to nudge *beisbol* from its pedestal as the country's favorite team sport, but it is still Panama's national pastime, has a passionate following, and produces some of the best players in the world.

The national baseball stadium **Estadio Nacional Rod Carew** (Corredor Norte, Camino de la Amistad, and Transístmica in Cerro Patacón on the northwest outskirts of the city, tel. 230-4255, www.estadionacional.com.pa or www.fedebeis.com, US$4), named after native son and Hall of Famer Rod Carew, is easy to get to. The stadium seats 26,000, but during a routine game between provincial teams, it may be nearly empty, making it easy to get close to the action and possibly see a major-leaguer in the making. Baseball is played only during Panama's summer (the dry season), though in season the stadium may host several games a week. The baseball season ends in May. Big concerts featuring international stars are sometimes held at the stadium.

HORSE-RACING

Panama has a well-established horse-racing industry. The national racetrack, **Hipódromo Presidente Remón** (tel. 217-6060, www.hipodromo.com, races Thurs., Sat., Sun., and holidays) is on the outskirts of the city about eight kilometers east of Punta Paitilla in the Juan Díaz area, on the way to the international airport. The quickest way to get there is via the Corredor Sur. It's also accessible from Vía España, which becomes Vía José Agustín Arango east of the city. The racecourse is just past the 45,000-seat national *fútbol* stadium, Estadio Rommel Fernández.

SNORKELING AND DIVING

Scubapanama (Avenida 6C Norte, tel. 261-3841 or 261-4064, www.scubapanama.com), Panama's largest dive operator, also rents and sells snorkeling and diving gear. Those who plan to do a fair amount of snorkeling should know that most of the equipment available on Panama's beaches and islands is mediocre at best. This is a decent place to buy some if you didn't bring your own.

Accommodations

Panama City offers good lodging options for most budgets. Finding an available room has gotten harder and harder in the last several years, but the city's hotel supply has finally caught up with the boom in tourism and business.

Advance reservations are a good idea, especially for midrange and luxury hotels. Try to book as far ahead of time as possible if visiting during holidays and the dry season. Panama City hotels tend to be terrible about answering email and responding to reservation-request forms on their websites. This is especially true of the lower-end lodgings. If you don't hear back in a few days, your best bet is to call.

WHAT TO EXPECT

Hotels often charge the same for one or two guests. Those traveling solo can sometimes save money by buddying up with fellow travelers, though often hotels charge more for two beds in a room. A third or fourth guest in a room is typically just a nominal additional charge, so small groups can often find deals even at the higher end of the scale. The midrange and high-end hotels often offer corporate rates and promotional deals that can be significantly cheaper than their standard rates. It never hurts to ask for the discount, which you can often get without so much as a business card. All prices listed include Panama's 10-percent room tax.

Hostels

Panama City is seeing a surge in hostels, and these tend to be the safest of the bare-bones accommodations. The best can be surprisingly pleasant, but dispel any notion of European- or even American-style youth hostels: Panama City hostels tend to be grungy, makeshift affairs installed in converted apartments. Many hostels are now serving as de facto travel agencies, helping guests with area tours and travel

throughout Panama and to Colombia and Costa Rica. Wireless access and use of Internet-enabled computers, luggage storage, and a modest, do-it-yourself breakfast are standard free extras at the city's hostels. Some hostels have air-conditioning, at least at night. They also increasingly have private rooms that can be pretty decent, especially for the price; these are popular and tend to fill up fast.

Panama City hostels are often on the move. Real estate is so expensive in the city that hostels often take up residence in an old apartment building that's waiting to be bought up, torn down, and replaced with a skyscraper. When that happens, the hostel owner packs up and moves on to the next building. Make sure you know where your hostel really is before you show up!

US$10-25

At the low end of the scale, every US$10 extra can mean dramatically better digs. For US$13, don't expect much more than a bare hostel room with a fan, though often even these places offer air-conditioning for a couple of bucks more.

US$25-50

Air-conditioning is universally available once the price gets up to around US$40–50 s/d per night; hot water kicks in at less than that. It's getting harder to find clean, safe, and comfortable rooms at this price, but it's still possible.

US$50-100

For US$60 s/d, it's possible to find some pleasant, clean hotels with reliable air-conditioning, hot-water bathrooms, and sometimes wireless Internet and satellite TV. Three-star hotel territory starts at around US$100 s/d. At that price, it's possible to find attractive rooms with good beds and amenities such as satellite TV, in-room telephones, free wireless Internet, in-room safes, a decent restaurant/bar, a small swimming pool (often on the rooftop), and so on. Some of these places are in high demand and should be booked several days or even weeks in advance if possible.

US$100-150

Many of the options for US$100–150 a night are so-called *aparthotels,* which offer furnished, usually large studio and one-bedroom apartments with a full kitchen and utensils, telephone, and washer and dryer either in the apartment or in a laundry facility on the premises. These also sometimes have a business center and small pool. They typically offer price breaks for long stays. These have proved popular and prices have climbed accordingly, but they still get booked solid with long-term visitors doing business in or moving to Panama.

Over US$150

Rack rates for luxury hotels are US$200–300 a night per couple. Guests may find these rates a good-value splurge at the very best places and excessive at others. Prices can vary wildly from day to day, and deals are often available. Booking far enough in advance—a good idea since these places are in great demand—can knock about US$100 off the rack rate. Luxury hotels universally offer high-speed wired or wireless Internet, but expect to pay at least US$15 a day for the privilege.

Panama City has begun to introduce a couple of closely related kinds of hotels: high-end apartment-style suites and condo hotels. The first are basically *aparthotels* for the luxury market. The second are time-share–style condos that can be rented out as hotel rooms when the owner is out of town.

CASCO VIEJO

A couple of hostels, a few lovely boutique hotels, and luxury apartments call Casco Viejo home. Apartments in Casco Viejo can often be rented for short periods, including by the night. The websites www.loscuatrotulipanes.com and www.arcoproperties.com are good places to start looking.

US$10-25

◖ **Luna's Castle** (Calle 9 Este and Avenida Eloy Alfaro, tel. 262-1540, www.lunascastle-hostel.com, US$13 pp in dorms, US$15 pp in a/c dorms, US$30 s/d in private rooms, breakfast included) opened in 2008 and has quickly become the Hilton of Panama's hostels. It's owned by the same guys who made Mondo Taitu (now under new ownership) and Hostel Heike in Bocas popular. Luna's Castle is in a lovely three-story colonial house with high ceilings and ornate balconies. French doors on the 2nd and 3rd floor open onto million-dollar views of Casco Viejo, Panama Bay, and the downtown skyline. Original fixtures include tile floors and a handsome wooden staircase.

On the ground floor is Relic Bar, a Casco Viejo hot spot that is open to all. For security in the evening, only hostel guests with wristbands are allowed upstairs into the hostel itself. The wristbands also entitle guests to discounts at some area restaurants.

The hostel has both dorms and private rooms. One dorm has four beds. The rest have 6–12 beds. All are mixed sex. Dorm rooms 7, 10, and 12 have ocean views. Number 10 is the most spacious. There are seven private rooms. A movie theater downstairs shows current releases to hostel guests, who can recline on three tiers of mattresses that serve as stadium-style seats. There's a lounge area, table tennis, and computers with free Internet access, as well as free wireless access for those with their own electronics. The included breakfast consists of (make-your-own) pancakes, bananas, coffee, and tea. The hostel also occasionally hosts art exhibitions and other cultural events.

Luna's Castle has a binder that contains up-to-date information for budget travelers on where to go and how to get around in Panama City and other backpacker destinations. The hostel also has maps of Casco Viejo and the rest of Panama City. They can help make arrangements for stays in other parts of Panama, including land transits to Guna Yala. Guests have access to lockers, free luggage storage, a book exchange, guitars, games, a communal kitchen, local and international calling, taxi shuttles to the international airport, a bar, parking, tour bookings, etc.

This is a top choice for budget travelers who want to spend time exploring Casco Viejo, meet other travelers, and get help with onward travel. On the other hand, it's a big, self-contained backpacker enclave, and it's not terribly convenient to other parts of the city. Travelers who want to meet locals and see other parts of the city on the cheap may find it easier to stay in more centrally located places such as Mamallena, La Jungla, or Pensión Las Torres.

This place is popular, so try to make reservations early. Luna's Castle only takes reservations two weeks in advance, but you can reserve through www.hostelworld.com earlier than that. The hostel does not take reservations for private rooms, the air-conditioned dorms, or for those arriving after 8 P.M.

Opened in 2005, **Hospedaje Casco Viejo** (Calle 8 and Avenida A, tel. 211-2027, www.hospedajecascoviejo.com, dorm beds US$11 pp, US$22 s/d with shared bath, US$25 s/d with private bath) offers 16 rooms in an old three-story house behind the Iglesia de San José (Church of the Golden Altar). All the rooms have ceiling fans only. None of the bathrooms has hot water. Some of the bedrooms have balconies. There's a tiny interior patio and a TV room for hanging out, a shared kitchen, a gated entrance with 24-hour reception, free wireless Internet, and lockers. This place could be great, but it tends toward the grungy side. In any case, the location can't be beat.

US$50-100

Magnolia Inn (Calle 8 and Calle Boquete,

tel. 202-0872, cell 6073-2773 or 6711-7108, U.S. tel. 786/375-9633, www.magnoliapanama.com, dorm beds US$16.50, private rooms start at US$88 s/d/t) opened in January 2012 offering "luxury" dorm beds and the most economical upscale rooms in Casco Viejo. It's a terrific addition to the neighborhood. The inn is the creation of a friendly gringo couple, Cherie and Reggie, and their teenage kids. They clearly love this place, which is housed in a gorgeous, listed house built circa 1900 and surprisingly intact, with marble floors, high ceilings, and period features such as an art deco staircase. The dorms are "luxurious" in that they have soft but thick mattresses, bedside plugs to charge one's electronics, air-conditioning, steps leading to the top bunks, lockers, and no more than 4–6 beds per room. They are certainly among the more civilized hostel accommodations in the country. The dorm rooms share clean toilets and hot-water showers. There's also a pleasant shared kitchen and lounge. There's a ballroom upstairs with a view of the cathedral towers. The inn sometimes offers ballroom dance classes there.

The inn has six private rooms with air-conditioning, TV, and private baths. These start at US$88 for rooms that sleep up to three people. The three nicest and biggest rooms are on the top floor and go for US$148.50 each. Room 3C has views of the cathedral, the rooftops of Casco Viejo, and the ocean.

Over US$150

A truly boutique hotel, **Canal House** (Avenida A and Calle 5 Oeste, tel. 228-1907 or 228-8683, toll-free U.S./Canada tel. 888/593-5023, www.canalhousepanama.com, starts at US$210 s/d including breakfast) offers some of the handsomest accommodations in the country. It is owned by the same company behind Las Clementinas. A four-story, 4,000-square-foot house built in 1893 and beautifully restored in 2005, it has just two suites and one guest room. The opulent furnishings manage to be both contemporary and in keeping with the colonial feel of the building. As its name suggests, the Canal House pays homage to the Panama Canal, down to the books in the library and the photos on the walls.

The master suite is the Miraflores (US$340), which features a huge bedroom with a king-size bed and walk-in closet, a sitting/dining area, a wraparound balcony, and a spiral staircase that leads to a loft study with a daybed, desk, and library. The Gatun Suite (US$270), on the top floor, has a king-size bed and a separate sitting room. The Pedro Miguel Room (US$210) is dramatically smaller, little bigger than its queen-size bed, but guests have access to the same common areas and services as other guests.

All three accommodations feature high-gloss hardwood floors, plasma-screen TVs with satellite TV, free wireless Internet, use of an iPad, and French doors that open onto wrought-iron balconies with fascinating views of the surrounding neighborhood. (Be sure to check out the view from the roof.) Management prides itself on personalized, attentive service, and it offers many extras for an additional fee, ranging from airport transfers and tours to secretarial services. This place books up well in advance, especially the least-expensive room (Pedro Miguel).

Casa de Horno (Avenida B and Calle 8, tel. 212-0052, cell 6561-3078, www.casadelhorno. net, starts at US$275 s/d, including breakfast) offers eight modern, spacious rooms in a historic, compact building. The designers have done an admirable job of striking a balance between preserving the old character of the place and fitting it with contemporary comforts. The original stone walls are exposed throughout, but the rooms have luxury features such as a modern kitchen with minibar and wine cooler, a sitting area, and 40-inch flat-screen TVs. All the rooms have balconies, and some look out of the cathedral. However, the rooms are not high enough up to have much of a view. The rooms

and common areas are filled with the rather romantic Portobelo portraits of Sandra Eleta, one of Panama's best-known photographers.

⬛**Las Clementinas** (Calle 11 and Avenida B, tel. 228-7613, http://lasclementinas.com, US$308–341 s/d) is another beautiful boutique hotel, though this one is on the very edge of what is normally considered Casco Viejo. It borders the considerably less charming part of the Santa Ana district. It is owned by the same company behind the Canal House. Housed in a 1930s-era apartment building, it features six large suites decorated in elegantly simple good taste. Each suite has somewhat different furnishings and art, but all have handsome hardwood floors and fully equipped kitchens. Like the Canal House, Las Clementinas offers many services for an extra fee.

This place is extremely popular and much-loved, so make bookings as far in advance as possible. Attached to the hotel is an attractive café (tel. 228-7617, 7 A.M.–11 P.M. Tues.–Sat., 7 A.M.–3 P.M. Sun.) that offers a two-course lunch for US$8.50.

CALIDONIA, LA EXPOSICIÓN, AND SANTA ANA

Most of the budget hotels are in and around the Calidonia/La Exposición district. This is a busy, older neighborhood near Panama Bay, with a high concentration of cheaper hotels, most of them in a 10-block area between Avenida Perú and Avenida Cuba.

Though a somewhat poor neighborhood, Calidonia is a bustling area and travelers generally feel safe enough here. Adventurous types can try one of the rock-bottom pensions along the pedestrian section of Avenida Central, but these are known hangouts for prostitutes and their customers and are not recommended. That area is busy day and night, which can add a sense of safety but makes for a noisy night's sleep. It's unquestionably a colorful place to stay, though.

In 2012, roadwork and the building of the

first phase of the new metro system were turning a significant chunk of Calidonia into a construction zone. Local businesses and residents were working around the chaos, but some of the places listed below may be affected by noise during your stay.

Some of the cheaper options in this neighborhood, especially those with the word "pension" or *"residencial"* in their names, are often used by local couples needing, shall we say, a little quality alone time. This isn't necessarily as tawdry as it sounds. While some twosomes are engaging in a financial transaction or adulterous liaison, others simply live in small houses with large families and never get any privacy at home.

US$10-25

The well-established **C Mamallena** (Casa 7-62, Calle 38 Oeste just off Avenida Central, cell 6676-6163, mamallenapa@yahoo.com, www.mamallena.com, starts at US$13 pp, a/c 9 P.M.–8 A.M.) has moved to a cool old, two-story house with a terrace. It's in a relatively quiet residential area of Calidonia and has good security. The hostel, which is partnered with the newer, instantly popular hostel of the same name in Boquete, is better-looking than most: The ceilings are high, the tile floors are lovely, and there's art on the walls. Movies are shown on a big-screen TV in the front living area. Facilities include two 8-bed dorms and one 12-bed dorm (the 12-bedder is actually less crowded). Stays include the ubiquitous pancake breakfast. There are also a dozen small private rooms with shared bathrooms (US$33 s/d) that are dark and a bit cell-like but basically okay, with semi-orthopedic mattresses, in a separate building set in a "rock garden" (i.e., gravel backyard), which also has attractive, custom-made wooden picnic tables and hammocks and serves as a common area for the hostel. The private rooms are popular and fill up fast. The hostel also offers good-value tours through its own travel agency, **Panama Travel Unlimited**

(tel. 395-5014, info@panamatravelunlimited, www.panamatravelunlimited.com). These include Panama City tours (US$25/pp) and day trips to Caribbean-side attractions (US$40/pp for either Portobelo and Isla Grande or Gatún Locks and Fuerte San Lorenzo). The agency also can arrange chartered sailboat cruises around Guna Yala for US$125–150 per person. There's a book exchange and shared kitchen. Airport transfers are available for US$30 per person for up to four people; the return trip to the airport is US$5 less.

It's a miracle the neighborhood institution that is **Pensión Las Torres** (Calle 36 and Calle Perú, tel. 225-0172, starts at US$15 s/d) still exists. How much longer can it possible endure? It consists of 24 rooms in a converted house, built in 1931, that retains its original Spanish tile and other old touches that give the place character and an almost Moroccan air. Prices have not gone up here in several years. A tiny fan-cooled room with shared bathroom goes for US$15 s/d. Large rooms with air-conditioning, satellite TV, and private hot-water bathroom are also available starting at US$18 s/d. Rooms are spartan but funky, and the beds are decent. If you think of it as a hostel that has only private rooms, you'll probably be pleasantly surprised. The staff are very friendly. This is a good budget place away from the normal tourist haunts. However, the rooms with private baths don't have bathroom doors, which can be awkward if you're sharing a room. The entrance to Pensión Las Torres is a bit hard to find, as it's hidden behind bushes.

The five-story **Hotel Ideal** (Calle 17 near Calle I, tel. 262-2400, $22–24 s/d) is one of the last remnants of a certain strain of wackiness that used to flourish in Panama City. The hotel remains a popular, if ramshackle, budget-lodging option. The ceiling and walls of the lobby are covered with mirrored discs. The rooms are old and a bit shabby (ask to see several), but they have good air-conditioning, private bathrooms with hot water, and TVs. Lockers in the lobby are US$0.25. There's a basic cafeteria and, next door, a self-service launderette (US$0.50–US$1 wash, US$1–1.50 dry, 7:30 A.M.–7:30 P.M. daily). The hotel is right across the street from a large public clinic, Policlínica President Remón, which contains a pharmacy (7 A.M.–7 P.M. Mon.–Fri.).

Hotel Andino (Calle 35 Este between Avenida Perú and Vía España, tel. 225-1162 or 225-0702, info@hotelandino.net, www.hotelandino.net, US$54 s, US$60.50 d) has 43 large, spartan air-conditioned rooms with satellite TV and wireless Internet access. The hotel was recently renovated and is now much more cheerful but twice as expensive as it was a couple of years ago. It's tucked away on a quiet street close to the bustle around Parque Belisario Porras. There's a bar/restaurant on the premises.

US$25-50

The three-story **Residencial Los Arcos** (Avenida 3 Sur and Calle 44 Este, tel. 225-0569, 225-0570, or 225-0571, US$44 s/d, a/c) offers simple but clean and tasteful modern rooms in a quiet neighborhood close to the action. Rooms can also be rented by the hour, but the place does not have a tawdry atmosphere.

The six-story **Hotel San Remo** (Calle 31 Este near Avenida Perú, tel. 227-0958 or 227-2840, www.hotelsanremopanama.com, US$36 s/d, a/c), across the street from Plaza Víctor Julio Gutiérrez (the national lottery plaza), opened in early 2003 and offers 60 simple but clean, modern rooms with decent beds and free wireless Internet access. The hotel also has a restaurant/bar, secure parking, and Internet and laundry service. This place is a good value, even if some of the rooms are quite small and look out on brick walls.

Hotel Centroamericano (Avenida Ecuador between Avenida Cuba and Avenida Perú, tel. 227-4555, www.hotelcentroamericano.com, US$55 s/d, a/c) was renovated in 2011. Its 61

rooms are much spruced up, if still quite simple. All rooms have satellite TV, wireless Internet, and in-room safes. They're proud here, for some reason, of having ice machines on every floor.

The only real problem with the **Hotel Arenteiro** (Calle 30 Este between Avenida Cuba and Avenida Perú, tel. 227-5883 or 225-3175, www.hotelarenteiropanama.com, US$30 s/d, a/c) is that it's five stories high but has no elevator. If you have a lot of luggage, ask for a lower floor. It offers 58 small, minimalist rooms with thin mattresses. It may remind you of a European pension. All rooms have satellite TV and phones. There's a restaurant/bar and a protected parking lot. Prices here have actually dropped dramatically recently, which may have something to do with the metro station being dug just a block away.

The **Hotel Acapulco** (Calle 30 Este between Avenida Cuba and Avenida Perú, tel. 225-3832, US$38.50 s/d, including breakfast and a/c) is an older but well-maintained six-story place with 55 clean, pleasant rooms, efficiently run by a proud, friendly staff. The beds are on the soft side but acceptable. All rooms have satellite TV and some have little balconies. There's a 24-hour restaurant. This is a decent option in its price range.

Euro Hotel (Vía España next to Hotel Bella Vista, tel. 263-0802 or 263-0927, info@eurohotelpanama.com, http://eurohotelpanama.com, US$55 s/d), the successor to the old Hotel Europa, opened at the end of 2004. It was spruced up by a renovation but is not terribly different-looking from its older self. It offers 103 rooms, a small pool, a bar, and a roomy cafeteria. Rooms are simple, plain, and dark but otherwise perfectly okay. The furnishings are older but in good shape, and the beds are firm. Don't waste money on the suites, which are just connecting rooms featuring bedrooms barely big enough to contain the bed.

The 60-room, five-story █**Hotel California** (Vía España and Calle 43, tel. 263-7736, hotelcalifornia@cwpanama.net, www.hotelcaliforniapanama.net, starts at US$44 s, US$49.50 d, a/c) has been known for many years as a place to get a decent room at a great price. Beds are somewhat hard, but rooms are nicely maintained, clean, and cheerful and have hot-water bathrooms, free wireless Internet access, safes, telephones, and satellite TV. Some have a bay view partly obstructed by high-rises. Rooms are somewhat small. The hotel is on loud, crowded Vía España and is not conveniently close to much, at least for pedestrians. Try to get a room at the back of the building, away from the road. There's a small gym and whirlpool tub on the roof. There's also laundry service and a bar/restaurant.

US$50-100

Hotel Roma Plaza (Calle 33 Este and Avenida 3 Sur, tel. 227-3844, reservas@hotelromaplaza.net, www.hotelromaplaza.net, US$71.50 s/d including breakfast) would be considered a decent two- or (on a good day) three-star hotel, if Panama used such ratings. Its rooms are light and airy and have dressing tables, satellite TV, and minibars. Some of the rooms smell of smoke, and a few are windowless; try to arrive early enough so you can switch rooms if you don't like the one you're shown. There's a pleasant 24-hour cafeteria, restaurant, bar, safe-deposit boxes, an attractive rooftop pool with a good view, a small gym, and free wireless Internet access. This place fills up. The hotel offers airport transfers for US$25 for two people, which is a few dollars less than the average taxi fare.

Hotel Costa Inn (Avenida Perú and Calle 39 Este, tel. 227-1522, costainn@cwpanama.net, www.hotelcostainn.com, US$66 s, US$77 d, including airport pickup and breakfast, a/c) is a seven-story hotel offering 87 rooms, a 24-hour bar/restaurant, a parking lot, room service, and a small rooftop pool with a good view of the city and the Bay of Panama. It was remodeled a few years back, and the rooms are now cheerful, with good beds and modern furnishings, satellite TV, and free wireless Internet. This place often has promotional deals, and the standard rates have not gone up in two years. It's popular with Latin American businesspeople. Free airport pickup at either the international or domestic airport is included. The hotel also runs a free shuttle that drops guests off at the airport (though only a couple of times a day, which may or may not coincide with your flight times). Both are unusual pluses for a hotel in this category. More recently the hotel has added a free shuttle service between the hotel and both the Albrook Mall and Multiplaza Pacific Mall.

The **Stanford Hotel** (off Plaza Cinco de Mayo, tel. 262-4933 or 262-4948, www.hotelstanfordpanama.com, US$47 s, US$62 d, including breakfast) now occupies what for many, many years had been the Hotel Internacional. It's been renovated and, though still a rather spartan place, it's spruced up and more comfortable than it's been in years. The beds are cheap but firm, and the rooms are fairly clean except for the smudged walls, which could use a lick of paint. Service is a bit disorganized, but friendly. The hotel's main appeal is its location right by Plaza Cinco de Mayo, at the entrance to the pedestrian section of Avenida Central, a plus for guests who want to be in the thick of an older, commerce-driven section of Panama City and away from the more touristy areas. There's a restaurant, a rooftop terrace, Internet-enabled computers in the lobby, and a neighboring casino.

US$100-150

Eco Inn Avila (Avenida Perú between Calle 36 Este and Calle 37 Este, tel. 394-1155 or 394-1160, www.ecoinnhotels.com, US$110 s/d, including buffet breakfast) was a good deal when it opened a couple of years back, but it has since been acquired by a small Latin American chain and prices have climbed steeply. It's now overpriced, especially given its scruffy neighborhood on the edge of Calidonia, close to

© WILLIAM FRIAR

A massive bust of Albert Einstein is a handy landmark in El Cangrejo.

Bella Vista, and a couple of blocks down from Hospital Nacional. Still, it's a clean, friendly, modern place in a newish six-story building. It's worth considering if special deals are being offered. Rooms are simple but attractive, with flat-screen TVs, in-room safes, and free wireless Internet access. There's basement parking and a restaurant (7:30 A.M.–10 P.M. daily).

EL CANGREJO AND VICINITY

Most of the midrange hotels, including nearly all the *aparthotels,* are in or around El Cangrejo, in the center of Panama City. They are mainly clustered together on busy Avenida Eusebio A. Morales/2 Norte or the rather quieter Calle D. Higher-end hotels are also beginning to appear.

US$10-25

La Jungla Hostel (Calle 49 Oeste between Vía Argentina and Vía Veneto, tel. 214-8069 www.hostallajungla.com, starts at $13 pp) is one of the city's more appealing hostels, not to

mention one of the cleanest. Run by the same folks who have Hostal Nomba in Boquete, it occupies the top two floors of a six-story apartment building in a relatively quiet residential section of El Cangrejo, three buildings up from Hotel Las Huacas (which is more familiar to taxi drivers). It sleeps up to 56 people in 6–10 person mixed-sex dorms with thin mattresses and four private rooms. Beds are US$13 in a fan-cooled room, US$3 more for air-conditioning. Women who'd like a single-sex dorm pay US$14. Private rooms start at US$32 s and US$43 d for a decent bedroom with shared bath; they cost a bit more with air-conditioning. Room 10, a curved room with lots of windows, is particularly popular. The nicest dorms and private rooms are downstairs, in the more chic part of the hostel. Baggage storage and towel rental are available for a buck a day. There's free wireless Internet access. The hostel also has snorkel equipment to rent and an in-house washer/dryer. There's a 10 percent discount for those who do local volunteer work (which the hostel can arrange). This is a laid-back, friendly place. There's a security gate, closed-circuit video cameras, 24-hour staffing, a shared kitchen, and a large terrace to hang out on. La Jungla may not be well-marked. If there's no sign, check the labels on the door buzzer.

US$50-100

Hotel Marbella (Calle D near Avenida Eusebio A. Morales, tel. 263-2220, www.hmarbella. com, US$88 s/d), near the Hotel Granada, is generally considered one of the better economy hotels. It's a clean, modern, five-story place on a pleasant residential street but close to a lot of urban action. The rooms are dark and austere, and most look out on blank walls. There's a restaurant on-site.

Hotel Las Huacas (Calle 49 Oeste, about halfway between Vía Veneto and Vía Argentina, tel. 213-2222, www.lashuacashotel.com, starts at US$80 s/d) is a pleasant, reasonably priced surprise tucked away on the backstreets of El Cangrejo. A renovation in mid-2010 replaced most of its rather kitschy safari trappings, and its 33 rooms now have a sleek, modern look. The rooms vary in size but all feature a mini-bar, free wireless Internet access, and a safe. Most have a small balcony.

The 53-room, seven-story **Hotel Milan** (Avenida Eusebio A. Morales, tel. 263-6130, hotelmilan@cwpanama.net, US$77 s/d) has the same ownership as the Euro Hotel. Built in 2004, it's nothing fancy and the mattresses are cheap, but it's clean, well maintained, and in a central and reasonably quiet location (at least as of this writing). Standard rooms are fairly large and have in-room safes. Small "economical" rooms are $11 cheaper but cannot be reserved in advance. It has a restaurant/bar.

US$100-150

Aparthotel Torres de Alba (Avenida Eusebio A. Morales, tel. 300-7130, www.torresdealba.

com.pa, starts at US$99 s/d) offers what are essentially small modern apartments, each of which has a bedroom, sitting room, full kitchen, safe, and washer and dryer. The place consists of twin 13-story towers and is mainly aimed at short-term residents. But even tourists who don't need all that stuff might consider staying here; it's simple but quite nice. There's a small gym, a pool that's borderline big enough for lap swimmers, and a parking garage in the building.

Rooms at **Sevilla Suites Apart-Hotel** (Avenida Eusebio A. Morales, tel. 213-0016 or 213-1312, fax 223-6344, www.sevillasuites. com, starts at US$110 s/d, including breakfast), built in 2000, are smaller and darker than those at the Torres de Alba, but the furnishings are quite nice. Accommodations lie closer to the hotel end of the apartment-hotel spectrum, but all the suites have mini-kitchens and wireless Internet access, and some have terraces. There's a small gym and pool. Two of Panama's best restaurants, Restaurante 1985 and Rincón Suizo, are right across the street, and several others are very close.

Coral Suites Apart-Hotel (Calle D, tel. 269-2727, fax 269-0083, coralsuites@coral-suites.net, www.coralsuites.net, US$132 s, US$154 d including continental breakfast) is a modern, nicely maintained place built in 2001. It features 63 rooms with very firm beds, full kitchenettes, satellite TV, in-room safe, ironing board, and a sitting area with table. There's room service, but no restaurant. There's a decent-size rooftop pool without much of a view and a small but reasonably equipped gym. Service is rather disorganized, but this is otherwise a good place.

A more recent addition to the row of business hotels on Calle D is the six-story **◖ Toscana Inn** (Calle D, tel. 265-0018 or 265-0019, www. toscanainnhotel.com, US$121 s/d, including breakfast). The rooms are decorated simply with a rather old-fashioned aesthetic, but the furnishings are new (the hotel opened in late

2009) and each room is equipped with a flat-screen TV, a minifridge, a safe, and firm beds. The corporate rate is about 10 percent cheaper; be sure to ask. Service is friendly and attentive. There's a small restaurant and bar, but no pool.

The three-story **Metro Hotel** (Calle D, tel. 202-5050, ventas@metrohotelpanama.com, www.metrohotelpanama.com, US$75 s/d, including continental breakfast) opened in November 2010 offering simple but clean and cheerful rooms. This place has a modern, colorful decor but is deliberately simple: it's for people who want a decent room in the center of town without paying a fortune. Entry-level rooms are little wider than the full-size bed, but the mattresses are good and the rooms feature a minifridge, safe, free wireless Internet access (guests are also welcome to use computers in the lobby), and tidy bathrooms. Another US$24 buys a room nearly twice as big, with two full beds. The hotel also offers parking and a laundry service.

The 166-room **Hotel Riande Granada** (Avenida Eusebio A. Morales near Vía España, tel.204-4444, granada@riandehotels.com, www.riandehoteles.com, starts at US$148.50 s/d) is one of the stalwarts of the Panama City hotel scene. Known universally as the Hotel Granada, for decades it was a top choice among the midrange hotels. It's needed a renovation for several years, and in 2011 it finally got it. A handsome makeover has resulted in more elegant, modern rooms but has also launched the Granada into a higher price bracket. The hotel has a casino, cafeteria, and swimming pool. It's part of the Riande chain, which also owns the Riande Aeropuerto Hotel and Resort near the international airport.

Over US$150

Victoria Hotel and Suites (Calle D, tel. 395-9000, fax 395-9001,info@victoriahoteland-suites.com, www.victoriahotelandsuites.com, rack rates start at US$193 s/d) is a modern,

nine-story business hotel that opened across the street from the Veneto Hotel and Casino in the autumn of 2010. It features 127 spotless rooms in a modern minimalist style with dark woods, blown-up photos of Casco Viejo, and all the amenities one would expect of a contemporary hotel in this class (32-inch flat-screen TVs, iPod docking stations, and 24-hour room service). The least expensive accommodations are the "deluxe rooms," which are spacious and have comfortable king-size beds. Request a room on a higher floor to get a view of the cityscape and a glimpse of the Pacific behind the towers. There's a tiny rooftop pool and gym, a lobby bar, and a restaurant. Service is friendly.

BELLA VISTA AND MARBELLA

Most of Panama's luxury hotels and a few hostels are found on or south of Vía España in the *area bancaria* (banking area) and the surrounding districts of Bella Vista and Marbella. Streets here are alive 24 hours a day.

Being conveniently close to both Vía España and the Calle Uruguay nightlife area makes this a popular location for travelers, who will definitely feel they're in the throbbing heart of Panama City. However, a great deal of skyscraper construction is going on in the area, increasing noise levels and generally disrupting the neighborhood.

US$50-100

Formerly a hostel, **San Roque Guesthouse** (Calle Ricardo Arias and Avenida 3 Sur, tel. 390-9554 or 390-9592, booking@hotelsanro-quepanama.com, www.hotelsanroquepanama.com, starts at US$60.50 s/d, a/c) has been given a cheerful sprucing up and is now a pleasant if cramped 20-room guesthouse squeezed between tower blocks right next to Restaurante Costa Azul. Prices vary depending on demand, but count on around US$60.50 for a stark, windowless, but clean and modern room with satellite TV and wireless Internet access. Three people can share a room for $75, and up to six people can shoehorn themselves into a room with three beds for US$100. There's a small, enclosed patio with a waterfall, which is a nice touch. Thick walls make this a relatively quiet oasis in the middle of a busy part of town. The owners are expanding, and a terrace restaurant was in the works in 2012. Given its location, this place is a good value, especially for small groups.

US$100-150

The corncob-shaped **Hotel Plaza Paitilla Inn** (Vía Italia in Punta Paitilla, tel. 208-0600, www.plazapaitillainn.com, US$126.50 s/d) was originally a rather upscale Holiday Inn. It's now at the upper end of the midrange hotels, and though it has aged considerably, it was renovated a few years back making rooms look rather spiffy, with new floor-to-ceiling windows that replaced fragile balconies. Many of the 272 rooms have dramatic views of Panama Bay and the city skyline, though skyscraper construction is eating away at these. The hotel has a casino and pool. The rates quoted here are technically promotional, but they're more likely to be on offer than the nominal rack rates. There is not much of interest to travelers within easy walking distance.

C Hotel Ejecutivo (Avenida Aquilino de la Guardia between Calle 51 and Calle 52, tel. 265-8011 or 264-3989, toll-free U.S./Canada tel. 866/876-0915, www.executivehotel-panama.com, US$104.50 s/d) has been a favorite with Latin American businesspeople for more than 30 years, and it's easy to see why. The Ejecutivo (eh-HEC-oo-TEE-voh), known as the Executive in English, is a solid value. (Several kinds of promotional discounts are routinely available—corporate, weekend, booking by Internet—that lower the cost by about 20–25 percent.) Rooms are similar to what you'd expect at a Best Western–style hotel: clean, pleasant enough, but nothing fancy. All come equipped with a refrigerator,

TV, coffeepot, telephone, desk, free Internet access, and balcony.

The hotel is centrally located just down from Vía España, and some rooms have terrific views of the lights of the city and Panama Bay, although these are disappearing thanks to the skyscraper-construction epidemic. The coffee shop offers big portions at low prices, and it's open 24 hours Thursday–Sunday. It's a popular place for breakfast. Guests are allowed to use some of the business center's facilities for free. Amenities include a tiny pool and fitness center.

Over US$150

Hotel Esplendor (Avenida Samuel Lewis and Calle Gerardo Ortega, tel. 209-9600, www.esplendorpanama.com, rack rates start at US$217 s/d) opened in late 2010 with 100 suites spread out over 42 floors. A number of newer towers in Panama City were intended to be condo towers and ended up being converted to hotels at the last minute, and this definitely feels like one of them. It's already showing signs of wear, and the service is less than gracious. On the other hand, suites have good beds, full kitchens, and are decorated in an understated, handsome style with all the usual amenities. They're spacious as well, ranging from 90 square meters for one-bedroom suites (US$217 for up to four people) to 110 for two-bedroom ones. Those on the higher floors have spectacular views of Panama City and the ocean; if you stay here, try for a place as high up as possible. One of the new arrivals on the city's culinary scene, Rausch Restaurant, is in the hotel. There's a small pool.

The 363-room **Hotel Continental and Casino** (Vía España and Calle Ricardo Arias, tel. 263-9999, www.continentalhotel.com, starts at US$130.30 s/d), right on busy Vía España, is another old Panama City landmark, but it's benefited from a tasteful remodeling that transformed it into an upscale business hotel. All the rooms are nice, but some are bigger and more elegantly appointed than others. There are quite a few categories (and prices) to choose from, so if you're not happy with what you booked, ask to see other options. The hotel has a restaurant, cafeteria, small pool, and casino. There are often promotional deals of various kinds here.

The **(C) Panama Marriott Hotel** (Calle 52 at Calle Ricardo Arias, tel. 210-9100, fax 210-9110, www.marriott.com, starts at US$192.50 s/d) is quite an elegant place, with 295 rooms, a fitness center, a spa, and a pleasant, upscale cafeteria, but no formal restaurant. There's also a deli with sandwiches and salads. Ask for a corner room; they're the largest of the standard rooms, which come with the usual business-hotel amenities. Corporate and other special rates are often available. There are six wheelchair-accessible rooms on the lower floors. This place is one of the most popular of the higher-end hotels. It's an attractive place in a central location, with lots of dining, shopping, and entertainment options an easy walk away.

Hotel Lé Meridien (Avenida Balboa and Calle Uruguay, tel. 297-3200, www.starwoodhotels.com, starts at US$196.90 s/d) is a member of the ever-expanding hotel portfolio of local developer Empresas Bern that also includes the InterContinental Miramar next door and the Gamboa Rainforest Resort. This one goes for a hipster-chic ambience reminiscent of a W Hotel, down to the electronic lounge beats pulsating through the shiny lobby. Its 111 rooms feature modern, minimalist furnishings that suggest a nicely appointed frequent-fliers lounge. There's a restaurant, a spa, and a small pool that, at least until the surrounding buildings are completed, may not be the most comfortable spot for female sunbathers, as it draws unwelcome attention from construction workers next door. The location is convenient for those with business in the financial district or who want to explore the Calle Uruguay nightspots, but it's a bit isolated otherwise, especially at night. If you ask reception to call you a cab, you'll get a tourist taxi that is authorized to charge several times the street-taxi rate. It should be easy to catch a cab on Avenida Balboa or up Calle Uruguay if you prefer.

Built in 1951, the **Hotel El Panamá** (Vía España next to Iglesia del Carmen, tel. 215-9000 or 215-9181, www.elpanama.com, starts at US$148.80 s/d) was for many years Panama's premier hotel. It has 330 rooms, including some cabanas by the large, attractive pool. The hotel has changed hands and been renovated repeatedly over the years, but one thing remains constant: The service is lousy. Because of its international name recognition, it still draws a lot of guests, many of whom are on package holidays. For the money, you can do better elsewhere without the potential hassle. However, frequent promotional offers can make the rates tempting, and the hotel is centrally located.

(C) Hotel DeVille (Calle Beatriz M. de Cabal near Calle 50, tel. 206-3100 or 263-0303, www.devillehotel.com.pa, starts at US$231 s/d, including breakfast) is an elegant, rather formal boutique hotel with four types of rooms: deluxe rooms, junior suites, two-bedroom duplex suites, and grand luxury suites. The "deluxe" is a spacious room with the simplest furnishings. It features a marble-tiled bathroom, high ceilings, a high-speed Internet connection, sitting area, and in-room safe. The junior suite is quite opulent, with highly polished dark woods, antique Vietnamese furniture inlaid with mother-of-pearl, a large bathroom with two sinks, a fax machine, and so on. The duplex suite resembles the junior suite but has an upper level with a bedroom and second bath. The grand luxury suite, oddly, isn't quite as luxurious as the duplex suites. Amusingly enough, given the ambivalent feelings toward Teddy Roosevelt in Panama, one of the suites is named for him. Even the fanciest suites, though more luxurious than the average overnight guest would need during a short stay, can be a decent value for families or groups. Art from local galleries is displayed in the lobby.

ACCOMMODATIONS **57**

The ultramodern ◖ **Radisson Decapolis Hotel** (behind the Multicentro Mall on Avenida Balboa, tel. 215-5000, toll-free U.S./Canada tel. 800/395-7046, www.radisson.com, rack rates start at US$163.90 s/d) is inspired by Europe and North America's trend-setting hotels. It's quite an impressive place that will appeal to those who prefer the sleek and streamlined over old-world elegance.

Opened in 2004, it's a 29-story concoction of brushed stainless steel and glass, including a glass elevator that goes to the 14th floor and is worth the ride just for the view. Traditional Panamanian elements—*mola* patterns, devil masks, ships—inform the modern decor. The standard rooms are quite large, sleek, attractive, and minimalist, with photo blowups of Panama's indigenous peoples over the beds and large windows looking out on the view. The view is spectacular on the ocean side, particularly on the higher floors, offering a panorama that encompasses Panama Bay, the towers of Paitilla, and, in some rooms, Casco Viejo.

Each room at the Decapolis has a safe, ironing board, hair dryer, coffeemaker, Internet connection, satellite TV, and English- and Spanish-language newspapers are delivered daily. Other features include the equally striking Fusion restaurant, a martini/sushi lobby bar, a tiny pool on the 4th floor with a hot tub and bar, and several executive floors, including two exclusively for businesswomen. The hotel's spa, Aqua, has some exercise machines and offers a full range of spa services, including facials, sauna, and steam baths. The hotel connects through a walkway with the glitzy Majestic Casino and the Multicentro Mall.

◖ **Hotel Riu Plaza** (Calle 50, tel. 378-9000, US$208 s/d) is my favorite among the latest crop of the high-end hotels. Opened in September 2010, it has 645 rooms spread over 34 floors. Rooms are spacious and well maintained, with bright but elegant decor, comfy beds, and nicely appointed bathrooms.

They remind me very much of the rooms in the Hotel Ciudad de David in, um, the city of David. Rooms look out over either Avenida Balboa or Calle 50. There's an inviting pool area with a decent-size pool and an artificial waterfall, a gym that for a change doesn't seem like an afterthought, an attractive bar/sushi lounge which is a nice spot to hang out in the evenings, a cafeteria, and a fancy Panamanian-fusion restaurant, Tastes. The lobby area is quite dramatic, with high ceilings and ornate furnishings that suggest a cross between a retro-modern train station and a business-class airport lounge. Front desk and concierge staff are prompt and professional.

From the outside, the **Bristol** (Calle Aquilino de la Guardia between Calle 51 and Calle 52, just down from the Hotel Ejecutivo, tel. 264-0000 or 265-7844, www.thebristol.com, rack rates start at US$390 s/d) is a nondescript, salmon-colored building that's easy to overlook, especially now that bigger buildings are going up all around it. Inside, however, the Bristol is a lovely boutique hotel. It's quite a luxurious place. Standard rooms are "deluxe," and they truly are. The furnishings are elegant, with local touches such as *mola* pillows and lamp bases made from Ngöbe-Buglé sandstone figurines. The attached Restaurante Barandas is attractive and one of Panama City's most ambitious. Service can be erratic here.

The **Hotel InterContinental Miramar Panama** (Avenida Balboa, tel. 206-8888, fax 223-4891, www.miramarpanama.com, starts at US$181.50 s/d) is on the middle of Avenida Balboa and has great views of the Pacific and the Panama City skyline. With the building of the Cinta Costera, however, it's no longer on the edge of the bay but rather on a landfill island between these two major traffic arteries. It's a 185-room luxury hotel that's part of the InterContinental chain and comes with the works: two restaurants, a largish pool, a health spa, tennis court, several bars, and so on. It's about due for an upgrade but is still a comfortable place to stay. All rooms have an executive desk, three phones, broadband access, minibar, safe, and other amenities. The best things about the hotel are its views and attractive pool.

The **Marriott Executive Apartments Finisterre** (Avenida 3A Sur and Calle Colombia, tel. 214-9200, www.marriott.com, starts at US$130 s/d for an executive suite) consists of 126 suites in a new tower built in 2010 just off Vía España across from the Iglesia del Carmen. The smallest and least expensive of these is the 600-square-meter executive suite, which features a king or two double beds, a couple of sofa beds, a 32-inch LCD TV, a dining area, and a fully equipped kitchen. The decor is understated and modern. Most of the suites have a view of Cerro Ancón (Ancon Hill). There's a three-story parking garage right in the building, a small fitness center, and a spa. There's a small restaurant and a fairly large pool, both located on lower floors. This is the sort of place affluent Latin American expat families might stay while shopping around for a luxury home.

EAST PANAMA CITY
Over US$150

Sheraton Panama Hotel and Convention Center (Vía Israel and Calle 77 across the street from the Atlapa Convention Center, tel. 305-5100, www.starwoodhotels.com, starts at US$141.90 s/d) has long had the most loyal clientele of the Panama luxury hotels. It's a huge complex with 362 rooms, three restaurants, a shopping gallery, an appealing casino that has expanded in recent years, an athletic club, a pool, a spa, and so on. This is the second-oldest luxury hotel in the city, after Hotel El Panamá, and it's changed hands several times through the years; it used to be called the Caesar Park, and its incarnation as a Sheraton is relatively recent. The hotel is on the eastern outskirts of town, quite a hike from everything but the

Atlapa Convention Center, the ruins of Old Panama, and the international airport. The popular indoor/outdoor grill **Restaurante y Parrillada Jimmy** (Vía Cincuentenario, tel. 224-1096, most items under US$10) is on the far side of the Atlapa Convention Center from the hotel. A counterpart to the plainer Restaurante Jimmy near the Hotel Continental downtown, it serves no-nonsense pastas, Greek dishes, seafood, and sandwiches. It's not worth making a special trip from elsewhere in the city, but it's one of the few options for those staying in this remoter part of town.

Amid great fanfare, controversy, funding crises, and an international incident or two, the **Trump Ocean Club International Hotel and Tower** (Calle Punta Colón, tel. 215-8800, U.S./Canada toll-free tel. 855/225-9640, www. trumphotelcollection.com, starts at US$251.90 s/d) has finally arrived. Sort of. Designed to resemble a gigantic sail—quite reminiscent of the Burj al Arab luxury hotel in Dubai—it was supposed to become a skyline-defining landmark for Panama City.

That might have happened, too, except it was erected in Punta Pacífica, just east of Punta Paitilla. So many other massive towers have already sprouted up all around the Trump building that it's barely visible from most angles. This also means that "rooms with an ocean view" might more accurately be described as "rooms with a view of skyscrapers and slivers of ocean." The rooms are spacious and luxurious, with all kinds of bells and whistles and deep, fluffy duvets on the beds. The hotel also buys into the current trend of putting bathtubs in the bedroom rather than in the, you know, bathroom.

Whether you love it, hate it, or feel a bit of both, it's definitely an impressive edifice. The hotel starts high up in the building, with the hotel's three-story "sky lobby." The public areas are attractive and dramatic, paying homage to Panama with touches like tables made from petrified wood extracted from Lago Gatún,

© WILLIAM FRIAR

The Trump Ocean Club International Hotel and Tower was designed to resemble a gigantic sail.

the bottom of which is filled with trees left standing when forests were flooded to create the artificial lake during the construction of the Panama Canal.

It's entirely possible never to speak a word of Spanish in the tower, as management appears to have cornered the market on employees who speak at least a semblance of fluent English.

Service fluctuates between friendly but slow to confused incompetence.

One of the snazziest things about the place is the large, open pool deck on the 13th floor. It features five swimming pools, including a couple of infinity pools. Other features include a good-size gym and spa and several restaurants.

Food

WHAT TO EXPECT

The restaurants are among the best things about Panama City. It's easy to find good food, pleasant surroundings, and a surprisingly wide variety of cuisine. Overall, Panama City is still waiting for a truly great restaurant, but there are quite a few good ones. There are plenty of solid options in every price range to keep short-term visitors happy.

Look out for the 10 percent service charge

on the bill; it's easy to double tip. The fad of placing bottled water on the table appears to be on the wane. These bottles are neither free nor necessary: Tap water in Panama is clean. If you're offered bottled water and don't want it, smile, shake your head, and ask for "Chagres" (CHA-gress) instead. (The Río Chagres is the source of Panama City's drinking water.)

For the higher-end restaurants, expect to pay about what you would for a similar place in the

United States. But it's also quite possible to stuff yourself on tasty, simple food for about US$2–3, if ambience means nothing to you. Panamanian *comida corriente* (literally, current food, meaning typical dishes of the day served cafeteria style) venues are scattered around the city, as are all kinds of American fast-food franchises.

Many of the upscale restaurants are found in two general areas on either side of Vía España: El Cangrejo to the northeast of the Hotel El Panamá, and the booming nightlife area around Calle Uruguay (also known as Calle 48 Este).

Make reservations at the fancier places, if only to be sure the restaurant is actually open. Even the best restaurants can be surprisingly empty, especially in the early evening. Things tend to get busier at lunchtime, when the upscale establishments draw a business clientele. Many restaurants are closed for lunch on Saturday and all day on Sunday or Monday.

Vegetarians may have to rely on the limited options at meat-eaters' restaurants. The safest bets are usually Asian or Italian places. Vegetarian restaurants tend to be low-end *comida corriente* places, serving food for a pittance. Vegans have especially limited options— Middle Eastern and Asian places are the best bet, followed by supermarkets. Those who eat kosher, though, have a few good options.

Restaurants are coming and going faster than ever in Panama these days. A good source of information (in Spanish) for new and notable restaurants is www.degustapanama.com.

CASCO VIEJO

Places to eat come and go especially quickly in Casco Viejo. It can be hard to find a decent place to eat on Sunday and Monday, and breakfast is tough any day. The **Super Gourmet Deli** (Avenida A between Calle 5 Oeste and Calle 6 Oeste, 8 A.M.–5 P.M. Mon.–Sat., 10 A.M.–4 P.M. Sun.) is a good option for breakfast or to grab a

René Café

© WILLIAM FRIAR

produce market, Calidonia

across the street from Parque Santa Ana, is a slightly grungy air-conditioned diner and a Panama City institution. This place has been here forever—the building it's housed in was erected in 1907, just four years after Panama became a country—and is a good spot for people-watching and soaking up the atmosphere of a slower, quainter Panama City from an earlier era. Food ranges from sandwiches to chop suey to pasta. The espresso drinks are palatable, and I've heard good things about the *sancocho*.

A Casa de Fernando (Calle 30 Este between Avenida Perú and Avenida Cuba, tel. 225-2378, 24 hours daily, under US$10) is a pleasant tavern likely to be of interest to those staying in the Calidonia/La Exposición area, mainly because it's got a central location and is open 24 hours. It serves an absurdly ambitious variety of food, including salads, soups, sandwiches, and all the usual meats, seafood, and pasta. It's not air-conditioned, but there are ceiling fans. This is a good find.

Indian

Indian restaurants have been slow to catch on in Panama City, despite a significant South Asian population. There are usually only one or two places in the entire city, and they don't tend to stick around long. They also tend to lay off the chilies in deference to the Panamanian palate, so ask for food to be prepared *picante* if you want it with a bit of a bite and *muy picante* if you prefer it moderately hot. Those who like it fiery are probably out of luck.

Restaurante Masala (Avenida 3 Sur and Calle 45, tel. 225-0105, 11:30 A.M.–3 P.M. and 6–10:30 P.M. Mon.–Sat., under US$15) offers the usual North Indian dishes, including ample vegetarian offerings. Food here is similar to an average takeout place in the United States or the United Kingdom. The kitchen must lack a proper tandoori oven, however, as the naan is more like fried bread. Its old home, a charming Bella Vista house, was bulldozed for yet another skyscraper, and its new digs are small and dark, but pleasant

© WILLIAM FRIAR

buying ceviche at the Restaurante Mercado de Marisco

enough and decorated with the expected Indian flourishes. Both table and floor seating is available. It's right next to Residencial Los Arcos.

Panamanian

Fast-food stands on Avenida Perú and Calle 35, near the Ministerio de Economía y Finanzas, cater to office workers who want cheap deep-fried goodies. They're convenient to those staying in Calidonia.

Restaurante Rincón Tableño #5 (Avenida Cuba near Calle 31 Este, tel. 227-5649, 5:30 A.M.–4:30 P.M. Mon.–Sat., 5:30 A.M.–2:30 P.M. Sun., under US$5) is a basic *comida corriente* cafeteria except that the waitresses wear pretty *pollera*-style blouses. The menu changes daily.

Pizzerias

Panama City has two branches of the beloved Napoli pizzeria. Napoli is famous for its clam pizza, but I've always been partial to its wonderfully charred, greasy pepperoni pies. There

are plenty of pastas and such on the menu, but people come here for the wood-oven–baked pizza. Plate-size individual pizzas are available for about five bucks.

The older and much plainer **Napoli** (Calle Estudiante and Calle I, one block from Avenida de los Mártires, tel. 262-2446 or 262-2448, 11:30 A.M.–11:30 P.M. Wed.–Mon.) is a good place to grab lunch during a walking tour of Avenida Central. It's a short walk up from the heart of Central. This branch has been around since 1962 and is an institution. It has an air-conditioned interior and an outdoor seating area where you can look out on what's left of the street life in this once bustling, now declining, area. The second branch is in Obarrio.

Seafood

Restaurante Mercado de Marisco (Avenida Balboa, tel. 377-0379, 11 A.M.–6 P.M. daily, closed the first Mon. of each month, mains around US$10) is just upstairs from the city fish market, which is at the west end of Avenida Balboa. It boasts that it has the "best and freshest fish and seafood in Panama," and one would hope so, given its downstairs neighbor. (The fish market is modern and fairly clean.) It's reasonably priced and offerings include ceviche, seafood soup, corvina, jumbo shrimp, and octopus in garlic sauce. The ceviche is particularly popular. If you don't see anything on the menu you like, buy your own fish downstairs and have it cooked here. The restaurant is a spartan place with little atmosphere, but there's a partial view of the bay and the Panama City skyline. The waitstaff are friendly and speak a little English. Since the area is a bit rough, it's best to come here at lunch. Come early or late to avoid the lunch rush, as this place fills up.

EL CANGREJO AND VICINITY

Some of the city's most established restaurants are in El Cangrejo, particularly along Avenida Eusebio A. Morales. Vía Argentina is mostly known as a relatively quiet place to go for breakfast, a cup of coffee and a snack, or typical Panamanian food.

Cafés

It's about time Panama City got a place like the **C New York Bagel Café** (off Vía Argentina, next to Einstein's Head, tel. 390-6051, 7 A.M.–8 P.M. Mon.–Fri., 8 A.M.–8 P.M. Sat., 8 A.M.–3 P.M. Sun.). It serves more than half a dozen decent coffees by the cup in a fittingly shabby coffeehouse atmosphere that's more San Francisco than New York, with thrift-store furniture and art on the walls. Full breakfasts are served all day for around US$6. The bagels actually taste like bagels, they try their hand at Tex-Mex, and US$4 gets diners wireless Internet access with no time limit.

Cafeterias and Diners

If you're just looking for a simple place for breakfast or a snack, try **Churrería Manolo** (Vía

Argentina 12 at Avenida 2B Norte, tel. 264-3965, 7 A.M.–1 A.M. daily, US$5). Though it's been given a rather austere remodeling, it still has an unpretentious coffee-shop atmosphere that has attracted both locals and resident foreigners for years. It's hard to explain the fondness for this place. The food quality goes up and down; the only things you can really count on are the churros. The yummiest churro is the *manjar blanco*—the filling is similar to condensed milk and looks disgusting, but it's so tasty it'll curl your toes. For a real sugar buzz, order the churros along with *chocolate a la española* (Spanish hot chocolate), which is thick and delicious. Mainly, though, Manolo is just a relaxing place to hang out on one of the few streets in the city that strike a nice balance between bustle and mellowness. After breakfast, sandwiches are the best bet. Other offerings include pasta, meat, and seafood.

East Asian

Panama City's longest-established Japanese restaurant is **Matsuei** (Avenida Eusebio A. Morales, tel. 264-9562 or 264-9547, www.matsueipanama.com, noon–11 P.M. Mon.–Sat., 5:30–10:30 P.M. Sun. and holidays, most items US$7–9), a small, simple place with a sushi bar that's been around since 1978. It has an extensive menu of sushi and sashimi, but far from budget prices. Cooked options include corvina prepared "Japanese style," tempura, and so on. The sushi's okay, but nothing special. This place is pretty consistent for Panama, where sushi places come and go. The *ebi* (shrimp) is tasty, but I don't recommend the California rolls. Imported fish is more expensive.

International

Restaurante 1985 (Avenida Eusebio A. Morales near Vía Veneto, tel. 263-8571 or 263-8541, www.1985.com, noon–11 P.M. Mon.–Fri., 6–11 P.M. Sat.–Sun.) is one of Panama's best restaurants, and one of its most expensive. It's under the command of Chef Willy Diggelmann, a long-established chef with an ever-expanding empire that includes Rincón Suizo, Caffé Pomodoro, and a rather pedestrian wine bar called the Wine Bar. It specializes in French cuisine and seafood but also offers German, Swiss, Spanish, and gourmet vegetarian dishes. The atmosphere is kind of floral country French, and not at all stuffy. This is a nice place for a splurge, as most dishes are in the double digits. If you're going by taxi, tell the driver you want to go to *restaurante mil noveciento ochenta y cinco,* or just point to this entry.

Rincón Suizo (Avenida Eusebio A. Morales near Vía Veneto, tel. 263-8310, www.1985.com, noon–11 P.M. Mon.–Fri., 6–11 P.M. Sat.–Sun.) is upstairs from Restaurante 1985, in the same building, and serves good Swiss and German food in a darker, cozier atmosphere. Offerings include raclette, *berner rösti* (fried potatoes), and cheese fondue. The food tends to be a bit cheaper here than at 1985.

Panamanian

Restaurante y Cafetería El Trapiche (Vía Argentina, tel. 269-2063 or takeout 269-4353, 7 A.M.–11 P.M. daily, US$4–9) has long been a local favorite for traditional Panamanian fare such as *mondongo* (tripe), *hojaldres* (fry bread), tortillas, tamales, and *ropa vieja* (shredded beef with rice). Those who want to sample a variety of things can go for the Fiesta Panameña (US$11). Breakfast is served until 11:30 A.M. and includes such hearty fare as scrambled eggs, steak, white cheese, and *carimañola* (a fried, meat-stuffed roll) for around US$5. There's an air-conditioned interior as well as seating outside on Vía Argentina.

Peruvian

The first time I visited ◧ **La Mar** (Calle Guatemala next to the PowerClub Gym near Vía Argentina, tel. 209-3323, www.lamarcebicheria.com, noon–3 P.M. and 7–11 P.M.

Mon.–Fri., 12:30–11 P.M. Sat., 1–9 P.M. Sun., mains US$10–20) none of the six types of ceviche on the menu were available. This might seem like a problem for a place that calls itself a *"cebichería Peruana"* (Pervuvian ceviche) restaurant. But the seafood here is so good one imagines the chef just hadn't found anything suitable in the market that day. Part of the growing culinary empire of the celebrated Peruvian chef Gastón Acurio, La Mar offers an extensive menu of Peruvian specialties, many of which will be unfamiliar to non-Peruvians. (The restaurant's website offers a Peruvian gastronomic dictionary, for Spanish speakers.) Originally opened as the high-end Astrid and Gastón, it has been reopened as a more casual but still sleek place with gray slate walls, shiny black tabletops, a ceviche bar, and a glassed-in kitchen. Service is also casual, for better or worse.

The waitstaff can make suggestions if you get overwhelmed, though unless you like organ meats beware of anything with *corazon de ternera* (calf heart), a Pervuian delicacy but not to everyone's taste. Seafood is definitely the way to go here, as the preparation is outstanding. The *especial macho,* for instance, is a buttersoft fillet of whatever mild fish is fresh that day on a bed of mashed potatoes and topped with tender calamari and shrimp that actually tastes like shrimp. It's delicious. The pisco sours are sweet and potent but very tasty. The desserts are also good, but so rich and sugary you can get diabetes just looking at them.

Machu Picchu (Calle Eusebio A. Morales, tel. 264-9308, noon–3 P.M. and 6–11 P.M. Mon.–Sat., noon–9 P.M. Sun.) is a pleasant, cozy, and moderately priced Peruvian restaurant with friendly service and decent seafood, which is its specialty. A good value here is to share a number of appetizers, which average around US$5. Try the Peruvian ceviche, which is prepared quite differently from Panamanian ceviche. The house wine is good, but consider sampling a pisco sour if you've never had one and are willing to risk a drink made with raw egg. Machu Picchu has a sister restaurant of the same name in Boquete.

Seafood

My favorite place for seafood is ◖Siete Mares (Calle Guatemala near Vía Argentina, tel. 264-0144, 11:30 A.M.–11:30 P.M. daily, US$16–24). One of the most consistent and consistently popular restaurants in the city, it's a cozy, tranquil place, and the service is good. An unusual house specialty is fried ceviche, a light and tangy appetizer. The fish is so tasty you won't need to order anything fancier than *corvina a la plancha* (grilled corvina). The restaurant has a modern look reminiscent of an upscale hotel lobby, including an artificial waterfall near the entrance. It does have one peculiar touch: chairs on rollers, like those you might find in a plush conference room. A pianist performs in the evening.

Steak Houses

Martín Fierro (Avenida Eusebio A. Morales, tel. 264-1927 or 223-1333, noon–3 P.M. and 6–11 P.M. Mon.–Sat., noon–10 P.M. Sun.) is a brightly lit place where decor runs a distant second to simply serving slabs of meat—grilled beef, chicken, and pork, either domestic or imported from Omaha, Nebraska. Expect to pay upward of US$25 for imported beef. The restaurant also serves pasta, seafood, and fish, but that's not why anyone comes here. Meals include access to a meager salad bar. If you really feel like punishing your heart, try the tasty *mozzarella frita* (fried mozzarella)—oh, go ahead, you're on vacation. Then try the quite good *tres leches* (three-milk) cake.

BELLA VISTA, MARBELLA, AND OBARRIO
Cafés

Crepes and Waffles (Avenida 5B between Calle Uruguay and Calle Aquilino de la Guardia, tel. 269-1574 or 305-6536, www.crepesywaffles.

com.pa, noon–11 P.M. Mon.–Sat., 9 A.M.–11 P.M. Sun., US$10) is a popular Latin American chain that serves—guess what?—in a sunny, modern, brick-and-glass building with an air-conditioned interior, outdoor terrace, and yuppie vibe. Only the 1970s soft rock mars the pleasant atmosphere. Its large selection of savory and sweet crepes include some vegetarian options. Other offerings include lots of coffee drinks, a salad bar, pita sandwiches, and other café goodies. There are newer branches in the Multiplaza Pacific and Albrook malls.

The menu at **Ozone Café** (Calle Uruguay near Calle 48, tel. 214-9616, www.ozonecafepanama.com, 11 A.M.–3 P.M. and 6–10 P.M. or so daily, mains average US$15) is almost comically eclectic: Among other things it features Indian, Iraqi, Indonesian, German, Lebanese, Senegalese, Italian, Tunisian, and Alabaman(!) cuisine. Of these, the Middle Eastern fare is probably the safest bet, and you'd probably also do okay with the pastas, salads, and grilled meats. The food is tasty, but the chef has a fondness for oil. This is a cozy, popular little place with a low slanting ceiling and little lamps that hang above the tables. The servers are gracious and attentive.

Cafeterias and Diners

The small Vía España branch of the **Niko's Café** chain is centrally located (Vía España to the side of the El Rey supermarket, tel. 223-0111, www.nikoscafe.com, 24 hours daily). These cafeterias have proven to be quite popular because of their wide selection of simple and tasty food, fast service, cleanliness, long hours, and cheap prices. A few dollars buy heaps of meat, starches, and some veggies from long rows of steam tables. Niko's also offers fresh sandwiches, soups, individual pizzas, and desserts. Most breakfast items are US$3 or less.

There are several cafeterias within a five-minute walk of the Hotel Continental, some of which are open 24 hours a day. The best known of these, though no longer open 24 hours, is **Restaurante Jimmy** (Calle Manuel María Icaza, tel. 223-1523, 7 A.M.–11 P.M. Mon.–Sat., US$5–7, many mains under US$10), just down from the hotel. It's a neighborhood institution with a spartan but clean and modern diner atmosphere since its 2003 move to new digs. It serves a wide range of items, including its own take on Greek food (pita, tzatziki, fried eggplant, *keftedakia*, and so on), which can be odd but rather tasty. Other possibilities include *sancocho* (a local stew), pasta, sandwiches, seafood, pizza, and various meats. There's another branch across the street from the Atlapa Convention Center on the way to the international airport.

The coffee shop of the **Hotel Ejecutivo** (Avenida Aquilino de la Guardia between Calle 51 and Calle 52, 24 hours Thurs.–Sat.) serves breakfast 24 hours a day in an unpretentious, friendly atmosphere. Offerings range from a full Panamanian-style breakfast with lots of fried things bad for your health to an all-you-can-eat breakfast buffet.

Rock Burger (Calle 53 Este, tel. 233-0725, 8:30 A.M.–10 P.M. daily) is a fast-food place offering decent burgers made to order for US$3.50 for a quarter pounder up to US$8.75 for a whole pound of beef. Those with more modest appetites can order "mini-rockers," or sliders, as gringos might know them as. The menu also includes a variety of sandwiches, including some served in pita or as wraps for US$3.50–6. Breakfast goes for US$3 or less. This place is popular with families. There are also Rock Burger outlets on Calle 50 and in Costa del Este.

There's a newer, rather sleek outlet of **Churrería Manolo** (Avenida 1D Sur and Calle Juan Ramón Poll C., tel. 214-3986, 7 A.M.–1 A.M. daily) in Obarrio. Check out this well-loved chain for its great churros, Spanish hot chocolate *(chocolate a la española),* breakfast, and sandwiches.

East Asian

Madame Chang (Calle 48 near Calle Uruguay, tel. 269-1313 or 269-9654, noon–3 P.M. and 6–10 P.M. Mon.–Sat., noon–10 P.M. Sun., US$15) has long been considered Panama's best and most upscale Chinese restaurant. But it appears to be going through a rocky period. It's still worth a go, particularly at lunch. Try the clams in black bean sauce to start. The *guabina* (a mild-flavored fish) steamed in soy sauce and Chinese vegetables, when done right, is light and delicious. The atmosphere is pleasant, with tile floors and peach walls and tablecloths, but it's not particularly dressy.

Sushi Itto (Calle 55 Este near Avenida 2 Sur/Samuel Lewis, tel. 265-1222 or 265-1136, noon–10 P.M. Mon.–Thurs., noon–11 P.M. Fri. and Sat., 12:30–10:30 P.M. Sun.), right next to the Reprosa jewelry store, is part of a Mexican sushi chain (yep, Mexican). It's a modern place with an extensive sushi menu as well as tempura, rice dishes, pastas, soups, and even a few Thai dishes. The sushi's okay. There's a second outlet in the Multiplaza Pacific Mall.

Guatemalan

◖ Hacienda Real (Calle 49 and Calle Colombia, tel. 264-0311, www.hacienda-real.com, noon–midnight daily, mains starting at around US$17), which opened in January 2010, is a bright new star on the Panama City dining scene. Though part of a Guatemala-based group of restaurants with branches around Central America, it doesn't feel like a chain restaurant at all. Decorating the place reportedly cost millions, and it shows. Great care has been taken beyond the decor as well. One of the waiters told me the parent company even has a kind of exchange program: Waiters from Guatemala were sent down to help get the Panama City branch off the ground, and the Panamanian staff were sent to Guatemala City to learn a bit about Guatemalan food and culture.

The food is tasty rather than outstanding, but the restaurant alone is lovely enough to justify a visit. It takes up three floors and has the feel of a Guatemalan coffee baron's opulent home. It specializes in grilled meats. Be sure to try the typically Guatemalan black beans with thick tortillas. The *choricero* starter includes these along with (delicious) french fries, a heap of chorizo sausage, and guacamole. It can easily feed two people with no need for a main course. The house flan is exceptional.

The colorful basement dining room shares its space with an open-plan kitchen, but the vaulted brick ceiling makes this room noisy, especially when filled with the business crowd holding power lunches. The glassed-in terrace two floors up is a quieter option, and it has a view of the leafy neighborhood and a sliver of sea. There are many other nooks and private rooms to choose from, as well as an attractive front patio with ceiling fans for those who'd prefer to dine alfresco.

International

La Posta (Calle 49 just west of Calle Uruguay, tel. 269-1076, www.lapostapanama.com, noon–2:30 P.M. and 6:30–10:30 P.M. Mon.–Sat., US$15–30) has become one of Panama City's favorite restaurants in the last few years. It serves imported and local seafood and meats along with a number of pastas. Some of us find the food uneven, but that's no reason not to visit it. It's in a sprawling old Bella Vista home, and it's been restored and decorated in a style very different from the much-missed Eurasia, which had a similar idea. La Posta is going for tropical elegance, with bamboo and wicker chairs, ceiling fans, old tile floors, and a long, elegant bar. Somerset Maugham and Hemingway would have felt right at home.

As its name suggests, **Fusion** (Radisson Decapolis Hotel, behind the Multicentro Mall on Avenida Balboa, tel. 215-5000, 6:30–10:30 A.M., noon–3 P.M., and 6–10:45 P.M. daily, most mains US$12–28) offers a fusion of different cuisine, especially Asian and Peruvian. This is easily the most striking-looking restaurant in Panama City. Be sure to sit inside the cone-shaped room, which shoots up for three floors and is dominated by a seven-meter bust that vaguely resembles an Easter Island statue and supposedly is meant to represent the fusion of the world's different races. The hotel's swimming pool is on the floor above it. The pool has a partial glass bottom, which allows light to stream through and gives the feel of dining in an underwater temple in Atlantis. Avoid the house wine. The passion fruit dessert is delicious.

Le Bistrot (Calle 53 Este, tel. 264-5587 or 269-4025, 11:30 A.M.–11:30 P.M. daily), tucked away in a nondescript office building across from the World Trade Center in Marbella, is a Panama institution that's been around for nearly 30 years. Year after year it's been one of the city's more consistent spots for fine dining and good service, especially compared to some of its trendier (and more expensive) rivals. The chairs on rollers may remind you of Siete Mares, which makes sense since they're both owned by the same folks. The decor is dated, but this is still a good place for a romantic dinner, as the banquettes and mood lighting offer lots of privacy. Food tends toward the usual array of seafood, fish, and meats, but it's quite well prepared. The *calamari a la plancha* (grilled squid) is a bit oily but delicious. Also try the *langostinos a la thermidor* (prawns thermidor), or the very tender *filete a la pimienta* (pepper steak). The *flan de queso* (cheesecake flan) is good if you still have room.

Italian

Tre Scalini Ristorante (Calle 52 in Bella Vista, tel. 269-9951 or 269-9952, www.trescalinipanama.com, noon–3:30 P.M. and 6–11 P.M. daily, mains around US$15) offers decent Italian food and friendly service in a cozy faux-Italian atmosphere. It's been around for more than two decades and is an old standby for many a Panama City dweller. There's a second Tre Scalini in the El Dorado district (Boulevard El Dorado and Calle Miguel Brostella, tel. 260-0052 or 236-5303), if you happen to find yourself out that way. Avoid the house wine at either place.

◖Vinoteca (Calle 57 and Avenida 1 Sur, tel. 223-7734 or 223-4676, http://vinotecapanama. com, noon–3 P.M. and 7–11 P.M. Mon.–Fri., noon–11 P.M. Sat., mains US$15–20) is a newer Italian restaurant that has risen from the ashes of one of Panama City's most venerable ones, Restaurante de las Americas. The new place is far more contemporary, both in ambience and service, and in my opinion the food is better. The service is good here: attentive, warm, and knowledgeable. The chef himself is often in the dining room, chatting with the young, affluent international crowd and helping with service.

"Vinoteca" roughly translates to wine cellar or wine collection, and the restaurant's own offerings include a decent and reasonably priced selection of Argentinean, Chilean, and Spanish wines kept in a glass-walled room visible from the dining room. The waitstaff know their wines and are helpful in recommending good pairings with food, which is a rarity in Panama. Wine is available by the bottle, glass, or *quartino*, a mini-carafe equivalent to a large glassful. The food is not out of the world or beautifully presented, but both the pasta and risotto are good. Seafood fans should try the *risotto di frutti mare.* The restaurant is small but has lots of hard surfaces (no tablecloths, tile floors), so it can get pretty noisy when full.

Napoli No. 2 (Calle 57 and Avenida 1D Sur, tel. 263-8799 or 263-8800, noon–midnight Tues.–Sat.) is the somewhat more upscale younger sister of the original Napoli pizzeria in the much more upscale neighborhood of Obarrio. It's air-conditioned and pleasant. The service is not so hot, but the food comes fast once you finally get to order.

Mediterranean

◖ Restaurante Beirut (Calle Ricardo Arias and Avenida 3 Sur, tel. 214-3815, noon–3 A.M. daily) has quickly become one of Panama City's favorite restaurants. Huge amounts of yummy, moderately priced Lebanese food are whisked to your table by the waitstaff, whether you sit in the air-conditioned interior or outside on the breezy covered terrace, which has fake stalactites dripping from its ceiling, creating a cave-like effect. The latter is the louder option, since the restaurant sits on a busy street across from the Marriott, but, especially in the evening—and most especially on a Friday evening—that's where the action is, and the people-watching is fun. The most economical way to eat here is to share. Go for one of the combination platters for around US$14; it consists of eight tasty items that can feed two reasonably hungry people. Even the pita is fresh and piping hot. The prices attract a younger crowd than one normally finds at this kind of restaurant, but everyone loves this place.

Habibi's (Calle Uruguay and Calle 48, tel. 264-3647, www.habibispanama.com, 11:30 A.M.–1 A.M. daily, US$10 or less) is a Lebanese café in a lovely old home that's been given an attractive modern makeover. It offers tasty Middle Eastern food, complete with hot pita bread. It's a popular place with a large front terrace for those who'd rather dine alfresco—a good option on dry-season evenings. This is also a good place for drinks and appetizers before a meal elsewhere.

The inexpensive **Athen's** (Calle 50 and Calle Uruguay, tel. 265-4637, 11 A.M.–11:30 P.M. Thurs.–Tues., under US$10) is a popular place for pizzas and for Greek salads, gyros, souvlaki, and other Greek dishes. It's a casual, fast-food kind of place with an air-conditioned interior and an outdoor terrace overlooking Calle 50 and Calle Uruguay. Each table has a phone customers can use to place an order, a gimmick undercut by the fact that the servers come around unprompted. The pizzas are just so-so. The pita sandwiches are huge and drowned in yogurt sauce but otherwise tasty. There's a second Athen's in the Obarrio neighborhood (Calle 57, tel. 223-1464) that's open on Wednesday when this branch is closed; its night off is Tuesday. A third one recently opened up in El Dorado, far away from the usual tourist haunts.

Panamanian

Restaurante-Bar Las Tinajas (Calle 51 near Avenida Federico Boyd, tel. 263-7890 or 269-3840, www.tinajaspanama.com, 11 A.M.–11 P.M. daily, US$10–15) is an unabashed tourist restaurant. It's worth checking out for its folkloric dance performances at 9 P.M. Tuesday–Saturday. Reservations are required for the show. The cuisine is Panamanian (and rather bland), and the restaurant is decorated to suggest a traditional town on the Azuero Peninsula. The quality of both the food and service can vary wildly here. Those who don't have time to travel around Panama to sample traditional Panamanian food and folklore can get a sense of it here, but those who plan to travel extensively around the country can have a less touristy experience elsewhere.

The upscale **C Restaurante Barandas** (Calle Aquilino de la Guardia between Calle 51 and Calle 52, tel. 264-0000 or 265-7844, 6:30 A.M.–11 P.M. daily) in the Bristol hotel is noted for its nouvelle Panamanian cuisine. Traditional Panamanian fixtures such as *carimañolas* (fried, meat-stuffed rolls), corvina, and yuca are given the fusion treatment, with unusual sauces and generally lighter, healthier recipes. The executive chef is Coquita Arias de Calvo, who has her own local cooking show, books, and magazine. She is sort of Panama's answer to Martha Stewart or Nigella Lawson. The dining room is formal and quite pleasant. Food is not always consistent here.

Tastes Fusion Restaurant (Hotel Riu Plaza, Calle 500, tel. 378-9000, 6:30–10:30 P.M. daily, mains US$14–31), in the Hotel Riu, is a newer place taking a stab at

Panamanian-fusion cuisine, and for the most part they do a good job with it. It's a surprisingly small restaurant for such a massive hotel, which helps the staff give gracious and attentive service. The atmosphere aims at modern and sophisticated without being too formal. Food presentation is fancy and a bit fussy—lots of deconstructed dishes assembled at the table—but it's a pleasant place to eat. The food can be hit or miss. It's open only for dinner.

Seafood

One of Panama City's old standbys has once again become a destination restaurant thanks to a recent move to flashy new digs. **C Casa de Mariscos** (Calle Manuel María Icaza, tel. 223-7755 or 264-2644, www.lacasadelmarisco-acha.com, noon–11 P.M. daily, most US$20–30) is an impressive-looking place with a polished stone facade, two-story ceilings, a plate-glass wall overlooking a small illuminated garden, and big, colorful paintings on its walls. The restaurant is still affectionately known to regulars as Acha in honor of its Spanish owner, Ramón Martínez Acha, who founded the original Casa de Mariscos in 1965 with his wife, Claudia Vásquez de Martínez. The seafood is well-prepared and delicious. For such a stylish and modern place, the restaurant holds on to some old ways it should have ditched by now, such as a pedestrian wine list and hairnets for some of its waitstaff. But it's still a good bet for a fancy night out.

Steak Houses

Market (Calle Uruguay and Calle 47, tel. 264-9401, noon–2:30 P.M. and 6:30–11 P.M. Mon.–Wed., 11:30 A.M.–11 P.M. Thurs.–Sat., 11:30 A.M.–9 P.M. Sun.), by the owner of the popular Restaurante La Posta, has been a favorite among Panamanian, gringo, and European meat lovers for the last few years. Market is known for its steaks (around US$30 for imported U.S. beef; about half that for tougher local beef from Chiriquí) and burgers (about US$7 for most, or more than double that for a colossal Angus beef burger). Burgers and beer are the best value. Market also does a pretty tasty Cobb salad and maracuya (passion fruit) pavlova. This is a fairly casual place with a large, high-roofed bar area, separated by walls of wine bottles from a slightly more formal dining area. The sound can be deafening when it's busy, such as a Sunday night, which is the traditional family night out for Panamanians who can afford it. Market also serves brunch on Saturday and Sunday.

An old standby, **Gaucho's Steak House** (Calle Uruguay and Calle 48, tel. 263-4469 or 263-1406, noon–3 P.M. and 6–10:30 P.M. daily) serves decent steaks for those who don't expect much more in a dining experience. Both the atmosphere (brightly lit, chain-steak-house vibe) and the food (this is a place for meat: you won't find much green outside the potted plants) are unadorned. The service tends to be fast and perfunctory. Though ostensibly an Argentine steak house, Gaucho's imports its meat from the United States. Expect to pay upward of US$25 for imported beef. Chicken and seafood are also on the menu, but that's not why people come here. For starters, try the *picado de chorizo* (a plate of sliced sausages); it's delicious.

Vegetarian

Me Gusta Comida Vegetariana (Calle Ricardo Arias, no phone, 7:30 A.M.–8 P.M. Mon.–Sat., portions US$0.60/each) has an ambience as plain as its no-frills food. It serves *comida corriente* cafeteria items and a few other goodies such as soy milk and veggie burgers. Its name, by the way, translates to the suitably plain "I like vegetarian food." It's near Restaurante Costa Azul, but probably not for much longer. It's a miracle it's survived the wrecking ball so far, as towers are sprouting all around it.

SUPERMARKETS AND SPECIALTY FOODS

Supermarkets are everywhere in Panama City, and in recent years their selections have vastly improved. They now more closely resemble mega-markets in the United States, with an array of imported and local goods, including a better choice of fresh produce (difficult growing conditions make much beyond tropical fruit hard to come by in the tropics).

Panama's biggest grocery-store chain is **El Rey**. It has close to a dozen stores in the greater Panama City area alone. The one on Vía España (tel. 223-7850, 24 hours daily) is centrally located and has a pharmacy and many other services. The more upscale **Riba Smith** supermarket has four locations in Panama City at last count. The most convenient for visitors are in Bella Vista (Calle 45, tel. 225-6247, 7:30 A.M.–9 P.M. Mon.–Sat., 8 A.M.–8 P.M. Sun.), on the Transístmica (tel. 299-3999, 7:30 A.M.–9 P.M. Mon.–Sat., 8 A.M.–8 P.M. Sun.), and in the Multiplaza Pacific shopping center (tel. 302-3793, 7:30 A.M.–9 P.M. Mon.–Sat., 8 A.M.–8 P.M. Sun.). The stores have buffet-style cafeterias as well. Riba Smith also does home (and presumably hotel!) deliveries with 24 hours notice and a modest minimum purchase.

Foodie Market (Bal Harbour shopping center in Punta Paitilla, 7:30 A.M.–8:30 P.M. Mon.–Fri., 8 A.M.–7 P.M. Sat., 9 A.M.–8 P.M. Sun.) is a small market that has good veggies and fruit.

Some of Panama's best coffee is at **Café Ruiz** (World Trade Center on Calle 53, tel. 265-0779, www.caferuiz.com, 7:30 A.M.–6 P.M. Mon.–Fri.). It's a café and shop that carries all kinds of roasts and flavors of coffee, both whole bean and ground. Attractive gift packages and mugs are available. Café Ruiz coffee is also available at some supermarkets, but the gourmet roast is available only at the Café Ruiz shops.

Felipe Motta in Marbella (Calle 53, tel. 269-6633, 9 A.M.–7 P.M. Mon.–Fri., 9 A.M.–6 P.M. Sat.) has a good selection of wines at prices comparable to what you'd find in the United States. It also has some gourmet foods and fresh bread and pastries.

Kosher Food

There's a kosher cafeteria/bakery, a kosher supermarket, and occasionally a kosher restaurant clustered together in Punta Paitilla. These have good, unusual (for Panama) offerings that may be of interest even to those who don't keep kosher. They are great options on Sunday, when many other places are closed, but expect crowds. **Pita-Pan Kosher** (Vía Italia, tel. 264-2786 or 265-1369, 7 A.M.–9 P.M. Mon.–Thurs., 7 A.M.–5 P.M. Fri., 9 A.M.–9 P.M. Sun., US$3.50–6) is an air-conditioned kosher cafeteria in the upscale Bal Harbour shopping center just off Avenida Balboa. It serves fish, salads, pasta, sandwiches, pizza, quiche, hummus with falafel, and so on. It even has kosher sushi. The food here is tasty. Another plus is that it serves pita and other fresh bread by the loaf. It's closed Friday evening through Sunday morning for the Sabbath.

Super Kosher (Calle 56 Este, tel. 263-5253, 8:30 A.M.–8:30 P.M. Sun.–Thurs., 8:30 A.M.–4:30 P.M. Fri.) is an upscale kosher supermarket one street north of the Bal Harbour shopping center. It has good veggies and products from the United States. There's a cafeteria inside that serves breakfast items, sandwiches, and other goodies, all kosher.

Information and Services

TOURIST INFORMATION

Panama's government tourism ministry, the Autoridad de Turismo Panamá (ATP), has its administrative headquarters at the Atlapa Convention Center next to the Sheraton Panama Hotel and Convention Center off Vía Israel, but it's not set up to deal with actual visitors. If you're eternally optimistic, you can try calling the office at 226-3544 or 226-7000. Until recently it was known as IPAT (Instituto Panameño de Turismo).

You will occasionally see ATP information booths around town, including ones at the ruins of Old Panama. There's also an information booth between Immigration and Customs at Tocumen International Airport that's sometimes staffed, though don't expect much more than a handful of hotel flyers. (Grab the business cards, if there are any—some of these offer 10 percent off at restaurants and businesses you might actually want to visit.)

Taxi drivers often double as tour guides. Don't expect a scholarly lecture on the sights, but it can be a reasonable way to cover a lot of ground. Agree on a price ahead of time.

MAPS

Tourist maps of Panama City are still a half-hearted affair. They tend not to be widely available, user-friendly, or terribly accurate or up-to-date, and they often seem little more than a guide to advertisers who paid to be put on the map, literally. Your best bets are the fold-outs that come with the free *Focus Magazine,* copies of which are easy to find in hotels and tourist-oriented sights around the city. City maps are sometimes for sale at bookstores, pharmacies, and Gran Morrison department stores. The stores also may carry one of several pictorial maps of Casco Viejo that have popped up in the last few years; these can make navigating around its maze of streets a bit easier.

HOSPITALS, POLICE, AND EMERGENCIES

Panama has begun offering free health insurance to tourists who enter the country by air. An explanatory leaflet should be distributed to passengers upon their plane's arrival.

The emergency number for the police (*policía*

nacional) is 104. The emergency number for the fire department *(bomberos)* is 103. Directory assistance *(asistencia al directorio)* is 102. The national operator can be reached at 101. To reach the international operator, dial 106.

The Panamanian government has a hotline for tourists who are lost, have been robbed, or are having any other problems (including with the police). The hotline's operators should be able to help tourists who speak English, Spanish, French, and Portuguese. The hotline number is 178.

The fire department *(bomberos)* has a reputation for arriving on the scene of an emergency before the police. Panama City finally has an official emergency medical response service. Dial 911 to call an ambulance (this is only for medical help; dial 104 for the police). This service, **Sistema Único de Manejo de Emergencias** (Unified System for the Management of Emergencies, www.sume911. pa), is slowly being rolled out around the country. This is a relatively new service. If an ambulance doesn't come quickly, your best bet may be to grab a taxi and get to the closest hospital.

Hospital Punta Pacífica and Hospital Nacional would be my first choices in an emergency, and both are central. There are private ambulance services in Panama City, though these are really aimed at already-existing subscribers. One to try is **SEMM** (tel. 366-0122 for emergencies, tel. 366-0100 for office, http://semmpanama.net).

Panama City has excellent medical facilities and excellent doctors and dentists, many of whom were trained in the United States and speak English. Even those without medical insurance can receive good care for far less than in the United States. It is illegal for foreigners to use government-funded *seguro social* (social security) hospitals and clinics, unless they work in Panama and have an employer who pays into the *seguro social* system. Attempting to do so is insurance fraud, which is a serious crime.

Centro Médico Paitilla (Calle 53 and Avenida Balboa, tel. 265-8800 or 269-0333, www.centromedicopaitilla.com) has long been considered Panama's best medical center. The **Hospital Nacional** (Avenida Cuba between Calle 38 and Calle 39, tel. 207-8100 or 207-8102, emergency room tel. 207-8110, 207-8136, or 306-3310, ambulance tel. 207-8119, www.hospitalnacional.com) opened a facility in 1998 and has been positioning itself as catering to the expatriate and foreign tourist market. The glittery new kid in town is **Hospital Punta Pacífica** (Punta Pacífica, tel. 204-8000, emergencies tel. 204-8184 or 204-8185, www.hospitalpuntapacifica.com). The hospital is affiliated with Johns Hopkins Medicine International, which provides advice and training from the acclaimed medical center in Baltimore, Maryland.

The pharmacy at the centrally located **El Rey supermarket** (tel. 223-1243) on Vía España is open 24 hours a day. **Farmacia Milani** (Calle 33 and Avenida Justo Arosemena/Avenida 3 Sur, tel. 225-0065), across the street from Hotel Roma Plaza in Calidonia, is also open 24 hours a day. **Farmacia Arrocha** is a large drugstore chain. Centrally located branches include one just off Vía España (Calle 49 Este, tel. 223-4505, 7 a.m.–9:45 p.m. daily), about midway between the Hotel Ejecutivo and the Hotel El Panamá, and one in the Albrook Mall (tel. 315-1728).

NEWSPAPERS AND PERIODICALS

All of Panama's daily newspapers are published in Panama City and are widely available at newsstands and in shops. Most are in Spanish (there are also long-established Chinese-language papers for the Chinese immigrant population). There are currently no stand-alone English-language daily newspapers, though some of the Spanish-language dailies are flirting with running stories in English, both in print and online.

Focus Magazine, a free magazine published twice yearly in English and Spanish, contains brief, enthusiastic articles on various attractions around the country, as well as maps, hotel and restaurant listings, and general tourist information. The same folks put out *The Visitor* (www.thevisitorpanama.com), a free, twice-monthly, bilingual tourist newspaper. Both are widely available at hotels and other locations that cater to travelers.

NATIONAL LIBRARY

Panama's national library, the four-story **Biblioteca Nacional de Panamá** (Parque Recreativo Omar off Vía Porras, tel. 224-9466 or 221-8360, 9 A.M.–6 P.M. Mon.–Fri., 9 A.M.–5 P.M. Sat.), may be of interest to those who want in-depth information on Panama. The collections include books by Panamanian authors or about Panama, and newspaper morgues dating from the 19th century. A wall of filing cabinets contains biographical information on prominent Panamanians and expatriates. The library is open to the public, but the stacks can't be browsed: Visitors search the electronic catalog on the 3rd floor and then request their selection from a librarian. All books must be perused on the premises; borrowing privileges have been suspended because too many people did not return books. There are several quiet, comfortable areas to read inside the library.

NAUTICAL CHARTS

Islamorada Internacional (Bldg. 808, Avenida Arnulfo Arias Madrid/Balboa Road, tel. 228-4348 or 228-6069, www.islamorada.com, 8 A.M.–5 P.M. Mon.–Fri.) is the place to go in Panama for nautical charts, books, software, instruments, flags, and pendants. It's actually in Balboa, in the former Canal Zone, across the street from the huge fountain of Arnulfo Arias. It lays claim to being the largest nautical bookstore in Panama. It also has general guidebooks to the Caribbean and elsewhere. Yachters can reach it in Balboa harbor at VHF channels 12 and 16; in Cristóbal try VHF 65 and 85, Radio Balboa. The staff speak fluent English here.

MONEY

Strangely enough for an international banking capital, until recently there were only two places in and around Panama City where visitors could exchange currencies. New places have begun to pop up around Plaza Concordia on Vía España and Vía Veneto next to Hotel El Panamá. But these deal mainly in euros and Colombian pesos, and they tend to be a bit casual and borderline shady, the kind of places where you can also cash checks and buy cheap watches.

Those who must exchange currency are much better off going to **Panacambios** (Vía España, tel. 223-1800, 8 A.M.–5 P.M. Mon.–Fri.), toward the back of the Plaza Regency next to Plaza Concordia. It's a Panama institution that's been in the same place since 1990. It's set back from the street and comes equipped with an armed guard and security gate. Panacambios carries every currency you can think of. How good the exchange rate will be depends on the currency: There's not much of a market to buy Colombian pesos, for instance, so you're probably better off spending them in Colombia than selling them here. The staff here are good-natured pros, and if you ask, they'll probably tell you if they can offer a good rate for whatever currency you have or want. Rates for euros and colones are more competitive, but in general they will be no better than those at a U.S. airport exchange counter—in other words, not a steal. Panama is dollar country.

The **Banco Nacional de Panamá** branch (7 A.M.–11 P.M. daily) in Tocumen International Airport has traditionally exchanged some major currencies, but in 2012 they had at least temporarily suspended this service.

The centrally located **Scotiabank** (Avenida Federico Boyd and Calle 51, 8 A.M.–3:30 P.M. Mon.–Fri., 9 A.M.–12:30 P.M. Sat.) in Bella Vista cashes travelers checks, something that can be quite a hassle in Panama.

Banks with ATMs are all over Panama City. For those staying in the Calidonia area, branches of **Banco Nacional de Panamá** (BNP) and **BBVA** (hours for both: 8 A.M.–3 P.M. Mon.–Fri., 9 A.M.–noon Sat.) are centrally located on a busy street. They both have 24-hour ATMs. The **HSBC** (10:30 A.M.–6 P.M. Mon.–Fri., 9 A.M.–3 P.M. Sat.) at the Multicentro Mall has unusually long hours during the week. Avoid the main BNP branch on Vía España; it gets absolutely packed.

Those who need to send or receive money the old-fashioned way can find **Western Union** (www.westernunion.com) outlets just about anywhere in Panama City. The main office is in the Plaza Concordia shopping complex (Vía España, tel. 800-2224, 8 A.M.–7 P.M. Mon.–Fri., 8 A.M.–5 P.M. Sat.). Other centrally located offices include a large center in the Albrook Mall (tel. 269-1055, 10 A.M.–7 P.M. daily), as well as an outlet next door in the Gran Terminal de Transportes. There's an outlet in the Super Empeñas San Ramón store in Calidonia (Calle 34 near Avenida Perú, tel. 225-1952, 7:30 A.M.–5:30 P.M. Mon.–Sat.). **MoneyGram** has about three dozen outlets in Panama City. The one at the Plaza Concordia is in the Bambi Empeños stores (Vía España, tel. 263-4293, 8 A.M.–6 P.M. Mon.–Fri., 8 A.M.–3 P.M. Sat.).

POST OFFICE

Panama's main post office is in Calidonia (Avenida Central between Calle 33 and Avenida Perú, 7 A.M.–5:45 P.M. Mon.–Fri., 7 A.M.–5 P.M. Sat.), across from the Basílica Don Bosco. There's a small **stamp museum** (tel. 512-0601, 8:30 A.M.–4:30 P.M.) in the complex that consists of a few recent first-day covers stuck on the wall of an office. Other post office branches include ones in the Plaza Concordia shopping center on Vía España and next to Restaurante Boulevard Balboa (Avenida Balboa near Calle 31). All are open the same hours as the main post office.

COMMUNICATIONS

Free wireless Internet has sprung up everywhere in Panama—in hotels, hostels, restaurants, cafés, you name it—and nowhere is this more true than in the capital. Often, for better and worse, there's no password protection, and it's just a matter of firing up your computer or phone and logging on. Even if you find a place that isn't yet wireless equipped, chances are you'll have a half dozen other signals from neighboring establishments to choose from, with proprietors who don't care if you piggyback. The Panamanian government is also rolling out a program of free Wi-Fi hotspots in public parks, hospitals, and schools around the country.

Internet cafés open and close constantly in Panama City, and the proliferation of free access throughout the city is bound to make the attrition rate even worse. Most are just bare-bones air-conditioned rooms with terminals, but the rates are good—usually around US$0.50–0.75 an hour. It's often possible to pay for just a half hour or 15 minutes. Some offer international calling at competitive rates (about US$0.20 a minute to Costa Rica or the United States, for instance). A few also send and receive faxes; domestic faxes tend to be reasonable, but sending an international fax can cost US$5 a page or more. Be sure to ask for rates ahead of time.

There are plenty of Internet cafés in the Calidonia area, where most of the budget hotels are. Many of these hotels also have Internet computers, often dollar-fed ones. A convenient Internet café is between the immigration office and Restaurante Pizzeria Romanaccio (Calle 29 Este between Avenida Perú and Avenida Cuba, no phone, 8 A.M.–midnight daily).

The Plaza Concordia shopping complex on Vía España has several places to access the Internet, the nicest of which is next to Western Union in the Cable and Wireless international call center (8 A.M.–9:30 P.M. Mon.–Sat., 9:30 A.M.–8 P.M. Sun.), which also charges standard rates for international phone calls. The Multicentro Mall also has call centers and Internet cafés. Passport-photo shops are in the same complex. There are plenty of other Internet places in the heart of Vía España. Centro Comercial Vía Veneto, the shopping center to the side of the Hotel El Panamá on Vía Veneto, has several 24-hour Internet cafés/international call centers. Names and ownership change seemingly overnight. Other Internet cafés in the Vía España area include a couple on Calle Ricardo Arias off Vía España, just south of the Hotel Continental.

Bytes Café/Sepia Restaurant (Vía Argentina, no phone, 7 A.M.–11 P.M. Mon.–Sat.) is across the street from and just north of the Vía Argentina branch of Churrería Manolo. It also places international calls.

Enterprising street vendors are now offering use of their cell phones to make local calls for around US$0.20, which can be more convenient than hunting for a pay phone. These are easiest to find in working-class commercial areas such as Calidonia, La Exposición, and Santa Ana.

However, those expecting to make lots of local calls are better off buying a local mobile phone that can be recharged with prepaid phone cards. Surprisingly good ones with clear sound and long battery life are widely available in shops throughout Panama for about $15–20, including a local SIM card, immediate activation, and US$2 in phone credit.

Internet cafés have been slow to come to Casco Viejo. But free wireless access is increasingly common in the area's lodgings and restaurants.

VISAS AND OFFICIALDOM
Panama City's main **Migración y Naturalización** (Immigration and Naturalization, Avenida Cuba and Calle 29 Este, tel. 207-1800, 777-7777, or 227-1077, tel./fax 227-1227, 8 A.M.–3 P.M. Mon.–Fri.) office is in Calidonia, close to most of the budget hotels. Visitors who need to change or extend

their visa should come here (and be prepared for a long day).

LAUNDRY
Lavamáticos (launderettes) are harder and harder to find in central Panama City (as opposed to *lavanderías,* which are comparable to dry-cleaning places in the United States). Hostels and both budget and business-oriented hotels often provide laundry service at quite reasonable rates; be sure to ask for prices ahead of time. Some hotels, especially *aparthotels,* have self-service washers and dryers. *Lavamáticos* generally charge around US$5–6 total to wash and dry a load. Washing in cold water is often a bit cheaper.

Lavandería Dry Clean (Calle Ricardo Arias near Avenida 3 Sur, 7:30 A.M.–7:30 P.M. Mon.–Sat.) is right next to Restaurante Costa Azul in Bella Vista.

Lavandería Fan Clean (tel. 399-2108, 7 A.M.–8:30 P.M. Mon.–Sat., 7:30 A.M.–5 P.M. Sun.) is across the street from Einstein's Head, about a block north of Vía Argentina in El Cangrejo.

Launderettes are scarce in Calidonia/La Exposición, but the midrange hotels often have laundry service. There's a *lavamático* in Casco Viejo (Avenida Central near Calle 8 Este, 7 A.M.–7 P.M. Mon.–Sat., 7 A.M.–3 P.M. Sun.) next to the cathedral. It charges US$0.50–$1 to wash, US$1 to dry.

SPANISH LANGUAGE COURSES
The Canadian-run **Spanish Panama** (Vía Argentina and Avenida 3B, tel. 213-3121, www.spanishpanama.com) is a well-established school in El Cangrejo that offers a range of private and group classes. In April 2010 it moved to new digs a few blocks away from its old home, which had been plagued by construction noise. Group classes that include airport pickup, lodging, breakfast, and (optional) salsa dance classes start at US$400/week. A one-week crash course (language instruction only) is US$180. Free weekly cultural and orientation activities

are also available. Spanish Panama is on Vía Argentina near the turnoff for Einstein's Head.

Casco Viejo now has a Spanish-language school. Run by former Peace Corps volunteers, **Casco Antiquo Spanish School** (Avenida A and Calle 4, tel. 838-5592, www.cascospanish. com) is in a crumbling old building with lots of character that houses several nongovernmental organizations that give the place the feel of a lively community center. Group lessons with two to three people are US$9.50/hour. Private lessons tailored to individual needs are US$12/hour. Intensive courses in groups of no more than six people start at US$195/week. Business-Spanish tutorials are US$18/hour. The school can arrange lodgings in local hostels and volunteer opportunities with the nongovernmental organizations in the building.

Getting There

Panama City, not surprisingly, is the country's transportation hub. It has its major international and domestic airports, its biggest bus terminal, its main ship ports, and plenty of rental car companies. Most travelers come to and leave the country through Tocumen International Airport, 25 kilometers east of Panama City. (It's pronounced "toe-COO-men," not "TOC-you-men," as many tourists and expats think.) The nearest cruise-ship port is at the end of the Calzada de Amador, which is near the Pacific entrance to the Panama Canal a few kilometers from downtown. The national bus terminal, for international, regional, and local buses, is the Gran Terminal de Transportes in Albrook. It's quite close to Panama City's domestic airport, Aeropuerto Marcos A. Gelabert, also in Albrook.

No roads or ferry service currently link Panama and Colombia; only airlines provide regular passenger service between the two countries.

DOMESTIC FLIGHTS

Panama City's small domestic airport, officially called **Aeropuerto Marcos A. Gelabert,** is near the Gran Terminal de Transportes in Albrook, a former U.S. Air Force base. It's just a couple of kilometers northwest of the heart of Panama City. Flights generally leave Panama City early in the morning, though some popular destinations have multiple daily departures scattered throughout the day.

Most taxi drivers won't know the airport by name: Ask to go to the Aeropuerto de Albrook. Emphasize that you want to go to Albrook to avoid being taken to Tocumen, the international airport. The fare from most parts of Panama City should be only a few dollars. It will generally make more sense, and even be more economical overall, to take a taxi directly to the airport than fool with making the short ride from downtown to Albrook by bus.

Air Panama (tel. 316-9000, www.flyairpanama.com) is the country's one remaining domestic carrier, following the sudden collapse of Aeroperlas in February 2012. Unless and until a new enterprise takes off, this is the only option for in-country flights. Air Panama was so inundated with new business following the demise of Aeroperlas that passengers were having to go to the airport to make and pay for bookings; the phone lines and website weren't coping. Air Panama flies to Bocas del Toro, Guna Yala, the Darién, David, the Islas Perlas, and a few other mainland destinations.

The airport terminal was undergoing a major overhaul in 2012, which in the short run was making for lots of noise, dust, and heat (the air-conditioning was switched off) but hopefully will improve facilities in the long run.

REGIONAL BUSES

Buses are the backbone of Panama's public transit system. They're frequent, fast, and cheap—at least by the standards of visitors. One-way fares from Panama City to most places in Panama are less than US$10. The longest and most expensive fare, to Bocas del Toro, is still less than US$30.

Most long-distance buses leave from the capital's **Gran Terminal de Transportes.** It's pretty *gran,* all right—huge and two stories high. Buses arrive on the top floor and leave from street level, which is where all the ticket booths are. Destinations are posted on each booth, and a schedule of hours and intermediate destinations is sometimes posted behind the ticket seller. The Gran Terminal now has a website (www.grantnt.com) listing details and prices for all destinations, which would be super swell if the list wasn't two years out of date.

There may be more than one bus headed to your destination at any given time. If a bus that has your destination as a final stop isn't convenient, look for one that has it as an interim stop. Those heading to Santiago, for instance, can buy a ticket at the Santiago booth or, say, the David booth since Santiago is on the way to David.

There's a US$0.10 departure fee for long-distance bus service. This fee can no longer be paid in cash. Passengers must get a rechargeable *Rapipass* smartcard at one of the booths near the exit turnstiles. There is no charge for the card (other than the US$0.10 exit fee), but passengers must present their passport or local identity card to the attendant, who will record the details. Card readers at the turnstiles deduct the US$0.10 fee from the *Rapipass* as passengers exit. Using the bathrooms in the terminal costs US$0.25.

Panama City and local area buses also operate from the terminal, including buses to Tocumen International Airport (look for the Tocumen, Corredor Sur bus). They leave from the ground floor, on the side facing the shopping mall. Destinations are signposted.

The ground floor has shops, pharmacies, a half-dozen banks and ATMs, a branch of the low-cost Niko's Café cafeteria, two U.S.-style food courts, places to take passport-size photos and laminate ID cards, a clinic, places selling cheap mobile phone and phone cards, and other businesses likely to be of interest to travelers.

Global Bank (10 A.M.–6 P.M. Mon.–Fri., 9 A.M.–2:30 P.M. Sat) has a 24-hour ATM. So does **HSBC bank** (9:30 A.M.–5:30 P.M. Mon.–Fri., 9 A.M.–1 P.M. Sat.), which is just opposite. There are now lots of ATMs in the terminal, but if there are crowds or you'd rather not withdraw money at a bus terminal, use one of the ATMs in the shopping mall next door. **Telxpress** (tel. 269-1055, 8 A.M.–8 P.M. daily) offers international phone call service at prices that tend to be excessive.

Schedule

Below are some bus destinations likely to be of interest to visitors. Bus schedules stay pretty stable, though the first and last bus of the day often change. Try to travel so you arrive at your destination during daylight hours, when it will be much easier to find local transport. Aim for *expresso* buses to your destination, as these can shave considerable time off a journey.

Almirante (port for Bocas del Toro archipelago) and Changuinola: One daily bus, at 8 P.M., though if that one fills up the company sometimes runs a second one at 8:30 P.M. The bus sells out so get to the station and buy tickets early. The ride takes about 10 hours. The company that runs this route has been adding and dropping a second departure, in the morning, for years now. If it's available and scheduled to leave later than about 7 A.M., any delay will mean you stand an excellent chance of missing the last water taxi to the islands and have to spend the night in either Almirante or Changuinola, or at a more attractive, but more remote and expensive, hotel called La Escapada. The last water taxi leaves at 6:30 P.M., and it sometimes fills up. It's safer to overnight on the bus and get to the islands during the day. It arrives at about 6 A.M. the next morning at the Almirante crossroads (US$27.80) and 7 A.M. at Changuinola (US$29). There's a two-suitcase maximum included in the fare.

Bayano: Every 40 minutes or so 3:20 A.M.–6 P.M. (US$3 to Lago Bayano, 2.5 hours).

Chitré: About once an hour 6 A.M.–11 P.M. (US$9.05, 3.5 hours).

Colón: Every 20 minutes or less 4:50 A.M.–10:10 P.M. for air-conditioned bus (US$3.15 for express, about 1.5 hours; the non-express bus using the toll road is US$2.15 but can be far slower). Look for the names ULTRACOLPA or EPACOC, the two companies that run the fancy air-conditioned buses. Avoid the cheaper but incredibly slow buses that skip the toll road and stop everywhere. Be very careful at the Colón bus station. Those who want to go to Portobelo or Isla Grande by public transportation should take a Colón-bound bus and transfer at Sabanitas, on the Transístmica (Boyd-Roosevelt Highway), well before reaching Colón.

Coronado: Every 15 minutes 6 A.M.–9 P.M. (US$2.80, 1.5 hours).

Darién: 4 A.M. and 4:15 P.M. Because of road conditions, Metetí (US$9, 6 hours) is usually the last stop. In the dry season, early morning buses sometimes make it all the way to Yaviza (US$14, about 7 hours). Add at least an hour to these estimates if the road is bad. For current road conditions, call the bus company that makes this run at cell 6792-9493 (Panama City) or cell 6841-4767 (Metetí).

David: Two well-established companies run large, long-haul, air-conditioned buses between Panama City and David. The fare is US$15.20 one-way, or US$18.15 for a one-way express bus. The trip theoretically takes about 6.5 hours, but buses frequently run late; express buses can shave up to an hour off that time. Buses generally stop at provincial towns along the Interamerican Highway, most notably Aguadulce, Penonomé, and Santiago. Other stops are made by request. In Santiago, buses usually take a half-hour break at the Pyramidal or Los Tucanes complex, both of which have a cafeteria, restaurant, bathrooms, pharmacy, ATM, and other services. Seats are assigned, and passengers can request seat assignments. For safety's sake, avoid seats at the front of the bus. Avoid sitting near the bathroom in the back. The companies frequently tinker with their schedules, so don't count on precise timing. However, buses leave virtually around the clock, and there is usually more than one option per hour during daylight hours. A third company, **Panafrom,** was running this route in 2012. They have six daily departures.

The largest of the three companies, with the most frequent trips, is **Terminales David-Panama** (tel. 314-6228, tel. 314-6395 for cargo, terminal@cwpanama.net). Buses leave every 60–90 minutes 5:30 A.M.–midnight. The last two buses, at 10:45 P.M. and midnight, are expresses.

Padafront (tel. 314-6264) has departures to David about every 1–2 hours approximately 6:45 A.M.–midnight. The last two buses, at 10:45 P.M. and midnight, are expresses.

El Copé: Every half hour 5 A.M.–6 P.M. (US$6.50, 3 hours).

El Valle: Every 30 minutes 7 A.M.–7 P.M. (US$4.25, 2.5 hours).

Farallón and Santa Clara: Every 20 minutes 5:30 A.M.–8 P.M. (US$3.95 to Santa Clara, US$4.70 to Farallón, 2 hours).

Las Tablas: About once an hour 6 A.M.–7 P.M. (US$9.70, 4 hours).

Paso Canoa (border crossing with Costa Rica): One of the companies that makes the Panama City–David run, Padafront, continues west to Paso Canoa, the main border crossing with Costa Rica. The trip takes 8–9 hours, slightly less for an express. Most travelers will be better off taking one of the international buses that continue to Costa Rica and beyond. But if you just need to make it to the border, Padafront leaves Panama City more frequently. Another possibility is to take any bus to David and switch to one of the small regional buses that run constantly between that city and the border.

Penonomé and La Pintada: Every 20–30 minutes 4:45 A.M.–10:45 P.M. (US$5.25 to Penonomé, 2 hours; US$6 to La Pintada, 2.5 hours).

San Carlos: Every 30 minutes 7 A.M.–7 P.M. (US$3.25, 2 hours).

Santiago: About every 30 minutes 2 A.M.–midnight (US$9.10, about 4 hours). Two companies, Expreso Veraguense and Sanpasa, work this route and compete aggressively with each other. Be prepared for *boleteros* (ticket touts) trying to get your business as you approach their counters.

Soná (for those going to Playa Santa Catalina): 8:20 A.M., 10:20 A.M., 12:45 P.M., 2:20 P.M., 4:20 P.M., and 5:45 P.M. (US$9.70, about 4.5 hours). Get a Santa Catalina bus or taxi in Soná. The last bus for Santa Catalina leaves Soná at 4 P.M.

BY CAR

The **Corredor Norte,** a toll highway with several entrances on the north and west outskirts of the city, leads north across the isthmus, ending at Sabanitas, not far from the outskirts of Colón, on the Caribbean coast. This is a far better option than taking the old, slow potholed Transístmica (also known as the transisthmian highway, officially it's the Boyd-Roosevelt Highway, though no one calls it that).

The **Corredor Sur,** another toll highway that begins just east of Punta Paitilla, leads to Tocumen International Airport, where it links with the Interamerican Highway. There, at a cloverleaf intersection next to Hotel Riande Aeropuerto Hotel and Resort, the Interamerican Highway (really just a two-lane road) continues east toward Cerro Azul and the Darién. This road passes through the Darién and finally ends at Yaviza, the beginning of the Darién Gap, through which no road has ever been built.

To all points west of Panama City—the beaches, mountains, Azuero Peninsula, Bocas del Toro, Costa Rican border, and the rest—there are only two ways to begin the journey by land: by crossing the **Puente de las Américas** (Bridge of the Americas) near the Pacific entrance to the Panama Canal or by taking the newer **Puente Centenario** (Centennial Bridge) across the canal near Pedro Miguel.

The Puente de las Américas is aging dramatically and has not been well maintained. There is also much more and much heavier traffic rumbling across it than it was ever meant to handle. As a result, it is literally falling apart. The Panamanian government launched a huge and enormously expensive repair project in early 2012, but it caused so much traffic chaos it was temporarily suspended. The project is expected to take until at least 2014 to complete. Try to avoid this bridge and take the Puente Centenario instead, especially during rush hours and at the start or end of the weekend.

West of either bridge, the road eventually connects with another toll highway, the **Autopista Arraiján-La Chorrera.** This is now a divided highway for much of the way to the western frontier, though most of the stretch between Santiago and David is still a two-lane road. Nevertheless, this entire ribbon of road is officially part of the Interamerican Highway.

Most Pacific-side destinations in the former Canal Zone are accessible from Panama City by taking **Gaillard Highway** (now officially known as Avenida Omar Torrijos Herrera), which borders the east bank of the canal and runs past the domestic airport at Albrook, the Panama Railway terminal at Corozal, Clayton, Miraflores and Pedro Miguel Locks, and so on. The road forks outside Gamboa. Left leads to the attractions around Gamboa before Gaillard Highway dead-ends in Gamboa itself. Right leads through part of Parque Nacional Soberanía, including part of the historic Las Cruces Trail, before intersecting the Transístmica, the old road linking Panama City with Colón.

Getting Around

Traffic in Panama City is bad and getting worse all the time. There are an estimated 450,000 cars here, which comes to one for every other man, woman, and child. Skyscraper construction, excavation work for the new metro system, flooded streets during bad weather, and major repair work on the main bridge spanning the Panama Canal have turned a congested city into one that comes to a near standstill at times.

If possible, avoid car trips during morning and evening rush hours, especially 8–9 A.M. and 4:30–6:30 P.M. A couple of toll roads that cut through the city—Corredor Norte and Corredor Sur—are a quick escape from some of the congestion, since they're priced out of reach of the average Panama City driver. Most tolls are less than US$2, so you'll save a lot of time and aggravation by taking them.

Taxis are inexpensive and easy to find at all hours, making them the transportation of choice even for Panamanians of modest means. Buses are frequent and even cheaper, but they are a far slower and less convenient way to get around most parts of the city. Panama City's new bus system, Metro Bus, is bringing modern mass transit to the city.

I don't recommend that those unfamiliar with Panama City, especially those unaccustomed to Latin American roads, attempt to drive in the city. It's a good way to spoil your day, if not your whole trip. Drivers are aggressive, streets are confusing and poorly marked, and there's a severe shortage of traffic signals, which most drivers treat merely as friendly suggestions in any case. Streets have been known to change from two-way to one-way literally overnight, without anyone bothering to change the signs. Other nuisances include the occasional stolen manhole cover.

Traffic in the former Canal Zone remains more orderly, but it too is increasingly showing the effects of chaotic road expansion and urban sprawl. Taxis, and in some cases buses, are convenient options for trips into the canal area, particularly for Pacific-side destinations such as the Calzada de Amador (Amador Causeway), Albrook, Miraflores Locks, and Balboa.

Adding to the confusion of getting around is the fact that many streets have multiple names. The names used in this chapter are generally those most likely to be recognized by taxi drivers and other locals. Some destinations, especially in the former Canal Zone, are much more likely to be known by proximity to landmarks than by any street name.

BY TAXI

Taxis offer by far the easiest way to get around the city. Panama reportedly has 40,000 taxis, and most of them are in Panama City jockeying for your business. Most are small Japanese cars that will take an individual just about anywhere in town for US$2 or less. Don't be put off by taxi drivers beeping their horns at you; it can be annoying, but it's just their way of finding out if you want a ride. All legal taxis in Panama, except tourist taxis with license plates that start with the letters "SET," must be painted yellow.

Taxis are not metered in Panama City (or anywhere else in the country), though they're being tested in the city and may eventually be installed. In the meantime, taxis charge according to a government-mandated zone system. The city is carved up into seven zones; fares are based on the number of zones crossed. The minimum fare is US$1.20, and each zone crossed is another US$0.40. The maximum standard fare for a single passenger traveling across all zones—from the Amador Causeway to Costa del Este, which is a very long ride— should be no more than US$3.60.

Each additional passenger adds US$0.50 to the fare, regardless of the distance. There's also a US$0.30 surcharge on Sunday, holidays, and late at night (10 P.M.–5 A.M.). Phoning for a taxi adds US$0.50 to the fare. Most taxi drivers are honest and decent, even if their driving is a bit nuts.

Asking the fare ahead of time is one way to know what you're in for, but it also betrays your ignorance of the going rate to your destination. Another common strategy for trips within the city limits is just to hand the driver US$2 at the end of the ride; if the legitimate fare is more than that, they'll most definitely let you know, but they're less likely to think they can scam you. Taxi drivers are required to present the zone chart on demand, though anyone likely to rip you off is likely to have a fake zone chart as well.

A bigger concern recently has been taxi drivers who refuse to take a fare because the destination is not convenient or profitable. Such a tactic is understandable, but it's illegal. The government has been cracking down on the so-called *no voy* ("I'm not going that way"). If this happens to you, report the culprit at tel. 502-0591.

Don't be alarmed if your driver stops to pick up another fare heading the same way. It's a normal practice, but tell the driver not to do it if it makes you uncomfortable (though expect to pay extra for the privilege of a private ride).

The bashed-up bodies of the average cab will give you some sense of how these Mad Maxes drive. Pulse-pounding near misses are common; think of it as local color. Fortunately, traffic congestion and moderate speeds mean most actual mishaps end up as fender benders.

Fares for rides outside the central city, for instance into the former Canal Zone, go up according to distance, but not as quickly as one might think. A ride as far as Gamboa, on the Panama Canal about halfway across the entire isthmus, costs around US$30. Taxis can also be hired for day tours, but bear in mind that few taxi drivers speak much English or are particularly knowledgeable tour guides, though

all know the city well. There are no standard rates—it depends on the distance, the mood of the driver, and your bargaining skills, but about US$7–8 an hour is a decent rule of thumb.

A few larger, air-conditioned cabs lurk around the more upscale hotels and are allowed to charge several times what the smaller guys do. They are tourist taxis, recognizable by the "SET" license plates. You can always just walk down the street to find a cheaper ride if you can do without air-conditioning and the sense of safety that comes from riding in a bigger hunk of metal.

Taxis are almost always easy to find, but radio taxis can be called as well. Hotels and restaurants will usually be happy to make the call for you.

BY RENTAL CAR

The major U.S. car rental agencies have outlets scattered around Panama City as well as at the international and domestic airports. Several outlets are within a few blocks of the Hotel Continental and Hotel El Panamá on or near Vía España.

Driving is likely to be the best way of getting to the beaches within a couple hours of the city. And for exploring both the nearby canal area and distant locations, it's a reasonable alternative to taxis, buses, and organized tours. Most of the rental agencies are within easy walking distance of each other near the Hotel El Panamá.

Avis Rent A Car (Calle D, tel. 278-9444, www.avis.com, 7 A.M.–9 P.M. daily) is near the El Cangrejo branch of Churrería Manolo, not far from the Hotel El Panamá. At last count it had five other branches in the Panama City and Panama Canal areas.

Budget Rent A Car (central reservations tel. 263-8777, www.budgetpanama.com) has two branches in the Vía España area. The larger one is on the western end of Vía España itself (tel. 263-9190, 7 A.M.–10 P.M. daily), just before Calle Gabrielle Mistral in Bella Vista. The other is at the entrance to the Hotel El Panamá (tel. 214-6806, 8 A.M.–5 P.M. daily).

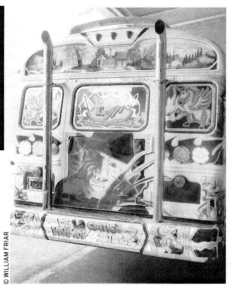

© WILLIAM FRIAR

Panama City's colorful *diablos rojos* buses are being phased out.

Hertz (tel. 210-9213, www.hertz.com, 8 A.M.–5 P.M. Mon.–Fri., 8 A.M.–4 P.M. Sat.) has an office at the Marriott Hotel. Including the international airport, Hertz at last count had five outlets in Panama City. For other locations, check their website.

National Car Rental (Vía Veneto and Avenida 2A Norte, tel. 265-5092, www.nationalcar.com, 8 A.M.–5 P.M. Mon.–Sat.) has an office in El Cangrejo, but the main outlet and car park is some distance away on Calle 50 (tel. 265-3333, 7 A.M.–10 P.M. daily). For other locations, check their website.

There's a **Thrifty Car Rental** (Vía España, tel. 214-7677) near the southern end of Vía España, opposite Budget Rent A Car.

ORGANIZED TOURS

All of Panama's major tour operators have their headquarters in Panama City, and they all offer Panama City tours. They're more of an afterthought for the ecotourism outfits, though, so those looking for a group tour might consider going with a more traditional tour company that offers city tours as a more or less daily business, or simply book through your hotel.

Because Panama City is a relatively compact place, half-day and full-day tours typically give an overview of the entire city, including the ruins of Panamá La Vieja (Panamá Viejo), parts of the reviving colonial district of Casco Viejo, and at least a drive through the major sections of modern, central Panama City. The full-day tours in particular usually find time for a visit to the area of the Panama Canal close to the city. This part of the tour inevitably includes a visit to Miraflores Locks and sometimes throws in stops at the handicrafts market next to the YMCA in Balboa and the Panama Canal Authority's Administration Building, a historic structure perched on a hill that has impressive murals depicting canal construction days in its rotunda and offers dramatic views of the former Canal Zone. All three canal stops are worthwhile, so look for tours that include more than just Miraflores Locks.

Pesantez Tours (tel. 366-9100, 223-5374, or 263-7577, www.pesantez-tours.com) is a long-established tour operator with a reputation for dependable service. Other possibilities include **Panoramic Panama** (tel. 314-1581 or 314-1604, www.bedandbreakfastpanama.com), which is affiliated with La Estancia, a popular bed-and-breakfast in the former Canal Zone; **Ecocircuitos** (tel. 315-1305, U.S./Canada toll-free tel. 800/830-1521, www.ecocircuitos.com); and **Gray Line Panama** (tel. 323-2333 or 323-3328, www.grayline-panama.com).

Expect to pay US$80–110 per person for a half-day tour and US$110–165 for a full-day tour. Larger groups pay less per person. Lunch is sometimes included. The exception is Panoramic Panama, which charges the same rate, US$110, for half-day city and canal tours for either one or two people, which is more

terminal. As you face Niko's Café, the entrance to this little sub-terminal will be on the right. Look for a sign that says SACA or COOP SACA.

Clayton: Every half hour 5:30–10 A.M., noon, every half hour 1:30–5 P.M., 6:30 P.M., and 8 P.M. Monday–Friday. On weekends the bus leaves at 6:45 A.M., 8 A.M., 10 A.M., noon, 2 P.M., 6:30 P.M., 9 P.M., and 10:45 P.M. The price is US$0.35.

Amador: Every half hour from about 6 A.M.–8 P.M. The price is US$0.25; US$0.50 in the evenings or on weekends and holidays.

Gamboa: Roughly every 1–2 hours 5 A.M.–10:45 P.M. Monday–Friday and 6:45 A.M.–10:45 P.M. Saturday and Sunday. The price is US$0.65. This bus can drop passengers off at Pedro Miguel Locks, Paraíso, Parque Nacional Soberanía, Summit Botanical Gardens, and other destinations en route to Gamboa for US$0.25–0.65.

Miraflores Locks (take the Paraíso, Gamboa, or Clayton bus): Buses run on the same schedule as the Clayton bus. Most buses do not go all the way to the locks—they only do so at shift changes for canal workers, which means the 5:30 A.M., 6:30 A.M., and 2:30 P.M. buses. All other buses stop along the main road, and passengers must walk about one kilometer to get to and from the locks. The schedule is inconvenient for visitors since they are not allowed into Miraflores until 9 A.M. and the visitors center closes at 5 P.M. In other words, plan to hoof it. Fortunately, it's a scenic walk.

BY METRO

You're likely to see many torn-up streets throughout Panama City during your visit, some of which cause major detours and traffic congestion. In the works is a modern metro system, Panama City's most ambitious transportation project yet. Line 1 of the Metro is expected to be completed sometime in 2014. Additional lines will be added in coming years.

The Line 1 stops will be Albrook (connecting with the Gran Terminal de Transportes), Curundu, Plaza Cinco de Mayo, Marañon, Santo Tomás, Iglesia del Carmen, Vía Argentina, Fernandez de Cordoba, 12 de Octubre, Pueblo Nuevo, San Miguelito, Pan de Azucar, and Los Andes. (Station names may change.) The stops between Albrook and Vía Argentina are likely to be of most interest to visitors, since they cover the heart of Panama City.

East of Fernandez de Cordoba, the Metro emerges from underground and runs on an elevated track through the suburbs to Los Andes, where the line ends at a shopping mall. Officials promise a ride along the entire line will take just 23 minutes. The fare price had not been announced at the time of writing.

THE PANAMA CANAL AND CENTRAL ISTHMUS

The Panama Canal is one of the most awe-inspiring of all human endeavors. Built across the isthmus of Panama at one of its narrowest and lowest points, it is 80 kilometers (50 miles) long, extending from Panama City on the Pacific Ocean to the city of Colón on the Caribbean Sea. To the bafflement of many a visitor, the Caribbean entrance is northwest of the Pacific entrance.

What was once the Canal Zone ran the length of the canal, extending eight kilometers on either side of it. The U.S. civilian townsites and military bases are now abandoned or being engulfed by the surrounding urban centers, though some of the forested lands have been set aside as protected areas.

The canal itself is so impressive it's easy to overlook nature's equally astonishing handiwork on its banks and in its waters. Parque Nacional Soberanía is one of the most accessible tropical forests in the world. It and the surrounding forests have some of the best bird-watching in the country. There's also a surprisingly decent chance of coming across largish mammals, including three species of monkeys (white-faced capuchins, Geoffroy's tamarins, and howlers), sloths, kinkajous, coatimundis, and capybaras (the largest rodent in the world) in the extensive moist tropical forests still standing here. Even jaguars and harpy eagles are not unheard of, but the chances of spotting either are extremely slim. You may also see a green iguana or two.

COURTESY OF THE AUTORIDAD DEL CANAL DE PANAMÁ

HIGHLIGHTS

◖ **Miraflores Locks:** The most accessible set of locks at the Panama Canal offer a close-up look at one of the world's great engineering feats (page 92).

◖ **Balboa:** This historic townsite offers a glimpse of what life in the former Canal Zone was like (page 95).

◖ **Amador Causeway:** This beautiful breakwater has spectacular views of Panama City and the Panama Canal (page 97).

◖ **Panama Canal Transit:** One of the world's top cruising destinations is also an affordable day trip (page 99).

◖ **Panama Railway:** Travel from ocean to ocean in an hour on this historic and highly scenic rail line (page 100).

◖ **Parque Nacional Soberanía:** This species-rich tropical forest is just a few minutes' drive from downtown Panama City (page 112).

◖ **Portobelo Ruins:** Wander the battered remains of one of the most important, pirate-pestered ports in the Spanish Empire (page 131).

LOOK FOR ◖ TO FIND RECOMMENDED SIGHTS, ACTIVITIES, DINING, AND LODGING.

THE PANAMA CANAL

Though less visited than the Pacific side, the Caribbean end of the Panama Canal and the nearby coastline are rich in history and even richer in natural beauty. Evidence of the former includes the well-preserved ruins of Spanish forts, built to protect looted Incan treasure, and some of the most awe-inspiring structures of the canal. The area's natural attractions can be found among the mangroves, coral reefs, beaches, and forests that still abound with wildlife. Scuba diving and snorkeling are popular and easily accessible in the warm Caribbean waters, home to brilliant tropical fish and ancient shipwrecks. All this begins within a two-hour drive of Panama City.

PLANNING YOUR TIME

It's possible to visit **Miraflores Locks, Pedro Miguel Locks, Gaillard Cut,** and the townsites of **Balboa** and **Ancón** in a single day. A good way to end that day is with an evening walk and a meal or a drink on the **Amador Causeway (Calzada de Amador).** A quick visit to **Gamboa** can be tacked on, but really exploring that area takes a second day. A **Panama Canal transit** is an all-day event; taking the **train** across the isthmus requires a half day to a full day, depending on the return trip. **Isla Taboga** is better for a day trip than an overnight visit, and those planning to see other islands can skip it altogether.

Most visitors to the Caribbean side go just

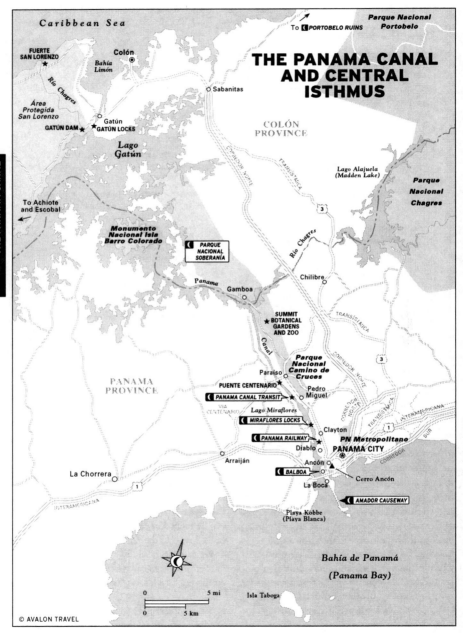

THE PANAMA CANAL AND CENTRAL ISTHMUS

Caribbean Sea

To ◖ PORTOBELO RUINS

Parque Nacional Portobelo

FUERTE SAN LORENZO ★

Bahía Limón

Colón ◉

○ Sabanitas

COLÓN PROVINCE

Área Protegida San Lorenzo

Río Chagres

GATÚN DAM ★ ○ Gatún ★ GATÚN LOCKS

Lago Gatún

Lago Alajuela (Madden Lake)

Parque Nacional Chagres

To Achiote and Escobal

Monumento Nacional Isla Barro Colorado

◖ PARQUE NACIONAL SOBERANÍA

Panama

Gamboa ○

Río Chagres

Chilibre ○

SUMMIT BOTANICAL GARDENS AND ZOO ★

PANAMA PROVINCE

Canal

Parque Nacional Camino de Cruces

Paraíso ○

Pedro Miguel ○

PUENTE CENTENARIO ★

◖ PANAMA CANAL TRANSIT ★

Lago Miraflores

◖ MIRAFLORES LOCKS ★

Clayton ○

PN Metropolitano

◖ PANAMA RAILWAY ★

Diablo ○

PANAMA CITY ⊛

Arraiján ○

Ancón ○

◖ BALBOA ○

La Chorrera ○

La Boca ○

Cerro Ancón

◖ AMADOR CAUSEWAY ◗

Playa Kóbbe (Playa Blanca)

Bahía de Panamá
(Panama Bay)

N

0   5 mi
0   5 km

Isla Taboga

© AVALON TRAVEL

for the day and return to Panama City at night. It's possible to take in **Portobelo,** the attractions near the Caribbean entrance to the Panama Canal (most notably **Gatún Locks** and **Gatún Dam**), and **Fuerte San Lorenzo** in a single day. However, it would be a long day, with lots of driving, and it's probably too ambitious for those relying solely on public transportation. Consider striking either Portobelo or Fuerte San Lorenzo off the itinerary; it'd be hard to do both. If at all possible, take the train across the isthmus at least one way. It's the most scenic and pleasant way to make the trip.

The Panama Canal is in the middle of a multibillion-dollar expansion that will include two new sets of giant locks, one on the Pacific and one on the Caribbean side of the isthmus. It's expected to be completed in 2015.

Spending the night somewhere on the Caribbean side is pretty much a must for those who want to add an outdoor activity such as scuba diving, birding, or boating to a visit. One approach for a longer visit is to stay a night or two on **Isla Grande,** stopping at Portobelo on the way over and visiting San Lorenzo and the canal-area attractions on the way back to Panama City.

Rainfall is far heavier on the Caribbean than the Pacific side of the isthmus. It averages 3.2 meters in Colón, nearly twice as much as in Panama City. For those not metrically inclined, that's more than 10 *feet* of rain a year. The dry season is also not as well-defined on the Caribbean as it is on the Pacific side. In Portobelo, one of the wettest spots in Panama, it rains nearly year-round.

The Former Canal Zone

The Pacific side of the former Canal Zone contains two of the Panama Canal's three sets of locks and the beginning of the approximately 14-kilometer Gaillard Cut through the Continental Divide, the toughest part of the canal to dig and the most dramatic to see. One of the new post-Panamax locks is also being built here.

The area also contains most of the former zone townsites, as they were known, which were home to the civilian employees of the canal and their families. These include Ancón, Balboa, La Boca, and Diablo. It's home also to what were once its most important U.S. military bases, including Howard Air Force Base, Fort Clayton, Fort Amador, Quarry Heights, Albrook Air Force Base, and Rodman Naval Station.

The Amador Causeway has become a major nightlife and tourism destination. Albrook is now a fairly upscale suburban residential area (and home to Panama City's domestic airport and bus terminal). Parts of Clayton have been converted into something called La Ciudad del Saber (The City of Knowledge), which attracts international academic and research institutions. The latest area to see development is Howard, which is gradually being rebranded as Panama Pacifico. Business parks, condominiums, an airport (there's already a huge airfield from its U.S. Air Force days), and more are being planned for the area.

But much of the former zone has become a series of ghost towns awaiting a development plan, or are being plowed under to make way for suburban housing, port facilities, highways, and industrial complexes.

SIGHTS

The Canal Zone attractions run along the east bank of the canal and are easily accessible from Panama City.

Pacific Side Locks

Work on the new post-Panamax locks on the

THE PANAMA CANAL

THE PANAMA CANAL

NEW LOCKS FOR A "POST-PANAMAX" WORLD

COURTESY OF THE AUTORIDAD DEL CANAL DE PANAMÁ

Giant locks and new access channels are being added to the canal.

The Panama Canal is in the middle of a multibillion-dollar expansion program due to be completed in 2015. Its centerpiece will be two new sets of locks, one near each ocean, located to the west of the current ones.

The chambers of the existing locks are enormous: each is almost 305 by 34 meters. The new ones will be colossal: nearly 427 by 55 meters. Each set of the new locks will contain three chambers, beside which will run basins in tiers meant to capture and reuse water used during transits. (The existing locks lose millions of gallons of freshwater to the sea with each lockage; the canal's watershed would

have to be greatly expanded to use a similar system for the new locks.) New access channels are also being dug, and existing ones widened and deepened.

Expansion work is well under way; though until the new locks are finished, there won't be much to see but giant holes in the ground.

The project is meant to allow "post-Panamax" ships to transit the canal (Panamax ships are specifically designed to fit through the existing canal). But not everyone is convinced the project will succeed, or even that it's necessary. Of course, the first time around there were plenty of doubters, too.

Pacific side of the canal had not even begun as this book went to press. But presuming work is completed on schedule, they should be finished and hard at work raising and lowering colossal ships by 2015.

◖ MIRAFLORES LOCKS

Miraflores Locks (Esclusas de Miraflores), completed in May 1913, stand at the Pacific entrance to the Panama Canal. They link the Pacific Ocean with the artificial Miraflores

The original locks controls have been replaced by a computerized system, but the old control boards have been left in place.

and theater. The 1st floor of the museum contains a history of the canal, starting with the failed French effort and continuing through its completion by the United States. The 2nd floor is an ecological exhibit that stresses the importance of the Panama Canal watershed and displays on the flora and fauna found within it. The 3rd floor shows the operation of the canal and includes a full-scale pilot-training simulator and a topographical canal map. The 4th floor has route maps that stress the importance of the canal to world commerce.

The restaurant has a terrace right on the edge of the locks, making it a great place to come for lunch or dinner. There's also an outdoor snack bar on the ground floor.

PEDRO MIGUEL LOCKS AND GAILLARD CUT
The Pedro Miguel Locks, about a 10-minute drive farther down Gaillard Highway from Miraflores, raise and lower ships in one 9.5-meter step, linking Miraflores Lake and Gaillard Cut. These locks are not open to the public, but they're visible through a chain-link fence. Those in the area may want to stop briefly and take a peek. There's also a partial view of the beginning of Gaillard Cut (also called Culebra Cut), where the canal was dug right through the Continental Divide. It's a dramatic sight, though the widening of the cut has made it a bit less so by pushing back and lowering the rocky peaks through which the waterway runs. Farther up the road is the Puente Centenario, an elegant suspension bridge over the canal that was inaugurated in 2004. There are good, if quick, views of the cut from the bridge.

Cerro Ancón
ADMINISTRATION BUILDING
The agency that runs the Panama Canal, now known as the Autoridad del Canal de Panamá (Panama Canal Authority), is headquartered in an imposing building perched on a small

Lake, raising and lowering ships 16.5 meters in two impressive steps. Of the canal's three sets of locks, these are the easiest to reach from Panama City and the best equipped to handle visitors. Recently, guards have become strict about not letting visitors onto the grounds until the visitors center opens at 9 A.M.

The massive **Centro de Visitantes de Miraflores** (Miraflores Visitors Center, tel. 276-8325, www.pancanal.com, 9 A.M.–5 P.M. daily, including holidays, entire complex: US$8, US$5 for kids ages 5–17, younger kids free, ground terrace and shops only: US$5, US$3 for kids) is an out-of-place monolith from the outside, but inside it's rather impressive. It contains a four-story museum, an observation deck, a theater that shows documentaries on the canal in English and Spanish, and a restaurant with good views of the locks. Hold on to your ticket to be admitted to the museum

© JIM GUY

The Administration Building on Cerro Ancón is the headquarters of the Autoridad del Canal de Panamá, which runs the Panama Canal.

hill on the side of Cerro Ancón. Known simply as the Administration Building (Edificio de Administración), it's worth visiting for a couple of reasons. First, there are dramatic murals inside the building's rotunda that depict the construction of the canal. These were painted by William B. Van Ingen, a New York artist who also created murals for the Library of Congress and the U.S. Mint in Philadelphia. They were installed in January 1915 and underwent a restoration in 1993. The four major panels of the mural show excavation at Gaillard Cut and the construction of Miraflores Locks, the Gatún Dam spillway, and a set of lock gates. They give a sense of what a staggering task the building of the canal was.

Second, there's a sweeping view of part of the former Canal Zone, especially the townsite of Balboa, from the back of the building. Walk through the doors at the rear of the rotunda, but they may lock behind you; in that case just

walk around the outside of the building to get back to the front entrance.

In the foreground are what were once Balboa Elementary School (on the left) and Balboa High School (on the right). The marble monolith between them is the Goethals Monument. The long, palm-lined promenade is the Prado. Each section of the Prado has the exact dimensions of a lock chamber: 1,000 by 110 feet. In the distance are the Bridge of the Americas and Cerro Sosa (Sosa Hill). Those feeling energetic can walk down the long flight of stairs and explore the townsite of Balboa.

Note the large bronze plaque at the foot of the steps. It's dedicated to David D. Gaillard, who led the excavation of Gaillard Cut. The plaque was moved here from the side of a mountain that was leveled during widening work. It was designed by the sculptor James Earle Fraser, who also designed the Buffalo Nickel and is best known for his moving sculpture *End of the Trail.* There's a replica of the plaque at the Miraflores Visitors Center.

Visitors are free to explore the rotunda any time of the day or night, but other parts of the building are off-limits without an appointment. Sign in with the guard at the door.

ADMINISTRATOR'S HOUSE

The Administrator's House, a wooden mansion set in a well-tended garden, is a short drive or an easy, pleasant walk farther up the road from the Administration Building. When the road forks, head left. During construction days this was the home of the canal's chief engineer. It originally sat overlooking what is now Gaillard Cut, allowing the chief engineers (first John F. Stevens, then George W. Goethals) to keep an eye on the excavation even when they were home. In 1914 it was taken apart and moved by train to its present location. It has been the home of the canal's chief executive ever since. Visitors are not allowed in the house, but they can walk around the front entrance. It's also pleasant to walk down Lion Hill Road, the winding, jungle-shrouded road to the right as you face the house. The grounds are enclosed by a green chain-link fence for security.

TOP OF CERRO ANCÓN

There's an impressive view of Casco Viejo, Panama Bay, and the modern city skyline from the top of Cerro Ancón (Ancon Hill). Walk behind the communications tower to get a look at the entrance to the Panama Canal, the Bridge of the Americas, Miraflores Locks, and the townsite of Balboa. It's also possible to walk up to the giant Panamanian flag, which was one of the first things to go up in the former Canal Zone after the ratification of the treaties that turned the canal over to Panama. This spot has the best view of the Panama City skyline. The U.S. military dug a tunnel into the heart of the hill, the entrance to which still stands in Quarry Heights, as a secure command post during times of crisis.

The road to the top starts at the entrance to Quarry Heights, once the headquarters of the U.S. Southern Command. Those driving should head up the road that goes past the Administration Building, then take a right when the road forks at the Administrator's House. Go past the guard house, then make a left past the headquarters of the environmental nonprofit ANCON. Access from this point on is by a one-way road. Guards at either end of the road tell you when it's safe to go, but honk the horn around curves anyway. The top of Cerro Ancón is two kilometers up from the Quarry Heights gate.

◖ Balboa

Those who want a sense of what life was like in the former Canal Zone should consider spending an hour or two wandering around the townsite of Balboa. The unofficial capital of the Canal Zone, it was the most formally planned of the zone communities. Today it's being squeezed between a container port and highway overpasses, and many of the old apartments are either unoccupied or have been converted into offices, but it retains much of its peculiar utilitarian elegance.

GOETHALS MONUMENT

This marble monolith at the base of the Administration Building was erected in honor of George W. Goethals, the chief engineer of the canal from 1907 to its completion in 1914. The three tiers of the fountain symbolize the three sets of locks. The monument was controversial when it was erected; some complained it didn't fit into the community's design.

CENTRO DE CAPACITACIÓN ASCANIO AROSEMENA

Along the palm-lined promenade of the **Prado** are what were once **Balboa Elementary School** and **Balboa High School**. Both are now offices used by the Panama Canal Authority. Parts of

THE OTHER SIDE

In the old Canal Zone days, those on the Pacific side of the canal spoke of the area around the Caribbean entrance as "the Other Side." (Naturally, those "other siders" in turn tended to apply that term to those on the Pacific side.) The Atlantic side felt like another world, even though it was less than 80 kilometers away. There were just two ways to get there by land: by the railroad or by a pothole-riddled highway known as the Transístmica. As kids, many Pacific siders, including this one, rarely made what seemed like an epic journey to the Caribbean side: swim meets and the annual football jamboree against our archrival, Cristóbal High School, were about it.

In those days we all thought in terms of the Atlantic rather than the Caribbean side, though the latter is more accurate. Even in a tiny world, the Atlantic side was minuscule, and it got less attention. The canal's headquarters was on the Pacific coast, close to Panama City, and that's where the action was. As a result, the Caribbean communities tended to be tight and socially active. With fewer diversions, Atlantic siders had to find ways to entertain themselves.

Residents lived in townsites with names such as Cristóbal, Gatún, Coco Solo (birthplace of John McCain), Margarita, and Rainbow City, dotted among which were U.S. military bases, such as Fort Sherman, Fort Gulick, and Fort Davis. Cristóbal was literally across the street from Colón, and partly for that reason the boundaries between the Canal Zone and Panama were especially fluid on this side.

When the gringos left, much of the Canal Zone became a virtual ghost town, and this is especially true of the Caribbean side. Whole townsites have grown silent, and in some places the tropical forest is taking over again.

the old high school, now known as the Centro de Capacitación Ascanio Arosemena (tel. 272-1111, 7 A.M.–4:15 P.M. Mon.–Fri.), are open to visitors. Outside is a breezeway dedicated to the Panamanians who died during the 1964 Flag Riots; their names are inscribed on the pillars. Just inside the building is a display that attempts to walk a delicate line between the still-polarized views on what exactly happened during the riots, the bloodiest and most controversial conflict between the United States and Panama until the 1989 U.S. invasion.

Lining the halls on this floor and the one above is a wealth of rare artifacts from both the French and U.S. canal efforts, including railroad ties and pickaxes, clippings from 19th-century newspapers, bonds sold to finance the disastrous French effort, fascinating black-and-white prints dating from the 1880s, maps, Canal Zone stamps and seals, and historic china and silverware from the Canal Zone governor's house. On the 2nd floor is the

Biblioteca Roberto F. Chiari (10 A.M.–4 P.M. Mon.–Fri. for researchers). This is the library of the Autoridad del Canal de Panamá (Panama Canal Authority), housed in what was once the high school library. It contains all kinds of technical and historical books and documents on the Panama Canal and Panama. It's not technically open to the general public, but those who fancy themselves researchers can certainly stop by and sign in.

STEVENS CIRCLE

Farther down the Prado is Stevens Circle, a rather drab monument to John Stevens, the canal's chief engineer between 1905 and 1907 and its master designer. On the left is the **Balboa post office.** Directly across the main road is what's left of a cafeteria that used to feed canal workers around the clock. Next to it is the **Teatro Balboa,** once a movie theater and now host to occasional concerts and other performances. Across the street from that is the former commissary for canal employees, now offices.

BALBOA ROAD

Heading down Avenida Arnulfo Arias Madrid (also known as Balboa Road) in the direction of Amador and Panama City, you'll see the **Union Church,** an ecumenical church still in use. Just past it is an enormous and rather weird **fountain** built in honor of Arnulfo Arias Madrid, who was elected (and overthrown) president of Panama four times. It was built by Mireya Moscoso, Arias's widow, after she became president in 1999, and depicts Arnulfo flashing a "V for victory" sign at figures representing the Panamanian people, who are struggling to their feet.

◖ Amador Causeway

The beautiful breakwater known as the Amador Causeway (Calzada de Amador) extends more than three kilometers into the Pacific, calming the waters at the entrance of the Panama Canal and preventing that entrance from silting up. It was built from soil dug from the canal and connects three islands: **Naos, Perico,** and **Flamenco.**

The causeway has gorgeous views. On one side the majestic Bridge of the Americas spans the Pacific entrance to the canal, so there's always a parade of ships gliding underneath it or waiting their turn in the anchorage. On the other side is the half-moon of Panama Bay, ringed by the ever-growing Panama City skyline.

The causeway is a nightlife destination for locals, and huge amounts of money are being poured into it in the hopes it will lure international visitors. In the last few years, restaurants, bars, and shopping centers have gone up in this area, as have a hotel, cruise-ship terminal, marina, convention hall, and amphitheater. Most of these have been built on Isla Flamenco on one end of the causeway and in Amador proper on the other. (Amador was formerly a U.S. army base called Fort Amador.)

The causeway itself has gotten an

THE PANAMA CANAL

© THOMAS GORISSEN/WWW.THOMASGORISSEN.COM

The Amador Causeway is popular with families, especially on the weekend.

understated and elegant makeover, with new streetlights and a renovated walking path that left the palm trees along it intact but added benches for those who need a rest. Near the entrance to the causeway is a row of flags of many countries, though the U.S. one is conspicuously absent; flying the stars and stripes anywhere in Panama, especially at a former gringo army base, would be loaded with controversial symbolism.

Amador and the causeway can get packed with visitors on the weekends, particularly dry-season Sundays. The popularity of the bars and restaurants causes traffic jams on the two-lane road on weekend nights.

For those without cars, the main way to get around here is on foot, though it can be a long walk in the sun from one end of the causeway to another. Fortunately, most of the attractions are clustered at the end of the causeway, on or near Isla Flamenco. There's a bike and scooter rental place at the entrance to the causeway. It may also be possible to flag down a passing taxi or bus for a quick ride up or down the causeway.

Avoid the taxi concession at the Flamenco Shopping Plaza. It's aimed at cruise-ship passengers and their prices are outrageous. (The hourly rate is nearly 10 times the norm.)

MUSEO DE LA BIODIVERSIDAD (MUSEUM OF BIODIVERSITY)

Designed by architect Frank O. Gehry, who is married to a Panamanian, this ambitious museum project (www.biomuseopanama. org) is meant to do for Panama what Gehry's Guggenheim did for Bilbao, Spain. The overly exuberant even maintain it will one day be a greater draw than the canal. This level of hype is a lot for any building to live up to, let alone one that is more modest in scale than the Bilbao Guggenheim and some other Gehry projects.

The museum's completion has been delayed for years by funding shortages, and the expected opening date has been pushed back

several times. The museum should finally open its doors during the life of this book, but I'll believe it when I see it.

In the meantime, the museum has been offering talks and a look at scale models of what the finished product will be like. The schedule varies, but in the dry season has included visits at noon and 5 P.M. on Saturdays and Sundays and talks in English at 1 P.M. on Sundays. Entrance fee is US$2.

For safety reasons, visitors younger than 18 are not allowed, and adults must wear long trousers and closed-toe shoes. Construction can cause the cancellation of planned visits.

EL CENTRO DE EXHIBICIONES MARINAS

There's a long-established little museum, El Centro de Exhibiciones Marinas (Punta Culebra on Naos, tel. 212-8000, ext. 2366, rainy season hours: 1–5 P.M. Tues.–Fri., 10 A.M.–6 P.M. Sat. and Sun.; dry season hours: 10 A.M.–6 P.M. Tues.–Sun., US$5 adults, US$1 children), toward the end of the causeway, that's well worth a visit. Try to call ahead of time, as opening and closing hours shift erratically.

This nicely designed marine exhibition center is run by the Panama-based Smithsonian Tropical Research Institute. Exhibits set up along a beachside path explain the extensive natural and human history of the area and touch on that of Panama in general. There's a small outdoor aquarium and an air-conditioned observation building. Free telescopes are set up along the path; check out the ships waiting to transit the canal. At the end of the path are a few hundred square meters of dry forest, once common all along the Pacific coast of Central America, but now mostly wiped out since it's easy to burn. It's amazing what you may find in this little patch of forest. There are lots of iguanas, and the last time I was there I saw a shaggy three-toed sloth walking upside down along a branch just a few meters above my head. The center is on Punta Culebra toward the

THE PANAMA CANAL

The Panama Canal is one of the world's great engineering feats.

end of the causeway. At the public beach on the first island, Naos, make a right when the road forks. There should be large signs.

Panama Canal Transit

A transit of the Panama Canal is unforgettable, and you don't have to buy a cruise to have the experience. These days the most popular way to do it is with **Panama Marine Adventures** (tel. 226-8917, www.pmatours.net, adults US$115–165, children under 12 US$65–75) on the *Pacific Queen*. This is an air-conditioned 119-foot vessel equipped with a snack bar, souvenir shop, and television monitors on which cruisers can watch documentaries on the canal when they need a break from the action on deck. Transits take place on Thursdays, Fridays, and Saturdays during the high season (January through March). The rest of the year transits are Saturday only. Transits do not normally go all the way through the canal from ocean to ocean. Instead, they go through two

sets of locks, Miraflores and Pedro Miguel, and Gaillard Cut. Transits begin or end at Gamboa, depending on whether it's a northbound or southbound transit. (Direction of the transit is marked on the company's website calendar.) Customers check in at Isla Flamenco on the Amador Causeway at 9 A.M. The tour includes land transportation between Isla Flamenco and Gamboa. The partial transit takes 4–5 hours. The price includes pickup at the Flamenco marina on the causeway, lunch and soft drinks, and a bilingual guide.

One Saturday a month the company offers a full transit. This starts at Flamenco at 7:30 A.M. and goes through the entire canal, ending at Colón, after exiting Gatún Locks. The transit takes 8–9 hours. It includes all the partial transit services plus a continental breakfast and land transportation back from Colón and Isla Flamenco.

Another group that offers transits is **Canal and Bay Tours** (tel. 209-2009 or 209-2010, www.canalandbaytours.com), with a similar schedule and identical prices (except for the partial-transit kids' fare—it's US$5 cheaper). It uses the 96-foot-long *Isla Morada* and 115-foot-long *Fantasia del Mar,* old ferryboats that made the run to Taboga for many years. The company has spruced them up. They recently introduced a partial Friday-night transit, which gives a very different perspective on the canal. The locks are brightly lit by high-mast lighting, turning night into day, and the rest of the canal is lit well enough to see what's going on.

Transits generally start early in the morning, but it's impossible for either company to promise exact end times. Scheduling is entirely up to the Panama Canal Authority.

◖ Panama Railway

The Panama railway (tel. 317-6700, www.panarail.com, adults US$25 one-way, children 12 and under US$15 one-way), the descendant of the famed Panama Railroad built for the 49ers during the California gold rush, ran constant daily trips back and forth across the isthmus during the Canal Zone days. It ran along and sometimes over stretches of the Panama Canal, was billed as the world's fastest and cheapest transcontinental journey, and was used as a commuter and cargo train.

Currently, the train makes one daily passenger trip, leaving the Pacific side of the isthmus at 7:15 A.M. and returning at 5:15 P.M. It's quite a step up from the utilitarian train of the old Canal Zone days: The cars in this one have dark wood paneling, leather banquettes set around tables, large observation windows, and waitresses in conductors' outfits who serve coffee and muffins. Seats are limited and most are set aside for daily commuters, so make reservations if possible. If not, show up early. Be sure to ask if there's space in the glass observation car. Sometimes there is only standing room on the between-car platforms available, which is actually quite pleasant since the ride is short and the spacious platforms offer great views and nice breezes.

The train doesn't quite go from ocean to ocean. The Pacific terminus is at the old Canal Zone townsite of Corozal, about a 15-minute drive away from downtown Panama City. The Caribbean terminus is at Colón. The train is an express and makes no stops en route. The trip lasts about an hour.

Those who take the train from Panama City to Colón can either hire a taxi and spend the day exploring Caribbean-side attractions, such as the nearby Gatún Locks, Fuerte San Lorenzo, and the Colón Free Zone, until it's time for the return train, or else catch a bus back to Panama City at the Terminal de Buses in Colón. However, the logistics of this are a bit dicey. Those who can afford it should instead arrange a tour that includes the train trip and a car that meets your group at the Colón station. Typically, not many taxis meet the train; beware of phony cabs. Only get into a licensed taxi, which will be painted bright yellow and have a license plate that matches the number painted on its side.

The bus terminal is a five-minute walk straight past the end of the rail line. It may be possible to find a cab there as well. Do not cross the road into Colón, as it is unsafe.

ENTERTAINMENT AND EVENTS

Amador Causeway has become a nightlife destination for Panama City dwellers, and on the weekends traffic there can be a nightmare. Panama's biggest concert venue is also in Amador, and there are a few other places to see live music and theater. During the dry season, a **concert series** is held on the steps of the Panama Canal Administration Building in Balboa on Tuesday and Thursday evenings.

Bars and Clubs

There are plenty of places to booze and schmooze in Amador. **Flamenco Shopping Plaza,** the shopping and dining center on Isla Flamenco, has several shoebox-size bars/nightclubs on the ground floor at the back of the complex. Each has a different theme—e.g., sports pub, Egyptian, *ciber*—but they're pretty interchangeable. Sometimes people dance a bit, but the clubs are usually too crowded for that. These are mostly places to have a drink and hook up.

Some of the restaurants on the 2nd floor of Flamenco Plaza have live music groups on weekend nights and Sunday afternoons. Chances of hearing "Margaritaville" are good, though the combos I've heard haven't actually been that bad. A folkloric dance group sometimes performs in the plaza when a ship is in port.

More ambitious clubs come and go elsewhere on the causeway and on the mainland around the Figali Convention Center, but these rarely last long. Those with their own transportation or a patient taxi should just trawl along and follow the crowds.

Performing Arts

Amador's glitzy **Panama Canal Village** (tel. 314-1414) contains the Figali Convention Center, Panama's largest venue for extravaganzas. It hosts major international rock and pop acts—ones that have gotten local fans revved up in the last few years include Metallica, the Red Hot Chili Peppers, Shakira, Paulina Rubio, and the Jonas Brothers.

Teatro Balboa (tel. 228-0327), an aging former movie house off Stevens Circle in the heart of the former Canal Zone townsite of Balboa, hosts concerts and the occasional play and special event.

The **Theatre Guild of Ancon** (tel. 212-0060, www.anconguild.com) is the only English-language playhouse in the country. It somehow survived the demise of the Canal Zone's once-thriving community theater scene and still puts on the occasional play. The rickety old wooden playhouse is next to the police station at the base of Cerro Ancón, just off Avenida Frangipani and Manzanillo Place. Jennifer Aniston's dad, John Aniston, was an actor at the theater in the 1950s.

SHOPPING

Balboa has a couple of good places to buy handicrafts. The first is the **Centro de Artesanías Internacional** (behind the YMCA on Avenida Arnulfo Arias Madrid/Balboa Road, 9 A.M.–6 P.M. Mon.–Sat., 10 A.M.–5 P.M. Sun.). It houses many stalls selling handicrafts from all over Panama—including tagua carvings, *molas,* cocobolo figurines, handwoven baskets, and Panama hats—as well as some from other parts of Latin America.

The tagua carvings, cocobolo figurines, and handwoven baskets are made by the Emberá and, especially, the Wounaan. They're incredibly labor-intensive, so don't expect good-quality ones to come cheap. This is especially true of the baskets, which are internationally famous. A so-so basket about the size of a softball costs at least US$25. Rainforest Art, a Wounaan-run stall at the very back of the center, is the first place to look for high-quality works.

Those who won't feel satisfied with a visit to Panama unless they buy a Panama hat (actually made in Ecuador) will find some good-quality ones here. Ask for the stall of Segundo Reyes. His best ones sell for US$100–200. He also has some coarser ones that start at a tenth of that. All hats come in attractive balsa boxes and make good presents. They need blocking, but you can have it done at home.

A newer *artesanía* is in the YMCA building itself, and those who work there aggressively lure in lost visitors who've heard there's a handicrafts hall nearby. By all means take a look, but don't be confused and miss out on the much bigger and better selection at the main artisans' center.

Farther up Avenida Arnulfo Arias Madrid/Balboa Road, on the right as one heads toward Avenida de los Mártires, is the **Centro Municipal de Artesanías Panameñas** (8 A.M.–6 P.M. daily). It's run by Gunas and has a wider and better selection of *molas.* You can probably strike a better bargain here, since they see less

THE PANAMA CANAL

business. The Guna women sewing *molas* and wearing *mola* blouses aren't doing it for show. That's really how they dress and what they do.

Most of the original shops at the **Flamenco Shopping Plaza,** at the end of the causeway, closed down in the last couple of years. Little wonder: The shops were hidden behind the plaza's restaurants and many visitors didn't even know they were there. Optimistic newcomers may have taken their place by the time you visit. The small cruise-ship terminal across the parking lot has a few services, including a duty-free shop that's open only to cruise-ship passengers in transit.

SPORTS AND RECREATION
Amador Causeway
The Amador Causeway is a popular place for walking, running, or biking. It's especially pleasant to ramble about in the morning and early evening, when the weather is cool and the light is gorgeous.

A well-run bike-rental place, **Bicicletas Moses** (tel. 211-2579, 8 A.M.–9 P.M. daily), is at the beginning of the causeway, where the international flags are flown. It's right next to Restaurante Pencas. It rents mountain bikes, tandem bikes, fun cycles (they resemble Hot Wheels–style tricycles), and other wheeled transport by the half hour and hour. Expect long lines on dry-season weekends. They also rent scooters. There's a nearby ATM if you need cash. They also rent baby carriers.

You may see people splashing around in the little beaches along the causeway; don't join them. These days it's such a health hazard it's actually illegal, as nearby signs warn visitors.

Cruises
Canal and Bay Tours (tel. 209-2009 or 209-2010, www.canalandbaytours.com) offers three-hour cruises of Panama Bay once a month, generally on a Friday or Saturday. The trip departs from the Amador cruise-ship terminal on Isla Flamenco. The fare is US$25.

Marinas
The **Flamenco Yacht Club** (Isla Flamenco, tel. 314-0665) is a well-equipped marina that offers moorings, repairs, maintenance, and supplies for everything from small pleasure boats to mega-yachts.

Golf
Summit Golf and Resort (tel. 232-4653, www. summitgolfpanama.com), 14 kilometers north of Balboa, is an upscale golf course, hotel, and spa that welcomes nonmembers. It's a 6,626-yard, par-72 course that was given a major makeover a few years back. It has a modern circular clubhouse with pretty views of rolling countryside, as well as a restaurant and bar. Greens fees are US$120 for 18 holes including cart, though they sometimes offer twilight fees for those willing to play as it's getting dark. Club rental is about US$50. Summit is 7.5 kilometers north of Miraflores Locks. The turn-off is on the right 1.5 kilometers before the left turn toward Gamboa.

ACCOMMODATIONS
Hotels and B&Bs are coming at last to the Pacific side of the canal area. There are now a few appealing places, but many travelers still prefer to stay in downtown Panama City, which is quite close by.

Ancón and Balboa
Simple but pleasant and quiet B&Bs are beginning to pop up in the old Canal Zone towns of Balboa and Ancón. The latter is on the side of Cerro Ancón and now includes the former U.S. Army base of Quarry Heights, formerly the headquarters of the U.S. Southern Command. Evidence of the latter still exists in the form of The Tunnel, a high-security command post drilled straight into the side of Cerro Ancón that was used for strategic planning in times of crisis.

These areas have the advantage of remaining quiet, tree-shrouded residential neighborhoods that are right next door to the urban chaos of

Panama City. Tranquil as this area is, it's important to exercise some caution, especially at night. Streets can be dark and deserted, and the incidence of home break-ins has shot up with the demise of the Canal Zone. Violent crime is unlikely, however. The places listed here all have good security, including locked gates.

US$50-100

■ **Dos Palmitos** (532B Guayacan Terrace, Ancón, tel. 391-0994, cell 6581-8132, in Europe: 331/4542-4007, Skype: Dos Palmitos, www.dospalmitos.com, US$82.50 s, US$96.80 d, including breakfast) is an appealing B&B in former Canal Zone housing of the older, two-story wooden variety. It features four small rooms, all of which are clean and have a simple but attractive decor, new bathrooms, comfortable beds, flat-screen TVs, free wireless Internet, hardwood floors, and air-conditioning.

This is not a posh place; it's a home that's been converted into a simple B&B. But it's immaculate and run well by a hands-on owner and is a good base for independent travelers who want to explore this part of Panama. It's a hidden gem. The neighborhood is not as well tended as it was in the old Canal Zone days, but this is still a quiet residential area, especially given that the crowded streets of Panama City are just a short walk away. There's a shared kitchen and common area with an Internet computer. Breakfast is served on a back terrace overlooking a walled garden. You're more likely to hear birdsong than traffic.

Dos Palmitos is owned and run by Angeline, a Dutch journalist with an interest in the history of Panama and the canal—be sure to notice the historic photos on the wall, as well as the framed newspapers and stock certificate from the era of the French canal fiasco. She speaks French, Dutch, English, Spanish, and German. She lives on the ground floor of the house, so she's often around. She can arrange tours at very reasonable prices, including day

trips to El Valle and Santa Clara and Gamboa. Best of all is a tour that overcomes the problem of getting back from the Caribbean side after taking the Panama Railway across the isthmus. For US$130 for two people (not including the US$25 per person train fare), guests are dropped off at the train in Corozal, picked up in Colón at the end of the ride, taken to Portobelo and Fuerte San Lorenzo, and then driven back to Dos Palmitos. (Guests can request a side trip to visit Gatún Locks, which they should definitely do.) That's a good price for a very full day.

The well-established and very popular **La Estancia** (Casa 35, Calle Amelia Denis de Icaza, tel. 314-1581 or 314-1604, www.bedandbreakfastpanama.com, starts at US$82.50 s/d, including continental breakfast, a/c) is a 12-room bed-and-breakfast in Quarry Heights, the former headquarters of the U.S. Southern Command, on the side of Cerro Ancón. The building was once used as apartments for military personnel and thus is a bit stark and utilitarian, but the owners have made attempts to soften the place.

Rooms have telephones and private bathrooms. Three have their bathrooms down the hall but come with a balcony and hammock to make up for that slight inconvenience. Most rooms have a queen-size bed. There's a common area for guests to relax in and free wireless Internet. The place is surrounded by trees, and there's a partial view of the Panama Canal and the Bridge of the Americas from some of the balconies. Two of the rooms are actually fair-size apartments with sitting rooms, kitchenettes, and a small patio. These go for US$108.90 a night, including breakfast. Guests can use the washer and dryer.

The owners can arrange tours through their own tour company, Panoramic Panama. To get to La Estancia, take the first left up the hill after passing the guardhouse at the entrance to Quarry Heights. The bed-and-breakfast is 400

THE PANAMA CANAL

meters past the guardhouse in a peach-colored, three-story building on the right.

Opened in 2008, the 🌙 **Balboa Inn** (2311a Calle Las Cruce, Balboa, tel. 314-1520, www. thebalboainn.com, $85 s, $95 d, including breakfast, a/c) is in what had once been a house for Panama Canal employees in the old Canal Zone days. The area is still a quiet residential neighborhood where you can hear the sounds of chirping birds in the surrounding trees rather than squealing traffic and construction. Security includes a locked gate in the front. Since the inn is near the base of Cerro Ancón, the occasional cute little *ñeque* shows up in the backyard. This is a good option for those who are happy to be somewhere in-between both the canal and the city. It has nine rooms, all with private bath, TV/ DVDs, safes, and free wireless Internet. Rooms are simple with rather thin mattresses, but each has been decorated with cheerful nature murals. A couple of the rooms upstairs have windows on two sides that let in lots of light. The friendly and competent staff can help arrange tours and give restaurant advice. Guests are welcome to use the kitchen. English, Spanish, and German are spoken here. This is a good find.

La Boca

La Boca means "the mouth," an apt name for a town bordering the Pacific entrance to the Panama Canal. There is not much to interest visitors in this former Canal Zone residential area.

US$50-100

The **Canal Inn** (opposite the campus of Universidad Maritima Internacional de Panamá, tel. 314-0112, cell 6612-7168, franzwald1@cwpanama.net, www.canal-inn.com, US$77 s, US$88 d, including breakfast, a/c) is an old Canal Zone building that has been converted into a pleasant B&B. It's across the street from what used to be Canal Zone College, at the foot of the Bridge of the Americas and near the banks of the canal.

It offers 17 simple but cheerful rooms of different sizes, all with wireless Internet access. There's a breakfast nook and common lounge area, and the whole place has been painted in bright colors and decorated to make it as homey and cozy as the old utilitarian Zone architecture will allow. It's cute. There's a small swimming pool out front.

This is a very quiet, almost deserted area, but heavy traffic rumbling over the bridge keeps it from ever being entirely silent. To get there, take the turnoff to La Boca in Balboa between the Union Church and the police station. Continue straight, then make the first left after the gas station. Continue on to the old Canal Zone College, which is now a maritime university. The Canal Inn will be on the right.

Albrook

Albrook is a former U.S. Air Force station that has become a popular destination for reasonably well-off Panamanians and foreign expats to live, mainly because it was quiet and not too built-up. It's much more developed now, especially around its main entrance, but it's still pretty quiet and leafy. That also makes it a rather isolated spot for most visitors, though it's also home to Panama City's domestic airport, main bus terminal, and one of its largest malls. There is one place to stay, though hotels are also in the works for the mall/bus terminal area.

US$50-100

Albrook Inn (14 Calle Hazelhurst, tel. 315-1789 or 315-1975, www.albrookinn.com, starts at US$99 s/d, including continental breakfast, a/c) is a two-story, 30-unit hotel opened in 2003 in a peaceful middle-class suburban neighborhood next to what had been the Albrook Officers' Club back when Albrook was a U.S. Air Force base. The standard rooms are small and simple with very firm beds and cable TV. Larger junior suites with a sitting room and sink start at US$110 s/d. There's a restaurant/bar in a backyard *rancho* (thatched-roof hut), a pool with hot tub, and both laundry service and a self-service washer and dryer. This is a good place if you can find a room with beds that aren't slabs of rock; try several.

Amador

Big, ambitious hotels have long been planned for Amador and the Amador Causeway (Calzada de Amador). They've been slow to come, but there are a couple of smaller, appealing options.

US$100-150

The well-established **Country Inn and Suites** (Amador, tel. 211-4500, fax 211-4501, www.panamacanalcountry.com/amador, starts at US$127 s/d including breakfast) is popular with visitors who want familiar surroundings close to both Panama City and the Panama Canal. You can't get much closer to the canal: It's literally on the edge of its Pacific entrance. It is on the water just past the entrance to Amador, before the causeway. It's a four-story, 159-unit hotel that resembles the other nondescript members of the chain. Standard rooms include cable TV, telephone, iron and ironing board, coffeemaker, free wireless Internet, and a balcony. It's worth paying the extra US$16.50 to get the view of the Pacific entrance to the canal and the Bridge of the Americas, the proximity to which is the most distinctive thing about this place. The hotel also has 53 suites of various kinds. There's a T.G.I. Friday's, an attractive swimming pool on the edge of the canal, a tennis court, a spa, and a business center. Tours of Panama City, the canal, and other attractions are easy to arrange from here.

OVER US$150

The Beach House (Isla Naos, Amador Causeway, tel. 380-1200, www.thebeach-housepanama.com, rack rates start at US$247.50 s/d, including breakfast) is a more upscale hotel that opened on the causeway itself in 2011. Tucked between Mi Ranchito and the ferry landing for Isla Taboga, it overlooks a little marina. It's quite small and has attractive modern rooms with good beds, well-appointed bathrooms, and balconies that face toward the city or Taboga. The city-facing rooms have spectacular views of the Bay of Panama and the skyline. Because it's so far up the causeway, the Beach House is quite isolated from Panama City and the rest of the former Canal Zone. It's a very quiet spot except on weekends, when the causeway is clogged with exercisers in the daytime and partiers at night.

Those without their own transportation will have to take taxis to get to and from the causeway. But there couldn't be a more convenient spot for those who want to visit Taboga, the Smithsonian's Centro de Exhibiciones Marinas, and, of course, the Amador Causeway itself. It is also convenient to the Museo de la Biodiversidad, whenever that finally opens. Stays include breakfast at the neighboring Mi Ranchito and access to a small swimming pool.

Clayton and Ciudad del Saber (City of Knowledge)

What was formerly known as Fort Clayton, a U.S. Army base, is now simply Clayton. The section of it closest to the canal is the Ciudad del Saber, known in English as the City of Knowledge. This is an ambitious, even admirable, plan to create a kind of research and academic park with institutions from around the world, and it has met with some success.

The rest of Clayton was largely abandoned in the last decade, but now development is coming fast.

US$25-50

The **Hostal de Clayton** (Building 605 B, tel. 317-1634 or 317-1264, cell 6631-0281 or 6572-5966, www.hostaldeclayton.com, starts at US$15 pp, including breakfast) consists of four rooms in old U.S. Army quarters in a particularly deserted part of Clayton. The rooms aren't terribly clean and the mattresses are thin, but the staff are friendly, the area is quiet, and the rates are good. Dorm rooms are US$15–19.95. Couples can share a private room for US$44.60. Free wireless Internet access, air-conditioning during the night, a rather barren backyard, and a basic breakfast are included. The hostel is about two kilometers from the main Clayton entrance. Taxis should charge US$5 from Albrook or US$25 from Tocumen. This place is far away from just about everything except Miraflores Locks.

OVER US$150

You are likely to encounter plenty of determined smiles at the newish **Holiday Inn City of Knowledge** (tel. 317-4000, www.holiday-inn.com, US$151.80 s/d). That's because it was built in conjunction with a hotel-management program, the Panama International Hotel School, at the Ciudad del Saber in Clayton, and its students and graduates run the place. The service can be a bit confused at times, but they definitely try hard. This Holiday Inn is an attractive, seven-story version, with good-size rooms that have minifridges, free broadband, and modern furnishings. There's a small pool behind the hotel, and a restaurant and bar. It's literally across the street from the canal and a short drive from Miraflores Locks. Expect to pay a bit more for canal-view rooms, the best of which are on the 6th floor. However, the hotel is not quite close enough to the canal to see much, especially since there are trees partly obscuring the view. The best views are from the stark event rooms on the top floor. The hotel is just off Gaillard Highway, about 10 kilometers from Balboa. It'll be on the right shortly before the main entrance to the City of Knowledge and the turnoff to Miraflores Locks.

West Bank of Canal and Playa Bonita

The area just over the Bridge of the Americas

is beginning to see tourist development. This is particularly true of the area that used to be known as Fort Kobbe, a U.S. Army base now known simply as **Kobbe** (sometimes spelled Koby, which is how it's pronounced), which hotel developers are trying to recast as Playa Bonita. A couple of big, fancy resorts have gone up here as have the beginning of what will likely be a number of condo towers.

Nonguests are not allowed on the grounds of the resorts. Locals and the backpacking crowd hang out instead in **Veracruz,** right next door, which has a few basic places to eat and drink and not much else, other than a reputation as a home to *maleantes* (thugs) which the resorts are anxious to keep as far away from their stretch of beach as possible. To do so, they've ringed their properties with gates and guards. Critics also argue that all beaches in Panama are public by law but these resorts' fences have cut off public access, effectively privatizing them.

These are the closest proper beaches to Panama City, and the only ones where you might feel safe sticking your toe into the water without the fear of pollution. The shoreline is pretty here, but the beaches are rocky and small, so don't expect vast expanses of gorgeous sand.

OVER US$150

The 300-room **◖ InterContinental Playa Bonita Resort and Spa** (tel. 206-8880 Panama City reservations, tel. 316-1463 at the hotel, www.playabonitapanama.com, US$265 s/d), which opened in 2005, is a fancy resort hotel in a spectacular spot near the Pacific entrance to the canal. It's part of a hotel group that includes the Miramar InterContinental and the Gamboa Rainforest Resort, among others.

This one is on a beach just west of the Bridge of the Americas. Guest rooms are in two five-story buildings designed so each room has a view of the sea, the ships waiting to transit the canal, and the islands of Taboga and Taboguilla in the distance. The beautifully landscaped grounds include a terraced fountain that flows down into five lagoon-shaped swimming pools of various sizes. These end in a small, rocky, half-moon beach. Now called Playa Bonita (formerly Kobbe Beach), the beach is not the greatest, but it's pleasant. This is the closest beach hotel from Panama City. It's an appealing, if pricey, place.

Standard rooms are attractive, with two double beds or one king bed, a safe, minibar, balcony, cable TV, coffeemaker, and wireless Internet access (US$10/day). The resort has three restaurants, including one in a large *rancho* by the beach. Bars are in the lobby and by the pool. A large, modern gym with plate-glass windows facing the ocean is open 24 hours a day. There's also an elegant full-service spa with a Southeast Asian tropical motif.

The resort is a short drive from Panama City, but it's quite secluded and there's nothing much around it. Only guests are allowed through the gatehouse, which is guarded more zealously than Panama's border crossings.

The ginormous **Westin Playa Bonita** (tel. 304-6600, www.starwoodhotels.com, starts at US$269.50 s/d) offers 600 rooms in three conjoined towers overlooking a strip of rocky beach. It has three swimming pools and an absolutely gigantic *rancho* bar restaurant on the grounds by the beach. Rooms are nice but rather plain, and the small bathtub in the bedroom is an odd touch. Room amenities include packets of bug repellent, a reminder that the *chitras* out here are ferocious, since the property is surrounded by mangroves. Not all rooms have an ocean view; getting one can involve a hefty upgrade fee. Service can be a bit chaotic, and the hotel is showing signs of wear and lack of maintenance.

It's definitely an attractive resort with sleekly modern public areas and inviting pools and grounds. Also, at least some among the concierge staff are impressively helpful and friendly; one makes it a point to remember the names of every guest he encounters.

FOOD

Despite all the development in the former Canal Zone, it's far from becoming a culinary destination.

Fortunately, downtown Panama City is quite close if the restaurants here aren't appealing.

There are plenty of places to eat on and near the causeway, though I've yet to have a memorable meal at any of them.

The **Balboa Yacht Club** (tel. 228-5196 or 228-5794) has risen from the ashes after a fire some years ago. It's roughly in its old location—despite the name, it's in Amador, above the water near the Country Inn and Suites. At this point it's a big *rancho* with a deck serving burgers, buckets of beer, and the like and blasting classic rock. It's popular with die-hard Zonians and yachters.

American chain restaurants (T.G.I. Friday's, Bennigan's, Subway) are also making inroads. Flamenco Plaza on Isla Flamenco and a newer complex on Isla Perico have an impressive number of theme restaurants squeezed into cramped spaces. Oddly, both have been designed so the parking lot is on the best real estate, with a view of Panama Bay and the Panama City skyline, while the restaurants are set so far back they really only have a view of the parking lot. Most are indoor/outdoor places. It's pleasant to sit outside in the evenings and enjoy the tropical breeze. There are also places to eat at the Gran Terminal de Transportes/Albrook Mall.

The food at ◖ **Centro de Visitantes de Miraflores** (Miraflores Locks Visitors Center, tel. 276-8325, noon–11 P.M. daily, US$10–15) is decent. It includes sandwiches, pastas, seafood, salads, and so on. But that's not the reason to come here. Dining on a terrace just a few meters from the locks of the Panama Canal is, to say the least, a novel experience. Diners can watch ships transiting day or night (high-mast lighting turns night into day at the locks). Come early or reserve a table against the railing, where the view is best. Service charge is included.

Niko's Café (tel. 228-8888, 7 A.M.–11 P.M. daily), at the end of the Prado next to Stevens Circle in Balboa, is one of a small chain of successful cafeterias in Panama City that offer simple, tasty food at rock-bottom prices. This one is in the heart of the old Canal Zone, between what was once the high school football stadium and the employee commissary, built on the site of a bowling alley. Reflecting its location, the cafeteria displays great panoramic black-and-white photos of the Canal Zone, U.S. military bases, and parts of Panama dating from the 1920s and 1930s. Much to the amazement of old Zonians, the seal of the Canal Zone is above the counter. About US$4 will get you heaps of food, which includes traditional Panamanian fare, sandwiches, soups, individual pizzas, and desserts. The café now has wireless Internet access.

Lum's Bar and Grill (tel. 317-6303, 11 A.M.–midnight daily, US$10–15), just off Gaillard Highway across the tracks from the railroad station in Corozal, is one of the last bastions of meat-and-potatoes Zonian spirit. Turn off the highway at the lovingly preserved Panama Railroad train cars. It's a converted warehouse that features a restaurant in the main room with pastas, salads, sandwiches, and the like. Attached to it is a sports bar with pool tables, ESPN, and, on some nights, live local bands. A favorite is a blues-rock outfit called Bitches Ghost, composed of Panamanians and gringo expats. These include Rod Richards, the original lead guitarist for the late 1960s/early 1970s rock band Rare Earth.

Restaurante Pencas (Amador, tel. 211-3671, www.pencas.com, noon–11 P.M. Mon.–Thurs., 12:30 P.M.–12:30 A.M. Fri.–Sat., noon–10 P.M. Sun.) is just past the Panama Canal Village. It's a large open-air place with tables on a raised deck near the water, and it has a view of the ocean and the Panama City skyline. The menu tends toward American comfort food and includes baby back ribs and other grilled meats, sandwiches, burgers, fajitas, pasta, and seafood. The *filete de canal frances* is a small but tender cut of beef. Restaurante Pencas sometimes hosts live music performances.

Mi Ranchito (Isla Naos, Amador Causeway, tel. 228-4909, 8:30 A.M.–midnight Mon.–Thurs., 8:30 A.M.–1 A.M. Fri.–Sat., mains US$7–12) is a simple but clean open-air place under a thatched roof on Naos, just past the turnoff to the Centro de Exhibiciones Marinas. It's the most popular place to eat on the Amador Causeway. It serves traditional Panamanian food, with an emphasis on fish and seafood at reasonable prices. It also has—wonder of wonders—a view of the bay. While many people have good experiences here, I've found the food to be just so-so—the corvina is not very flavorful and is drowned in sauce, and the soup is thin. Still, the location is good and a *típico* meal in pleasant surroundings can be had for less than US$10. The *patacones* (fried green plantains) are tasty.

INFORMATION AND SERVICES

The **Smithsonian Tropical Research Institute** (tel. 212-8000, www.stri.org) has its headquarters, the Earl S. Tupper Research and Conference Center, in Ancón. It's a large building on Roosevelt Avenue across Avenida de los Mártires from the Palacio Legislativo. It has a small **research library** (9 A.M.–5 P.M. Mon., Wed.–Fri.; 8 A.M.–5 P.M. Tues.; 9 A.M.–noon Sat.) that contains science periodicals and older research books and a **bookstore** (10 A.M.–4:30 P.M. Mon.–Fri.) with some hard-to-find books on Panama's natural history. Both are worth a visit for detailed information on Panama's flora and fauna. They are open to the public, but visitors must present an ID and sign in to get into the center. The center also has a cafeteria that serves lunch for less than US$5.

GETTING THERE AND AROUND

Taxis are the most convenient way to get from downtown Panama City to most of the destinations in the former Canal Zone, though they're easy to explore by rental car as well. Many tour operators offer day tours that include stops in

Balboa, Miraflores Locks, and the handicrafts market next to the YMCA. Exploring by bus requires a lot of connections.

By Taxi

Taxis from central Panama City to any of these destinations should cost less than US$5. But to explore more than one, it makes more sense to arrange a taxi tour. Agree on a price ahead of time.

By Bus

There are many buses from Panama City to specific canal-area destinations, but trying to explore the whole area by bus is time-consuming, and the fares quickly add up. Taxis are a more practical alternative. Those who want to stick with public transportation can take one of the SACA buses from the Gran Terminal in Albrook.

By Car

The Administration Building is in Altos de Balboa (Balboa Heights), a short drive from downtown Panama City. It's hard to miss. Balboa begins just down the hill from it.

Miraflores Locks are about a 20-minute drive from Panama City, just off Gaillard Highway. The entrance to Miraflores Locks is on the left past Clayton, which is less than 10 kilometers from Balboa. Pedro Miguel Locks are about five kilometers farther on. Just beyond Pedro Miguel is the beginning of Gaillard Cut, now sometimes referred to by its original name, Culebra Cut.

Amador begins near the east end of the Bridge of the Americas. Drivers coming from downtown Panama City can reach Amador by two roads. The older route is to drive through Balboa on Avenida Arnulfo Arias Madrid (also called Balboa Road) and onto the road between the YMCA and the huge statue of Arnulfo Arias. This leads straight to Amador. A faster and more direct route is to take a newer access road that links Avenida de los Mártires directly with Amador near the entrance to the Bridge of

the Americas; follow the signs and stay alert— the intersections come up quickly and can be dangerous. Once in Amador, stay straight to get to the causeway.

ISLA TABOGA

Taboga is the most easily accessible island from Panama City. It's just 12 nautical miles away, a trip that takes about an hour by ferry. It's a pretty, quaint little island. If you squint, its whitewashed walls, curving staircases, and flowering trees may remind you of a Greek island.

Taboga is home to a full-time population and attracts many weekend visitors. It's an appealing place that inspires a nostalgic affection somewhat out of proportion to its modern-day charms, especially for those who like deserted, pristine shores. Beaches here are okay, if a bit rocky, but they can get relatively crowded on dry-season weekends, and some trash washes up from Panama City.

Since Taboga's attractions can be explored in a day and there aren't many facilities on the island, you may not want to spend the night. But it is a good place for a day trip.

The ferry ride over is half the fun of a Taboga visit. It leads past the Pacific entrance to the Panama Canal, under the Bridge of the Americas, and along the causeway. You can occasionally see dolphins on the way over, and if you're very, very lucky, you may spot a humpback whale.

An awful lot of history has passed through Taboga since the Spaniards first came calling in the early 16th century. The current town was founded in 1524, and it claims to have the second-oldest church in the western hemisphere. Francisco Pizarro is said to have planned the destruction of the Incan Empire on Taboga. Its visitors have also included pirates, 49ers, and workers on both the French and American canals. Canal workers recovered from their illnesses at a convalescent hospital here that has long since disappeared.

There are no ATMs or banks on the island, so take all the cash you think you'll need.

THE PANAMA CANAL

Isla Taboga is known as "the island of flowers."

Sights

The main beaches are on either side of the floating pier, where the ferries arrive. The more attractive one, **Playa La Restinga,** faces Panama City. A right turn as you leave the pier leads along an ocean path shaded by tamarind trees. Avoid the stretch of beach on the far left as you face the ocean; the smell of sewage will tell you why. At low tide it's possible to walk across a sandbar from Playa La Restinga to the neighboring islet of El Morro. The sandbar disappears at high tide.

The town itself is quite attractive and worth exploring. There are two main roads, a high street and a low street, which are easy to walk on since there are few cars on the island. Both roads are to the left of the pier as you leave the ferry. When the jasmine, oleander, bougainvillea, and hibiscus are in bloom, you'll understand why Taboga is called "the Island of Flowers." Houses tend to be well-maintained and quaint.

When Paul Gauguin first left Europe for the tropics, he was so taken with Taboga that he tried to buy land here. However, he was broke and ended up having to help dig the Panama Canal instead, a job he detested. He never could afford Taboga's prices and soon sailed on. He eventually found Tahiti, and the rest is art history. There's a plaque commemorating his stay, from May to July 1887, up the high street by some picturesque Spanish ruins. Don't miss the lovely garden filled with a rainbow of flowering plants.

The cute whitewashed church in the center of town, **Iglesia San Pedro,** was originally made out of wood, erected after the founding of Taboga in 1524. It's supposedly the second-oldest church in the western hemisphere. Taboga is a hilly island that lends itself to walks past old gravesites, abandoned U.S. military bunkers, and the overgrown remains of Spanish fortifications. The cemetery, on the edge of the ocean toward the end of the road, makes for a picturesque amble.

It's possible to take a moderately strenuous

walk to the top of **Cerro de la Cruz,** which, as the name implies, is topped by a cross. There's a good view of the ocean from here. The south side of the island, together with neighboring Isla Urabá, is part of a national wildlife refuge that protects the nesting area of an important brown pelican colony.

Accommodations and Food

Until recently Taboga lacked decent places to spend the night; most people are content with a day trip. There are once again a few options, the most popular of which is **El Cerrito Tropical** (tel. 390-8999, cell 6489-0074, www.cerritotropicalpanama.com, starts at US$77 s/d, including breakfast, a/c), which is on a hill about a 10-minute walk from the ferry pier. El Cerrito is a B&B with three "B&B rooms" and three apartments. The apartments range from a one-bedroom for up to two people (US$110) up to a three-bedroom that can sleep six (US$297). The rooms are due for a sprucing up, but the place has a relaxed vibe, like staying at a friend's beach house. The B&B rooms are simple but cheerfully decorated, with private bathrooms and a shared balcony. These range in price US$77–104.50. Your hosts are Cynthia Mulder, a Canadian, and her husband Hiddo, who is from the "Dutch Caribbean." They can organize a range of tours, including fishing, snorkeling, and exploring the island. El Cerrito's website has good information on the island and how to get around. Also check out www.taboga.panamanow.com.

The B&B has an attractive two-terrace restaurant (7:30–9 A.M., noon–2 P.M., 5:30–7 P.M.) with lovely views of the ocean and ships at anchor waiting to transit the canal. Most items are US$7.50–12.50.

Vereda Tropical (tel. 250-2154, www.hotelveredatropical.com, starts at US$71.50 s/d) is a surprisingly attractive if rather peculiar-looking hotel. It's sort of a cross between a mock Spanish colonial and a nautical-themed building. Rooms are pleasant and clean, and the more expensive ones have air-conditioning and balconies with a view of the ocean. It's worth springing a bit more to get the ocean view. The place is perched at the top of a hill, which gives its terrace restaurant, which is shaded by bougainvilleas, great ocean views. It's open 7:30–10:30 A.M., 12:30–4 P.M., and 6:30–9 P.M. Most dishes are US$11–16, and include pizza, seafood, and pasta. It's the only pizzeria on the island, but it's not very good. The view makes up for a lot, though.

■   **Mundi's** (cell 6476-0610, 8:30 A.M.–4 P.M. daily, US$8–13) serves the best food on Taboga. It's a simple little open-air place right above the water, to the right as one exits the ferry ramp. It has good yuca, good corvina, and friendly service.

Restaurante Acuario (cell 6801-6394 or 6763-8896, 8:30 A.M.–9 P.M. daily, most US$8–13) is on a balcony of a house above Playa Honda, to the left as one leaves the ferry pier. It's a basic seafood place with prices that aren't basic enough. It charges US$10, for instance, for a not very tasty shrimp cocktail.

Getting There and Around

Ferries to Isla Taboga leave from Isla Naos on the Amador Causeway. A taxi from Panama City to the pier should cost about US$4–5. There is parking near the pier for those who drive.

El Calypso (tel. 314-1730 or 390-2403) uses two ferries of different size, the *Calypso Queen* and *Calypso Princess.* The fare is US$7 one way and US$12 round-trip.

El Calypso ferries make the trip to Taboga at 8:30 A.M. Monday–Friday, with a second ferry at 3 P.M. Monday and Friday. On weekends and holidays they leave at 8 A.M., 10:30 A.M., and 4 P.M.

Trips from Taboga back to Amador are at 9:30 A.M. Monday and Friday, with a second ferry at 4:30 P.M. Monday–Friday. The weekend and holiday schedule is 9 A.M., 3 P.M., and 5 P.M.

Ferry schedules are more theoretical than real; service is erratic. Make a reservation or show up early on dry-season weekends and holidays to be sure of getting a ticket—this is a popular day-trip destination for Panamanians. The ferry requires passengers to arrive at least an hour ahead of time. Also, since there's no assigned seating, board early to claim a spot out of the sun—it's easy to get fried before even reaching the beach. There are few vehicles of any kind on the island, and it's easy to get around on foot. But if the heat or the climbs get to be too much, a taxi ride anywhere costs no more than US$1.50.

Gamboa and Vicinity

The townsite of Gamboa, on the banks of the Panama Canal about halfway across the isthmus, is surrounded by extraordinary natural beauty, especially given how close it is to Panama City. It's a gateway to world-famous birding trails, the tropical rainforest of Parque Nacional Soberanía, the powerful Río Chagres, botanical gardens and a zoo, and the huge, artificial Lago Gatún. That lake is at the heart of the canal and contains Barro Colorado Island, one of the world's foremost natural laboratories for the study of tropical nature.

Though Emberá and Wounaan people still live up the Río Chagres, Gamboa is the headquarters of the canal's engineering and dredging divisions and has a modern infrastructure. Gamboa today has few services, accommodations, or places to eat.

Lago Alajuela (formerly Madden Lake) is a second artificial lake northeast of Gamboa that supplies water for the canal. Some people like to visit its impressive Madden Dam, but because it's not entirely safe, tourists should avoid it.

SIGHTS
Parque Municipal Summit (Summit Botanical Gardens and Zoo)
These gardens (off Gaillard Highway a few kilometers before Gamboa, tel. 232-4854, 9 A.M.–5 P.M. daily, US$5) are worth a quick side trip on the way to or from Gamboa. They were created by the Panama Canal Company in 1923 for the study of tropical plants and turned over to the Panamanian government in 1985. The place has deteriorated in recent years, but some efforts are being made to fix it up. At last count there were 4,000 plants representing 366 species still growing in the gardens.

Summit Gardens also has a small zoo that contains tapirs, caimans, jaguars, and other large animals. Many of their cages are tiny and antiquated, which will disturb many visitors.

The harpy eagle compound, Summit's showcase, is more encouraging. The harpy eagle is the world's most powerful bird of prey; it can grow up to a meter long from bill to tail. Sadly, it's also endangered. The bird is indigenous to Panama, and a major purpose of the compound is to try to get the birds to reproduce in captivity. The specimens here are magnificent, with thick plumage, fearsome hooked bills, and steely talons. They look like stoic high chiefs.

◖ Parque Nacional Soberanía
This is a true tropical forest, and it's one of the most accessible in the world. Its 22,000 hectares extend along the east bank of the Panama Canal, ending at Lago Gatún near the town of Limón. The wildlife is amazing, especially considering how close the park is to population centers. Among its inhabitants are 525 species of birds, 105 species of mammals, 55 species of amphibians, and 79 species of reptiles.

All its well-maintained trails are a short drive from Panama City on the Gaillard Highway, making it quite feasible to go for a morning hike during which there's a chance of encountering such tourist-pleasing critters as sloths, coatimundis, toucans, and kinkajous, and then be back in the heart of the city in time for lunch in an air-conditioned restaurant.

A section of the famous **Camino de Cruces (Las Cruces Trail),** which has a history dating to the 16th century, runs through the park. To reach it by car, continue straight when the Gaillard Highway forks just past the railroad overpass with "1929" carved in it. The road, now Madden Road (don't expect a street sign), will pass through a forest, which, sadly, is often strewn with litter. There's a parking area and picnic tables on the left after 6.3 kilometers. The trailhead is well marked. It's possible to hike this trail for about five or six hours to the Chagres and even camp along it. For just a glimpse of this storied trail, walk at least five minutes along it and you'll come to a section where the ancient paving stones that once lined the trail have been restored. In the dry season, you may have to brush aside dead leaves to find them. (Use your boot to do this, not your hand, as there are still some poisonous snakes in the forest.)

All the other trails are on the road to Gamboa. Back near the 1929 overpass, turn off the Galliard Highway toward Gamboa. The first major trail will be the wide, flat **Plantation Road.** It's a right turn off the highway; follow the Canopy Tower signs. The entrance to the trail is on the left at the base of the road leading to the Canopy Tower.

Farther along the main road is **Sendero El Charco** (literally, pond trail), also on the right. This is a very short (844 meters) trail with a little waterfall near the entrance. A barbecue area on the premises attracts hordes of families on the weekends.

The best trail for viewing birdlife is the famous **Pipeline Road (Camino del Oleoducto).** To get there, cross over the one-lane bridge leading into Gamboa. Continue straight. After about three kilometers the road will fork; take the left fork onto the gravel road. The swampy area to the right, just before Pipeline Road, is worth checking out on the way back from an early-morning birding trip. At around 8–9 A.M., as the forest warms up, there's an excellent chance of spotting capybaras, the world's largest rodents, on the far side of the clearing. A couple of kilometers past this area there's a Parque Nacional Soberanía sign indicating you've reached Camino del Oleoducto. Make a right here and park.

For the first six kilometers or so, the forest is mostly secondary growth. You'll see dozens of species of birds if you arrive early. There's a slight chance of finding anteaters, howler monkeys, white-faced capuchins, Geoffroy's tamarin, green iguanas, agoutis, coatimundis, or two- and three-toed sloths. Serious birders will want to continue past this area into old-growth forest, where there's a possibility of seeing such rare specimens as yellow-eared toucanets, crimson-bellied woodpeckers, sirystes, and other gorgeous birds that will impress even those who don't know a russet antshrike from a slaty-winged foliage-gleaner. The unbelievably lucky may see an endangered harpy eagle, but don't count on it. Pipeline Road continues for many kilometers, but the bridges over streams are not well-maintained these days. Bridge collapses can curtail a long hike. Get here by dawn to see this famous birding road in all its feathered glory.

About 1.6 kilometers in from the entrance to Pipeline Road is the **Panama Rainforest Discovery Center** (tel. 264-6266 in Panama City, tel. 314-9386 or 314-9388 in Gamboa, www.pipelineroad.org, 6 A.M.–4 P.M. daily), a new interpretive center and observation tower in the middle of the forest. The tower is a modern steel structure 30 meters high, with rest platforms on the way up and a top platform that's just above the canopy. There is a kilometer of developed trails in the immediate area. The visitors center has restrooms and a gift shop that sells drinks and snacks. Admission to the complex is a whopping US$30 for adults and US$4 for kids younger than 12 during the premium time of 6–10 A.M., when one is most likely to see wildlife. The price drops to US$20 for adults and US$2 for kids after 10 A.M. But to have the best chance of seeing interesting wildlife, particularly birds, visitors should try to be on-site as soon as the tower opens. The center is open daily except for Christmas Day and New Year's Day. Recently it has been offering late afternoon hikes (4–6 P.M.), when the forest starts to come back to life.

Other than the Panama Rainforest Discovery Center, the rest of the Pipeline Road area, and the national park generally, is open to the public at a much more modest fee. Hiking and camping permits are available at the ANAM office at the edge of the park, inconveniently located well before any of the trails. It's on Gaillard Highway at the fork just past the narrow overpass; you can't miss the huge Parque Nacional Soberanía sign. The office is officially open 8 A.M.–4 P.M. weekdays, but the staff live in the little house behind the office so there should always be someone there to take your money. Entrance fee is US$5, which gives visitors access to all the trails for the day. The camping fee is another US$5.

Bear in mind there are no developed camping sites in the park (though there are some facilities at Sendero El Charco) and this is a tropical forest. Those planning an early-morning hike can probably pay on the way back without a problem. But otherwise ask about the conditions of the trails, especially Pipeline Road, before venturing out. The Camino de Cruces is quite a hike from the other trails; Gamboa-bound buses take passengers only as far as the fork to Gamboa, after which you'll have to hoof it for six kilometers unless you can flag down a ride. It's much more convenient to take a taxi from Panama City or go with a tour group.

Lago Gatún

Once the largest artificially made lake in the world, at 422 square kilometers Lago Gatún is still a plenty impressive body of water. It was formed by damming the Río Chagres near its mouth, at Gatún, and is an integral part of the Panama Canal. Transiting ships still follow the submerged riverbed of the Chagres, since it's the deepest part of the lake. It's long been a popular spot with boaters, water-skiers, anglers, and even scuba divers. The diving here is unusual, to say the least. A Belgian locomotive and 8 of its 40 train cars, abandoned during construction days, were recently salvaged from the bottom of the lake, and submerged trees and remnants of old towns are still there. Not surprisingly, however, the water is murky and in some places choked with vegetation. Divers find the experience rather spooky.

Caimans have always shared the lake with people, but there are a lot more of them now. The lake now also has crocodiles, so diving may not be the best idea.

The fishing here is terrific—the peacock bass population, accidentally introduced decades ago, is so out of control anglers are actually encouraged to catch them to restore some kind of ecological balance. It's not uncommon for an angler who knows the good spots to catch dozens of fish an hour.

A highlight of a Lago Gatún boat trip is a visit to the **primate sanctuary** scattered among more than a dozen islands in the lake, known collectively as the Islas Tigre and Islas Las Brujas. Here visitors can spot tamarins, spider monkeys, white-faced capuchins, howlers, and night monkeys swinging or peering from trees just a few meters from the boat.

Only visit the sanctuary on a tour led by a responsible naturalist group such as Ancon Expeditions. Do not feed or have any physical contact with the monkeys. All but the night monkeys have been rescued from illegal captivity, and the project is trying to reintroduce them to the wild. The last thing they need is more human contact. Besides, some can be

© WILLIAM FRIAR

a white-faced capuchin at the primate sanctuary in Lago Gatún

pretty aggressive, so don't get too close. Some boat tours of the area include walks through small, forested islands, some of which have spooky ruins from the old Canal Zone days. Douse yourself with insect repellent before exploring them; the mosquitoes can be voracious.

Barro Colorado Island

BCI, as it's commonly known, is one of the world's most famous biological reserves. Part of what makes it exceptional is that it's been left alone so long: It was declared a protected area in 1923, when such reserves in the neotropics were almost unheard of. Since then its flora and fauna have been more intensely studied than those of any other tropical area of comparable size. The island is administered by the **Smithsonian Tropical Research Institute** (STRI, tel. 212-8951, fax 212-8026, www.stri. org), which is based in Panama.

Barro Colorado Island was actually a hill until 1914, when the damming of the Chagres River to create Lago Gatún made that hill an island. The flooding of the lake left only 15 square kilometers of tropical forest on the island, but they contain 480 species of trees (more than in all of Europe), 70 species of bats, 384 species of birds, 30 species of frogs, 47 species of snakes, and on and on. Just accounting for the insects on the island is an overwhelming task. Take ants, for instance: More than 200 species have been identified so far.

Day visitors, as opposed to research scientists, can walk on only some trails, usually an interpretive loop that takes 2–3 hours to traverse at an easy clip. It's fairly flat most of the way, but it does get muddy at times. There's a short side trail off the main loop that's well worth taking. It leads to the aptly named Big Tree, a kapok *(Ceiba pentandra)* so huge other trees are growing on its branches.

Visitors are not allowed on the trails without an authorized guide. But consider buying *A Day on Barro Colorado Island* (Smithsonian), by Marina Wong and Jorge Ventocilla, anyway. It contains a trail guide and information on the island's flora and fauna that will help you get much more out of your visit. It's sold in a few places in Panama, including the little bookshop at STRI's main office in Panama City. The Gamboa Rainforest Resort may have it as well.

BCI has the kind of wildlife many visitors come to the tropics to see, including tapirs, coatimundis, sloths, ocelots, anteaters, collared peccaries, and three species of monkeys. Day visitors expecting a jungle crawling with creatures will likely be disappointed. One may see almost no animal life during a short visit to BCI.

The only mammals one is likely to encounter are agoutis and howler monkeys. It's actually hard not to stumble upon howlers. A 1977 census found 65 troops on the island, each with about 19 monkeys. Their numbers haven't changed much since.

Access to the island is strictly controlled. Visitors must arrange a tour through STRI or an STRI-approved tour operator, and the few spaces get booked up early. Cancellations are not uncommon, however, so last-minute trips are sometimes possible. Some tour operators offer trips to Barro Colorado Nature Monument, which includes the surrounding mainland as well as the island itself. Make sure the tour actually goes to the island if that's important to you.

STRI offers **tours** (tel. 212-8951, fax 212-8026, www.stri.org, Tues., Wed., and Fri. at 7:15 A.M.; Sat. and Sun. at 8 A.M.; US$70 pp, US$40 students). The cost includes the launch from Gamboa to BCI, a 2–3-hour hike with a naturalist guide, a tour of the visitors center, and lunch at the field-research station (vegetarian food is available). It may be possible to chat up a research scientist over lunch. Reservations should be made as far ahead of time as possible.

The launch to the island leaves from a pier in Gamboa, about an hour's drive from Panama City. It's imperative that visitors arrive early, as the launch to the island leaves on the dot

and there's no other way to get there. Visitors are responsible for their own transportation to Gamboa. A taxi from Panama City costs around US$30. The STRI website now has detailed information about the trip and a schematic map explaining how to get to the pier.

Río Chagres

This powerful river supplies most of the water for the Panama Canal and much of the drinking water for Panama City. It once flowed unimpeded across the isthmus, emptying into the Caribbean below the ruins of Fuerte San Lorenzo near the city of Colón. The damming of the river near Gatún Locks created the massive Lago Gatún, and today the river disappears into the lake at Gamboa and doesn't resurface until it approaches the Caribbean. But the upper reaches of the Chagres still wind their way through lovely rainforest. In the dry season, stretches of the river become little more than glorified puddles. In the rainy season, however, the Chagres can rise many meters in a single hour. Flash floods are not unknown.

The Emberá and Wounaan have been relocated from the Darién jungle in recent decades to live in communities along the banks of the river surprisingly close to Panama City. The one most visited by tourists is Parara Puru. While these are true Emberá who cling to some of their traditional ways, visitors should note that the village is rather touristy and the elaborate traditional costumes the people wear are put on for their benefit. Even the concept of a village is not a traditional part of Emberá culture; historically, families lived in relative isolation from each other.

Still, the trip up the river is beautiful and encounters with Emberá and Wounaan people are always interesting. Visits to the community include dance demonstrations, a walk through a botanical garden, and a chance to buy cocobolo figurines, tagua nut carvings, woven baskets, and other handicrafts. Those inclined can have themselves painted with traditional *jagua* (a kind of vegetable dye) designs, but bear in mind the dye takes up to two weeks to fade and can't be washed off. Several tour operators offer trips up the Chagres to Parara Puru. **Aventuras Panama** (tel. 260-0044 or 236-5814, www.aventuraspanama.com) offers an all-day excursion for US$110. The trip includes lunch in the community. River rafting is also possible on the Chagres.

SPORTS AND RECREATION
Canopy Tower

Unless the Canopy Tower (tel. 264-5720, U.S. toll-free tel. 800/930-3397, www.canopytower. com) is packed with guests, it offers day tours to anyone. There's a decent chance of seeing good-size mammals (other than your fellow visitors) and an excellent chance of spotting lots of birds. Possibilities include an early-morning (6:30–11 A.M.) or lunch (12:30–5 P.M.) visit for

COURTESY OF THE CANOPY TOWER

The Canopy Tower is a unique eco-lodge in Parque Nacional Soberanía.

US$95 that includes a two-hour guided walk and wildlife viewing from the tower.

Gamboa Rainforest Resort

You don't have to be a guest at the Gamboa Rainforest Resort (tel. 314-5000, www.gamboaresort.com) to use its **activities center** (8 A.M.–6 P.M. daily) or book its tours, which include bird-watching walks and night safaris on the lake. The resort rents kayaks, bicycles, and other toys. You can also charter fishing boats here, but expect to pay for it.

The **aerial tram** (7:30 A.M., 9:15 A.M., 10:30 A.M., 1:30 P.M., and 3 P.M. Tues.–Sun., US$40 pp) is one of the star attractions of the resort. It's sort of like a ski lift that takes passengers up about 80 meters to a hill, passing through the canopy of a patch of secondary forest along the way. A bilingual naturalist guide travels along in each four- or five-person gondola to spot and describe flora and fauna. Passengers can get off at the top and climb a 30-meter observation tower that offers panoramic views of the canal, the Chagres, and the surrounding forest. The trip takes a little over an hour, not including the stop at the observation platform. Don't get your hopes up about seeing too much wildlife; these canopy trams are a comfortable way to experience tropical forest, but a quick zip through the trees is unlikely to net many encounters with animals. For the best chance of seeing anything, take the first tram of the day, before most birds and jungle critters have slipped away. The rate is excessive for what you get, but if you're lucky enough to glimpse something special, you might feel it's worth it. Contact Gamboa Rainforest Resort for reservations and information.

Before or after a tram ride, it's worth wandering around the resort's **flora and fauna exhibits,** though combining this with the tram ride is an additional US$10 pp. They're housed in a series of structures on the road leading up to the tram and include an orchid nursery, a serpentarium with impressive native and non-native species, a butterfly house, and a small freshwater aquarium that also contains crocodiles, caimans, and turtles. The model Emberá village nearby is rather hokey, but it's a chance to meet a few Emberá and buy their tightly woven baskets and other handicrafts.

Fishing, Boating, and Adventure Tours

There's a small **marina** just outside Gamboa, near the one-lane bridge across the Río Chagres, where boatmen offer fishing tours on their basic *pangas*. Stop by at least a day ahead of time to work out a deal. Anglers need to be on the lake just before dawn; by midmorning the peacock bass stop biting. A morning of fishing costs about US$50. The captains can also take visitors on an exploratory cruise around Lago Gatún and/or the Chagres River. The price depends on distance.

A group called **Panama Canal Fishing** (tel. 315-1905, cell 6678-2653, www.panama-canalfishing.com) offers a higher-end, all-inclusive fishing experience on Lago Gatún. Trips are made on a roomy and comfortable Hurricane Fundeck 201. The cost is US$445 per boat and includes round-trip transfers between Panama City and Gamboa, a fishing guide and captain, picnic lunch and drinks, and all fishing equipment, bait, and lures. Boats can accommodate up to six anglers, at US$25 extra per person after the first two. Prices do not include sales tax.

Panama Canal Fishing is run by Richard Cahill and his wife, Gaby. Rich has worked for years as an accomplished naturalist guide with Ancon Expeditions, and is highly recommended. He's knowledgeable, reliable, enthusiastic, fun, and an all-around good guy. He's fluent in English and Spanish. The company also offers tours of the lake's primate sanctuary and the Panama Canal, usually as an add-on to the fishing trip.

Aventuras Panama (tel. 260-0044 or 236-5814, cell 6679-4404, www.aventuraspanama.com) offers rafting trips on the Río Chagres. The rafting is usually quite gentle, with mostly Class II rapids and a few Class IIIs. It's not intended for those who need big white water. However, this is still a long, fairly rigorous trip, and the Chagres, like any other powerful river, has seen its share of accidents and needs to be approached with respect. Clients are picked up from their hotel at 5 A.M. and driven into the highlands above Cerro Azul. From there, it's a 1.5-hour hike through the forest to the put-in spot. Rafters spend all day on the river, ending up in Lago Alajuela (also called Madden Lake) in the late afternoon. Clients are dropped back at their hotel around 7 P.M. The trip costs US$175 per person and includes breakfast, lunch, and transfers. Clients must be between the ages of 12 and 70. The company offers many other tours, including rafting trips on the Mamoní and Río Grande and a boat ride up the Chagres to visit the Emberá community of Parara Puru.

ACCOMMODATIONS AND FOOD

The few hotels in the Gamboa area are impressive, if expensive, places that are destinations in themselves. The only restaurants open to non-guests are at the Gamboa Rainforest Resort, though the Canopy Tower sometimes offers day passes that include a meal. There are also basic fast-food stands near the entrance to the main Gamboa pier that are open during work hours to feed Panama Canal dredging division workers.

Other lodging is beginning to come to this area. Three B&Bs have opened up in old Zone housing in Gamboa. **The Canopy B&B** (Harding Ave. and Jadwin Ave., tel. 833-5929, U.S. toll-free 800/930-3397, www.canopytower.com, US$88 s, US$132 d, including breakfast), not to be confused with the Canopy Tower, is meant as a more affordable alternative.

Ivan's Beds and Breakfast (111 Jadwin

Ave., tel. 6981-4583, cell 6981-4583, www. gamboaecotours.com, US$45 pp, including breakfast) is aimed at birders and other nature lovers, as it's quite close to Pipeline Road. **Mateo's Gamboa B&B** (131A Calle Humberto Zárate, cell 6690-0664, www.gamboabedandbreakfast.com, US$35 s/d, including breakfast) is run by a retired Panamanian couple.

It's also possible to camp in Parque Nacional Soberanía, but there are no facilities and this is a true tropical forest, with all the potential discomfort that that implies.

Canopy Tower

The Canopy Tower (tel. 264-5720, U.S. toll-free tel. 800/930-3397, www.canopytower.com, high-season Canopy Room packages US$229 pp, including meals and one bird tour, three-day minimum stay) is an old U.S. military radar tower that has been cleverly transformed into an impressive 12-room hotel and wildlife observation platform, high above the floor of the protected Parque Nacional Soberanía. Visitors can look out the window of their room right into the forest.

The rooms are simple but cheerful and comfortable, with teak louvered doors and other touches that soften the utilitarian feel of the structure. Each room has two single beds with ceiling fans and a good hot-water bathroom. Five single rooms have been added on the level below the canopy rooms, about 5.5 meters above the hilltop. Formerly guides' quarters, they are quite small (eight square meters, less than half the size of the canopy rooms), have a single bed, and share a bathroom.

The Blue Cotinga Suite (US$259 s/d in high season) is a large room (34 square meters) that can sleep three and has a private balcony with a hammock swing. This is the fanciest place to stay at the tower. The Harpy Eagle Suite, one floor down, is a bit smaller (27 square meters) and plainer, but the rates are the same for one or two people. It can sleep up to four.

The tower is not air-conditioned so as not to scare away wildlife and separate guests from the sound of the forest. However, the elevation is high enough that, with the screened windows open and the ceiling fan on, it's quite comfortable. The tower is made of metal and sound carries easily, so don't expect to sleep in late.

The rooms, however, are only a small part of a visit to the tower. Stays include all meals and a daily, guided tour into the national park on well-maintained trails. The food here is good, concentrating on simple but tasty local dishes.

One flight up from the canopy rooms are the dining and living room, which offer a near 360-degree view. Guests can continue up to the roof, which is a great place to watch the sun rise and set over the forest, listen to the roar of howler monkeys, and watch for owls and other nocturnal creatures at night.

The chances of spotting birds and wildlife can plummet during a rain, though they come out to dry afterwards. But the migration season, which occurs late in the rainy season, can be an exciting time to visit. This is when literally millions of raptors pass through Panama on their annual migration. Rates at this time (mid-September to mid-December) are higher than "green season" rates but lower than high-season ones.

Guests are likely to see more wildlife while lounging in the tower than they would on long hikes in remoter areas. Within five minutes of my first visit several years ago I saw a tití monkey (Geoffroy's tamarin) and a host of other creatures. By the end of my second visit a few years later, I had seen a kinkajou, a dozen coatimundi moms and babies, a sloth, an unidentified snake, and innumerable birds (short-tailed hawk, three toucans in a single tree, dusky-capped flycatcher, white-whiskered puffbird, white-shouldered tanager, blue-crowned manakin, and on and on). At last count, bird-watchers had identified 283 species of birds just from the tower and Semaphore Hill Road.

The Canopy Tower is 25 kilometers from

Panama City, about a half-hour drive. Those driving must take the left fork off Gaillard Highway after the railroad bridge and follow the road toward Gamboa. The well-marked turnoff to the Canopy Tower will be on the right 1.6 kilometers past Summit Botanical Gardens. There's a gate across the entrance to the tower road that you may have to open. Go up the one-lane, well-maintained road 1.7 kilometers to the tower. The tower is not wheelchair-accessible. Access to the top of the tower is by stairs—five dozen of them.

Make reservations, even for day trips, as far in advance as possible; the tower is world-famous and extremely popular.

Gamboa Rainforest Resort

The resort (tel. 314-5000, U.S. toll-free tel. 877/800-1690, www.gamboaresort.com, starts at US$198 s/d), which opened in 2000, is a peculiar mixture of an ecotourism resort, luxury spa, and theme park. Spread over its 137 hectares are a slice of tropical forest with an aerial tram running through the canopy, a full-service spa, a 107-room hotel, an entire neighborhood of one- and two-bedroom historic apartments converted from old Canal Zone housing, a huge swimming pool, tennis courts, three restaurants, traditionally dressed Emberá selling handicrafts at a pseudo-model village, an orchid nursery, a snake house, an amphibian exhibit, several aquariums, a butterfly house, and a marina.

The location couldn't be better: The resort was built right on the banks of the Chagres, one of Panama's most important rivers, and it is only a stroll away from Lago Gatún, where one can watch ships transiting the Panama Canal. It's bordered by Parque Nacional Soberanía, the major trails of which are just a few kilometers away, as is the Canopy Tower.

There are two basic kinds of accommodations. Those in the main building start at US$231 for a room with a balcony, air-conditioning, minibar, safe, cable TV, iron and ironing board, coffeemaker, and so on. Room quality is on a par with what one would find at a midlevel business hotel in the United States.

The price for the one-bedroom historic apartment is a comparative bargain at US$198 s/d. Whereas the rooms in the hotel are generic, these have character. They consist of renovated wooden buildings dating from the 1930s that actually housed Panama Canal employees and their families in the old Canal Zone days. The decor is simple and cheerful, from the rattan furniture to the historic canal clippings and sketches on the walls. All have sitting rooms and kitchenettes with microwaves, minifridges, and coffeemakers. They don't have a view of the river, but they're surrounded by trees.

All kinds of multiday packages are available that combine stays with golfing, bird-watching, spa treatments, ecotours, and so on. The resort's activities center rents mountain bikes, kayaks, pedal boats, and other gear.

The food at the resort is hit or miss. Of the three restaurants, **Restaurante Los Lagartos** (tel. 276-6812, 11:30 A.M.–5 P.M. daily) is the best option because of its terrific location. It's down the hill from the main hotel, built onto an attractive, open-walled wooden terrace that juts into the Río Chagres near where it empties into Lago Gatún. From their tables diners can sometimes see turtles, caimans, and the odd iguana sunbathing on the same log, peacock bass and tilapia nosing about in the shallows, and little blue herons and jacanas hunting for food among the floating vegetation. Even here the food tends to be mediocre, but the show put on by nature is exceptional.

The spa at the Gamboa Rainforest Resort is also open to nonguests and offers a wide assortment of treatments and packages at U.S. prices, varying from manicures and massages to a full day of pampering. The Gamboa Rainforest Resort is about a 45-minute drive from downtown Panama City.

GETTING THERE AND AROUND

The end of the road in Gamboa is about a 45-minute drive from Panama City. Taxis charge around US$30 one-way. Buses leave from the SACA bus section of the Gran Terminal de Transportes in Albrook. Gamboa-bound buses take passengers within reasonable walking distance of every attraction in the area except the Camino de Cruces. They're not close to each other, though, so it's not feasible to walk from one attraction to the next. Buses to and from Gamboa stop at designated bus stops along Gaillard Highway about every half hour during daylight hours, but this can be a time-consuming way to visit the various spots. Those who can afford it should consider hiring a taxi for a half-day or full-day tour.

Those driving from Panama City should head west on Gaillard Highway. Just past Pedro Miguel the road summits a small hill and then crosses under a narrow underpass, a railroad bridge with "1929" carved into it. The ANAM office that sells hiking and camping permits is at the fork. Going straight leads into Madden Forest, a part of Parque Nacional Soberanía. Here's where you'll find the Camino de Cruces (Las Cruces Trail). A left turn at the fork keeps you on Gaillard Highway and leads to Summit Botanical Gardens, Plantation Road, the Canopy Tower, and Sendero El Charco, in that order. Cross the one-lane bridge (caution—be sure to stop if the red light is on) into the town of Gamboa, where the road ends. An immediate right turn leads up to the Gamboa Rainforest Resort. Staying straight leads to the Isla Barro Colorado launch and Pipeline Road.

Colón and the Costa Abajo

The Colón province lies along the central Caribbean coast of Panama. Its capital is Colón, historically Panama's second-most important city. Though this area starts just 80 kilometers north of Panama City, it has long been neglected and has significantly fewer resources and facilities than the Pacific side of the isthmus. A few tour operators, especially dive operators, specialize in the area, but it is still relatively off the beaten track for most tourists. This is slowly changing, with new hotels, cruise-ship departures, and commercial projects in the works. These plans are serious enough to worry environmentalists, who fear especially for the important mangrove forests along the coastline. There is even talk of building a fanciful Dubai-style offshore city stuffed with high-rises next to Colón.

The coastline west of Colón is known as Costa Abajo ("lower coast"). It is a still a lightly developed area with rough roads and few visitors other than avid bird-watchers. But it offers the well-preserved ruins of a Spanish fort and lush tropical forest surrounding the mouth of the storied Río Chagres. These are all on the west side of the canal, across the swing bridge at Gatún Locks that is the only land link between western and eastern Panama on the Caribbean side of the isthmus.

The area is worth adding as a side trip on the way to or from, say, Portobelo or Isla Grande, or for those taking the Panama Railway across the isthmus. As a destination in itself, it's likely to be most appealing to those with an especially keen interest in the Panama Canal or Panama's piratical past.

The area's few main sights—Gatún Locks, Gatún Dam, and Fuerte San Lorenzo—are all clustered close together in a relatively small area southwest of Colón. So are its natural attractions, the mouth of the Río Chagres and the bird-watching spots around Achiote and Escobal.

THE PANAMA CANAL

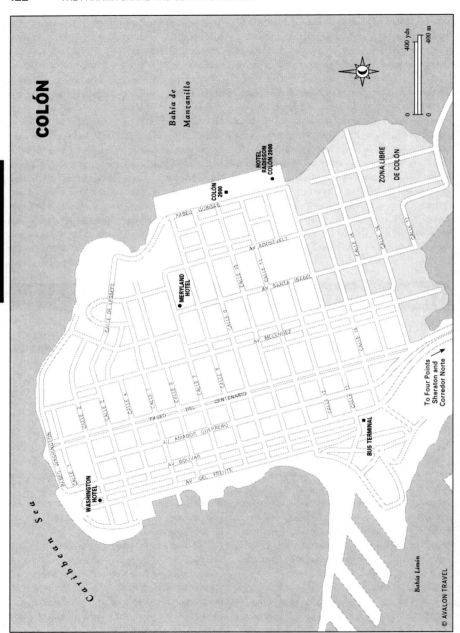

COLÓN

Bahía de Manzanillo

Caribbean Sea

Bahía Limón

HOTEL RADISSON COLON 2000

COLON 2000

PASEO GORGAS

AV. ROOSEVELT

MERYLAND HOTEL

AV. SANTA ISABEL

AV. MELENDEZ

ZONA LIBRE DE COLON

CALLE DE LESSEPS

CALLE 16

CALLE 15

CALLE 13

CALLE 14

CALLE 12

PASEO DEL CENTENARIO

CALLE 11

CALLE 10

CALLE 9

CALLE 8

CALLE 7

CALLE 6

CALLE 5

CALLE 4

CALLE 3

CALLE 2

CALLE 1

PASEO WASHINGTON

AV. AMADOR GUERRERO

AV. BOLIVAR

AV. DEL FRENTE

BUS TERMINAL

WASHINGTON HOTEL

To Four Points Sheraton and Corredor Norte

400 yds

400 m

© AVALON TRAVEL

SAFETY CONSIDERATIONS

Though the city of Colón (pop. 42,133, co-LONE in Spanish and kah-LAWN in English) has a long, colorful history, it should be avoided. It has little to offer tourists, and you can see all the region's sights without ever stopping here. More importantly, extreme unemployment and poverty give this crumbling city a terrible reputation as a place where muggings are common.

There's always talk about revitalizing Colón, but little ever seems to change for its poor residents. For the foreseeable future, sadly, visitors should stay well away from the city.

For those who insist on visiting, do not walk around Colón: Drive or take taxis everywhere. Shopping at the Colón Free Zone and Colón 2000 is reasonably safe.

HISTORY

For most of its history, Colón has been known as a place to avoid. Even the intrepid Columbus decided to steer clear of the area when he and his crew became the first Europeans to see Isla Manzanillo. All they saw was a pestilential swamp filled with mosquitoes, snakes, caimans, and who knows what else.

Throughout the Spanish colonial era, the Colón area was largely ignored. The Spanish built their forts at San Lorenzo to the west and Portobelo and Nombre de Dios to the east.

It wasn't until an American company began work on the Panama Railroad in 1850 that people started living and working on the island and built the foundations of the city of Colón. The railroad had its Caribbean terminus nearby, and a settlement sprang up to house the employees and cater to the 49ers, who were on their way to the California goldfields.

The town did not even merit a name until 1852, when it was dubbed Aspinwall in honor of one of the founders of the railroad. Panama was still a part of Colombia at the time, and officials in Bogotá rejected the name, insisting it be called Colón, the Spanish name for

Columbus. A feud over the name erupted between the Panama Railroad Company and Bogotá, resulting in much confusion until 1890, when the Colombian government began rejecting any letters with "Aspinwall" on the envelope. The railroad company finally gave in.

Colón's fortunes declined following the gold rush, but they revived again in the 1880s when the French began their doomed attempt to build a sea-level canal. Colón residents would later reminisce about this as a time when champagne was in far greater supply than the suspect local water. Then Colón burned to the ground in 1885 during the so-called Prestán Uprising and was rebuilt, primarily by the Panama Railroad Company. It wasn't until the French effort collapsed and the U.S. effort began that Colón began to be cleaned up and transformed into a modern city. The gringos installed sewers and plumbing, paved the streets, drained the swamps, and sanitized the whole place.

For the first half of the 20th century, Colón became a rather picturesque little city of three-story wooden buildings with long verandas, and white, neoclassical concrete buildings erected by the Isthmian Canal Commission. Front Street, which faced the railroad tracks and the port of Cristóbal, boasted elegant shops. As Panama City and the Pacific side of the isthmus grew in importance, Colón again deteriorated.

SIGHTS
Gatún Locks

On the Pacific side of the Panama Canal it takes two sets of locks to raise or lower ships 26 meters. Gatún Locks (visiting hours: 9 A.M.–4 P.M. daily), on the Caribbean side west of Colón, do the job by themselves. Each lock chamber is the same size as those on the Pacific—almost 305 by 34 meters—but there are three pairs of them on this side. That makes Gatún Locks absolutely massive, a little more than 1.5 kilometers from end to end. It's an impressive sight. It will probably still be impressive even when the new

AMINTA MELENDÉZ: COLÓN'S FAVORITE DAUGHTER

One special day in Colón's history is November 5. On that day in 1903, separatists in Colón used a young woman, 18-year-old Aminta Melendéz, to smuggle a message to conspirators in Panama City about a plot to disarm Colombian troops that had landed in Colón to put down Panama's incipient revolution. Melendéz was the daughter of Porfirio Melendéz, Colón's police chief and one of the separatists. To do so, she had to walk right past swarms of heavily armed troops, and capture would likely have meant her execution.

The plot was never acted upon, but Aminta's bravery is still celebrated every November 5 as part of Colón's independence festivities. Throughout her life, it was traditional for the president of Panama to visit her home to pay homage. Oddly, for a country that loves celebrations, this is not a national holiday, something that annoys Colón boosters.

post-Panamax locks are completed just east of these. They're scheduled to begin service in 2015.

As dramatic as the locks are, most visitors based on the Pacific side of the isthmus are satisfied with seeing Miraflores and perhaps Pedro Miguel without making a special trip just to see these.

An observation platform up a long flight of stairs gives an excellent view of the locks, the Caribbean entrance to the canal, and Lago Gatún. There's another observation spot downstairs. It has a small-scale model of the entire canal. Bathrooms for tourists are in the building behind the model.

The number of tourists visiting the locks is increasing, but free bilingual talks, like the ones offered at Miraflores, are still sporadic here. The best bet to catch a talk is when a cruise ship disgorges its passengers for a tour.

Gatún Dam

The huge (nearly 2.5 kilometers long) earthen Gatún Dam was built to create Lago Gatún (Gatún Lake), a vital part of the Panama Canal. It was the largest such structure in the world when the canal opened in 1914. The dam controls the flow of the mighty Río Chagres, a major obstacle to canal builders, and supplies electricity used at the locks and the surrounding communities. It's an awesome sight when the spillway is opened and the water comes roaring out. A small bridge runs right by the spillway, behind which there's a good view of the canal.

To get to the dam, cross over the swing bridge that spans the north end of Gatún Locks. The wait can be up to half an hour if a ship is transiting, but the bridge provides a fascinating fish's-eye view of the locks, since one actually drives through a lock chamber. Take the first left after the bridge and head up the road for about two kilometers.

There is a free car ferry across the channel that runs 5 A.M.–9 P.M. daily. But the wait can be as long as an hour, depending on ship traffic, for the three-minute ride. For safety reasons you're not even allowed out of the car. The ferry is meant primarily for heavy equipment and trucks too big for the swing bridge, which is far more interesting and comparatively speedy.

Fuerte San Lorenzo and Área Protegida San Lorenzo

This is one of Panama's newest protected areas. Its 12,000 hectares include a former U.S. military base (Fort Sherman), the impressive ruins of the Spanish fort of San Lorenzo, and four types of forest, including mangroves and freshwater wetlands. The United States left most of this forest standing, and with the departure of the military, all kinds of wildlife have returned even to formerly populated areas. The big question is what happens next.

Conflicting demands are being made on the area. On the one side are those who want to preserve this vital ecosystem, restricting its use as much as possible to ecotourism and scientific research. This area is a crucial link in the biological corridor that runs the length of Panama, especially since so much of the land to the east and west of it has already been deforested. That also makes it a linchpin in the even more important Mesoamerican Biological Corridor, which runs the entire length of Central America.

It seems likely that those pushing for conservation will be at least partly successful. In the short term, only organized groups are being allowed into most of the protected area. That's probably just as well for now, because visitors really wouldn't want to wander around here by themselves. Besides the usual hazards found in a tropical forest, there is unexploded ordnance in the area. The U.S. military conducted jungle-warfare training and had a firing range here.

The ruins of Fuerte San Lorenzo (full name: Castillo de San Lorenzo el Real de Chagres) are impressive and surprisingly intact. They sit on the edge of a cliff with a commanding view of the Caribbean coast and the mouth of the Río Chagres, which the Spaniards built the fort to protect. The Welsh buccaneer Henry Morgan won a bloody battle here in 1671, destroying the then-wooden fort before crossing the isthmus to sack Panama City. San Lorenzo was rebuilt as a strong stone fort in 1680, but the British admiral Edward Vernon still managed to destroy it in 1740. It was rebuilt yet again in 1768, with more fortifications added in 1779. These are the ruins visible today. The ruins, along with those at Portobelo, were declared a UNESCO World Heritage Site in 1980. Be careful wandering around the fort. There are few guardrails, and it's easy to walk right off a roof or a cliff.

The entrance to the area is 12 kilometers past Gatún Locks in the former U.S. military base of Fort Sherman; stay straight after crossing over the swing bridge at the locks. Fuerte San Lorenzo is another 11 kilometers up a rough but passable road. It's a left turn past the entrance to Fort Sherman. On the way to Fort Sherman, look for a water-filled channel near the road. This is the French Cut, a remnant of the doomed French effort to build a sea-level canal.

Once-popular Shimmy Beach, to the right as one enters Sherman, is covered in trash washed up from Colón—not the best spot for a swim. The turnoff to San Lorenzo is on the left. It's a 20-minute drive on a sometimes-rough road from here. Those without a four-wheel drive can ask about road conditions at the gate.

From this point on the road is surrounded by beautiful rainforest. It's easy to feel transported back in time and imagine conquistadors and pirates hacking their way through this jungle in their relentless pursuit of treasure. Follow the signs to the fort, which is where the road ends. Road conditions get fairly rough toward the end.

SHOPPING
Zona Libre de Colón

The Zona Libre de Colón (Colón Free Zone, most shops 8 A.M.–5 P.M. Mon.–Fri., a few open on Sat.–Sun.) is the world's second-largest free-trade zone, after Hong Kong. A free zone is an area where goods can be imported and exported free from customs duties. Each year about US$10 billion worth of goods move through its 1,000 companies, which employ an estimated 15,000 permanent workers and thousands more temporary ones. It opened in 1948.

This isn't just some sort of oversize shopping mall: It's a shopping city within a city, one far wealthier and better maintained than the real city that surrounds it. It's huge—400 hectares—and is one of the most important contributors to Panama's GNP. Goods come mainly from Hong Kong, Japan, and the United States and go mainly to Central and South America.

The Zona Libre is primarily aimed at international wholesalers, not consumers.

Individuals can shop at some stores there, but getting in and around the place, and getting purchases out, is a hassle. Think twice before going to the trouble: Many goods are just as cheap and far easier to get at airport duty-free stores or even at discount houses back home.

Private cars and taxis are not allowed inside the free zone, which is just as well because the streets inside it are permanently gridlocked with trucks. There are fairly safe parking lots just outside the zone.

Visitors need a permit to enter the Zona Libre. The office is on the right as you face the main gate. Have passports and return flight information handy. Be prepared for a long wait in line.

Good values inside the zone include 10-, 14-, and 18-karat gold, jewelry, cosmetics, liquor, and high-end handbags, scarves, watches, and stereo equipment. Gold jewelry is sold by weight depending on the purity.

One store worth checking out is **Motta International** (tel. 431-6000, www.motta-int. com), not far from the main entrance. Motta carries a little bit of a lot of things, including watches, perfume, liquor, electronics, clothing accessories, and crystal. Sample brand names: Cartier, Lalique, Montblanc, CK, Fendi, Limoges Castel, Baccarat, and Camusso. The atmosphere is pleasant and the service gracious.

Once you've made a purchase, you can't just waltz outside the Zona Libre with it. Remember, this is a free-trade zone and purchases are meant for export only. For those flying out of the country, stores will deliver purchases to the airport for pickup on the day of the flight. Stores tend to charge a minimum of at least US$15 for delivery and need at least two days.

Everyone leaving the zone is subject to search, and anyone caught with *contrabando* can be charged with a crime.

Colón 2000

This cruise port/shopping mall is on the eastern edge of Colón, close to the Free Zone. It opened in 2000 and was supposed to attract fleets of cruise ships to Colón and breathe life into the local economy. This has been slow to happen.

Since 2007, Royal Caribbean Cruise Lines has been making Colón 2000 a home port, with its *Enchantment of the Seas* offering cruises originating from the port. Some other cruise ships stop at the port as well. Besides a handful of duty-free shops and some souvenir-trinket stores, most of which are only open during cruise season, the complex includes an enormous Super 99 grocery store, a Western Union branch, Hertz and Budget car rental offices, an ATM, and a couple of places to eat. During the main cruise season (approximately Oct.–May), folkloric dancers perform for the tourists when a ship is in port. The place is pretty deserted when ships don't show up.

In spoken Spanish this place is called Colón Dos Mil.

SPORTS AND RECREATION
Bird-Watching

The central Caribbean coast is prime bird-watching country. The Audubon Society once identified 350 species on a single day during its annual Christmas Bird Count. Especially popular spots for birding include what is now the **Área Protegida San Lorenzo** and the **Achiote and Escobal Roads,** in Costa Abajo, west of Colón. The roads to Achiote and Escobal start just past Gatún Dam, though they can be tough to drive, particularly in the rainy season. Bird-watchers should go with an experienced guide.

Tours

Nattur Panama (tel. 442-1340, fax 442-8485, www.natturpanama.com) offers a popular tour, the Conquerors' Path, that includes a boat trip down the lower Río Chagres to Fuerte San Lorenzo, a tour of the fort, and a trip to Gatún Locks. The cost is US$85 per person with a four person minimum. It also offers tours of Portobelo, Gatún Locks, and Colón, as well as

The view from the pool at the Washington Hotel is rather unusual: ships at anchor on the other side of the seawall.

fishing and birding trips. The group has a nature lodge in Sabanitas.

ACCOMMODATIONS AND FOOD

Be prepared to be rather isolated, as it is not safe to wander far outside the hotels in and around Colón, and there's nothing much around the safer but more remote spots. It's generally a better idea to make the Pacific side your base and just make day trips around here.

Colón

There are several places to stay in or on the outskirts of Colón. The four listed here are the best and safest. Those staying in Colón should eat at their hotel. Otherwise, a reasonably safe dining option away from downtown Colón is **Café Iguana** (in Colón 2000, tel. 447-3570 and 447-3956, 10 A.M.–10 P.M. Mon.–Sat., US$5–12). In the Colón 2000 cruise port/shopping center, the café is upstairs and on the right as one faces

the complex. It's a simple but pleasant place to eat if the air-conditioner is working, with photos from the Panama Canal construction era on the wall and Middle Eastern music on the stereo. People come here for the Lebanese food, but other options include Mexican food, sandwiches, burgers, fish, meats, and pastas. If nothing on the menu looks appealing, there's also a Subway sandwich shop in the Colón 2000 complex, as well as a few other restaurants and cafés.

The **Meryland Hotel** (corner of Calle 7 and Santa Isabel next to Parque Sucre, tel. 441-7055, 441-5309, or 441-7127, www.hotelmeryland.com, US$44 s, US$55 d, a/c) was built in 2000 in a quiet, sparsely settled part of town. There's a long, narrow park outside and lots of schoolkids passing by on school days. It definitely feels like the safest spot to stay in town. It's a modern, clean place with cheerful neo-Spanish colonial decor, featuring lots of glossy tile and ornate iron fixtures. Amazingly, the paint in the rooms started peeling soon after the hotel opened. All rooms have cable TV and phones. The hotel has parking and an Internet café. There's room service from the restaurant (open until 10 P.M. Sun.–Fri., later on Sat.) on the premises. Rooms are dark and the beds need replacing, but this is still a decent value in an okay neighborhood if you need to spend the night in Colón. Some of the houses near the hotel used to be quarters for Panama Canal employees during the Canal Zone days.

The **Washington Hotel** (2nd St. at the northwest end of Colón, tel. 441-7133, US$61 s/d) is now officially known as the New Washington Hotel, but no one will ever call it that. Built by the United States in 1913 at the order of President William H. Taft, a frequent visitor to Panama during canal construction days, first as Secretary of War and then as president, on the site of a Panama Railroad Company guesthouse erected in 1870, it was once one of Panama's grand hotels. It has hosted two American presidents (Taft and Warren Harding), a British prime minister (David Lloyd George), Will Rogers, Bob Hope, Al Jolson, and others. Those glory days are long gone. The Spanish-inspired colonial building and common areas are still lovely, if tattered, with brass railings, wrought ironwork, chandeliers, painted wooden beams, and marble stairs. And the hotel is built right on the edge of the sea, with a view of ships at anchor waiting to transit the canal. But the new rooms are still drab and musty, with spongy beds. They're large, however, and come with a minifridge. Amenities include a bar, casino, nightclub, and a large pool right next to the seawall; sea spray sometimes splashes close to the pool. It's definitely worth a quick visit for those in the neighborhood, but most would probably prefer staying in the less historic but more comfortable surroundings of the Meryland Hotel, which has comparable rates.

The six-story, 103-room **Hotel Radisson**

Colón 2000 (Colón 2000, www.radisson.com, tel. 447-1135, US$152.90 s/d) is the most upscale place to stay in downtown Colón and the most convenient for those with a cruise to catch. It has good security and is in Colón 2000, which is kind of the city's Green Zone. The rooms are pleasant enough, if a bit musty, and there's a restaurant, bar, and small gym and pool, but the whole place gives off a kind of sluggish, sullen Caribbean vibe. Two rooms on the 2nd floor are available, for an extra fee, with a stark balcony that looks out over the pool, but I advise avoiding these: the pool fills up with partiers blasting music, making these potentially the loudest rooms in the hotel. Try for a room that faces away from the pool and the waterfront if peace and quiet are important to you.

The newish **◖ Four Points by Sheraton Colón** (Avenida A. Waked, Millennium Plaza, on the outskirts of Colón, tel. 447-1000, www. starwoodhotels.com, starts at US$137.50) is the fanciest place to stay on the Caribbean side of the canal area. It's a 15-story tower in a gated shopping complex, just off the main road leading into downtown Colón. It's in an industrial area right next to the Free Zone and close to nothing else, but it's certainly the most secure location you could hope for. The 230 rooms are spacious, attractive, and comfortable, with floor-to-ceiling windows, but not much to look out on (though some of us find it interesting to get a bird's-eye view on the city-within-a-city that is the Colón Free Zone). Service is friendly and attentive. Some of the rooms have a distant view of Limón Bay and the entrance to the canal. There's a restaurant, bar, and a small pool that's right next to the polluted Río Manzanillo. Good deals can be had here, depending on when you visit. It's a significantly nicer hotel than the Radisson, and when there's a deal available, it might even be cheaper.

Outside Colón

◖ Sierra Llorona Panama Lodge (tel.

442-8104, cell 6614-8191, www.sierrallorona. com, starts at US$55 s/d, including breakfast and a hike with local guide) is a lodge south of Colón that's popular with bird-watchers: Approximately 200 species of resident and migratory birds have been spotted in the surrounding forest. Hikes led by a local guide are available in the surrounding area, which includes the lodge's own private reserve. These are included with stays. Day-trippers can visit the lodge for a hike, lunch, and use of the facilities for US$20 for one or two people.

Sierra Llorona means "crying mountain," an apt name for a place that sees rain 286 days a year. Expect predawn rains even in the so-called dry season here. The plus side of all that precipitation is evident in the lushness of the 200 hectares of private primary and secondary rainforest surrounding the lodge. There are four kilometers of well-maintained trails that start about a 10-minute walk from the lodge. Scientists frequent the area to study its flora and fauna, some of which is not found elsewhere. A new species of frog, *Atelopus limosus,* was discovered here in 1995. This is its only known habitat.

The lodge is really a sprawling private house with a separate building a short walk down the hill. There are seven rooms of various sizes; none is anything fancy, but they're clean, cheerful, and comfortable. They do not have air-conditioning, TV, or telephones. The lodge sits on a ridge 300 meters above sea level. Even this modest elevation is enough to give the place pleasant breezes in the morning and evening and views of the Caribbean, Limón Bay, and, at night, the lights of Colón.

Sierra Llorona is near the small community of Santa Rita Arriba (not to be confused with nearby Santa Rita). If you're coming from Panama City, it's reached by a right turn off the Transístmica a couple of kilometers before Sabanitas.

The **Hotel Meliá Panama Canal** (Avenida de Las Naciones Unidas, tel. 470-1100 or 470-1916, www.solmelia.com, US$126.50 s/d), a Spanish-owned 258-room resort, has a striking location on the forested banks of Lago Gatún near the Área Protegida San Lorenzo in Espinar (formerly Fort Gulick), close to Colón and Gatún Locks. But it's not yet an area that attracts many tourists, and the base itself is still largely a ghost town.

The hotel was built from the remains of the U.S. military's notorious School of the Americas, which had a reputation for training Latin American dictators and torturers. Its parentage notwithstanding, it's quite an attractive hotel, with bright and cheerful Spanish-Mediterranean decor that tosses in a splash of Italian rococo. Rooms are large, with Spanish tile floors, cable TV, tasteful decoration, lots of dark wood, a minibar, and incredibly hard beds. Guests have also complained of wafer-thin walls, indifferent or rude service, and musty, poorly maintained rooms. Amenities include an impressive swimming pool, pleasant restaurant, piano bar, casino, business center, and so on. Its restaurant is wildly inconsistent.

The hotel offers tours to Gatún Locks, motorboat and kayak rentals on Lago Gatún, fishing trips, and other activities. Package deals, especially on the weekend and during the rainy season, are often available.

The hotel is not far from Gatún Locks. To get here from Panama City, turn left before the Cuatro Altos overpass outside Colón. Stay straight on this road, which snakes to the right, then back left, for about 1.5 kilometers. Take the second left onto Avenida de Las Naciones Unidas. Look for the Sol Meliá sign.

INFORMATION AND SERVICES

The Colón 2000 cruise port/shopping center has a few facilities of interest to tourists. The **Super 99** supermarket has a Citibank outlet and ATM, a cafeteria, and a pharmacy (10 A.M.–6 P.M. Mon.–Fri., 11 A.M.–3 P.M. Sat.). The store also carries everything from phone cards and cheap mobile phones to camping supplies.

The complex also has a **Western Union office**

(tel. 441-7308, 9 A.M.–5 P.M. Mon.–Sat.). The **Colombian consulate** (tel. 441-6170 or 441-0114) is in an upstairs office nearby. **Budget** (tel. 441-7161) and **Hertz** (tel. 441-3272) rental car offices are open approximately 8 A.M.–5 P.M. Monday–Saturday. Duty-free shops (cruise passengers only) and souvenir shops may only be open during cruise-ship season.

There is a marina, **Shelter Bay** (tel. 433-3581, www.shelterbaymarina.com), at Fort Sherman, just west of the canal entrance. It has a simple restaurant/bar serving burgers and such with nothing more than US$10. There's a small pool/whirlpool tub, table tennis, and free wireless Internet access, but there's little reason for anyone other than yachters to go all the way out there.

GETTING THERE AND AROUND

A quick and easy trip coast to coast is literally a 500-year-old dream. The dream has finally been realized with the completion of the Corredor Norte from Panama City to Sabanitas, not far from Colón. Depending on Panama City and Colón traffic off the highway, the trip should take no more than 1.5 hours, probably less. Expect it to take nearly twice that long via the old Transístmica. It's not worth it just to avoid the minimal toll.

Most visitors explore the area with a taxi guide or a tour operator. Look for tours that include at least a one-way train trip.

By Bus

The **Terminal de Buses de Colón** (on Avenida Bolívar, Colón's major shopping drag, and Calle 13) is a busy place and should be relatively safe, at least during the day, but be alert for pickpockets and backpack thieves. Any bus marked Costa Abajo can take you to Gatún Locks and the attractions west of them, including the bird-watching areas around Achiote (fare: US$1). For La Guaira and Nombre de Dios, look for buses that say Costa Arriba,

though be sure to confirm the bus is really going all the way to your destination. Below are details on a few of the more popular routes.

La Guaira: 9:30 A.M., 11:30 A.M., 1:30 P.M., 3:30 P.M., 4:30 P.M., and 5:30 P.M. The fare is US$2.85. Return buses leave La Guaira every hour or two 5:30 A.M.–1 P.M. The Sunday schedule is different, with buses running at 9:30 A.M., 12:30 P.M., and 3:30 P.M., returning at 10 A.M., 11 A.M., noon, 1 P.M., 2 P.M., and 4 P.M. This schedule changes a lot, so use these times only as general guidelines.

Nombre de Dios: 6 A.M., 9 A.M., 10 A.M., 11 A.M., noon, 1 P.M., 3 P.M., 4 P.M., and 5:45 P.M. Monday–Saturday; 9 A.M., 11 A.M., 1 P.M., 3 P.M., and 5:45 P.M. Sunday. The fare is US$2.75. Return buses run once an hour 4 A.M.–3 P.M.

Panama City: Buses leave every 20 minutes or so 4:30 A.M.–10 P.M. The fare is US$1.80, or US$2.50 for the express bus. Try to get the express, which takes about 1.5 hours. The slower buses can take up to twice as long to cover the same ground when traffic is bad.

Portobelo: 16 buses daily 6:15 A.M.–9 P.M. The fare is US$1.30. Return buses run about every half hour 4:30 A.M.–6 P.M.

By Taxi

A taxi anywhere within Colón should cost about US$1. Take taxis everywhere. To visit area tourist attractions, consider hiring a taxi by the hour. Watch out for fake taxis: Real taxis are yellow, and their license plate numbers match those painted on their doors.

Now that more cruise ships stop at Colón 2000, the taxis have organized into cooperatives and have established standard fares for tours, which they carry around as a laminated sheet. It's easy to find a taxi at Colón 2000 during cruise-ship season, though it may be difficult at other times. Fares are excessive, but there's some semblance of order and all rates are negotiable; you can make a deal for less if there are more taxis than passengers around.

Taxi cooperative fares are US$3 for trips within Colón or to the Free Zone; Gatún Locks tour for US$80, or US$160 for Gatún Locks and Portobelo (1–4 people), US$180 for a tour of the Pacific-side attractions, including Miraflores Locks, Casco Viejo, and Old Panama (1–3 people); and transfers to Tocumen International Airport (US$100 for one person, US$120 for two).

By Car

To get to Colón and Costa Abajo from Panama City, take the **Corredor Norte** toll highway to the end of the line. Cars have to finish the journey north on the old **Transístmica** (also known as the Transisthmian Highway or the Boyd-Roosevelt Highway).

At the Cuatro Altos (literally, four stops) intersection, turn west (left) to get to Gatún Locks, Gatún Dam, and the Costa Abajo attractions. Stay straight for Colón. Roads aren't well marked, and highway construction, especially the new overpass at Cuatro Altos, has jumbled things up considerably.

Portobelo and the Costa Arriba

The stretch of coast east of Colón is known as Costa Arriba, which includes Portobelo, Nombre de Dios and its neighboring villages, and La Guaira, the jumping-off point for Isla Grande. For most of the way this is a lovely drive: It's quite striking to zip along the lush, quiet coastline and suddenly come upon the ruins of ancient Spanish forts.

Though the Spanish ruins scattered all over this seaside town hint at its long history, it still may be hard to believe that Portobelo (pop. 3,867) was one of the most important ports in the Spanish Empire. Today it's sleepy and impoverished, the decaying houses of its current residents built near or in some cases into the crumbling stone ruins. It truly comes alive only on October 21, for the celebration of the Festival del Cristo Negro (the Black Christ Festival).

The town's poverty can be a bit intimidating, but visitors shouldn't have any problems if they come here during the day and stay alert. Portobelo is one of the wettest spots on the isthmus.

A large swath of this area is part of Parque Nacional Portobelo, whose boundaries extend into the surrounding waters. The park is under increasing development pressure, however, as are the natural treasures that are not even nominally protected. Settlers are rapidly cutting down much of the lush forest in this area, and cookie-cutter suburban housing is going up along the beautiful coastline.

SIGHTS
◖ Portobelo Ruins

During the Spanish colonial era, the Costa Arriba became one of the most strategically important areas in the entire Spanish Empire. It was here that most of the incredible treasure of the Incas was brought after being shipped up from South America. All that wealth made the Caribbean coast a target of pirates and buccaneers for hundreds of years. The Spanish fortresses were constantly under siege and were captured several times.

Entering Portobelo from the west, the first Spanish structure you'll encounter is **Castillo Santiago de la Gloria,** on the left side of the road. It's the last incarnation of a fort that was built, destroyed, rebuilt, and tinkered with for more than 150 years and never ended up defending the town particularly well. These ruins date from 1753.

In the town itself is **Castillo San Gerónimo,** which dates from the same period. The nearby customs house, the **Real Aduana de Portobelo,** was restored in February 1998 by the Spanish government. The little museum inside the

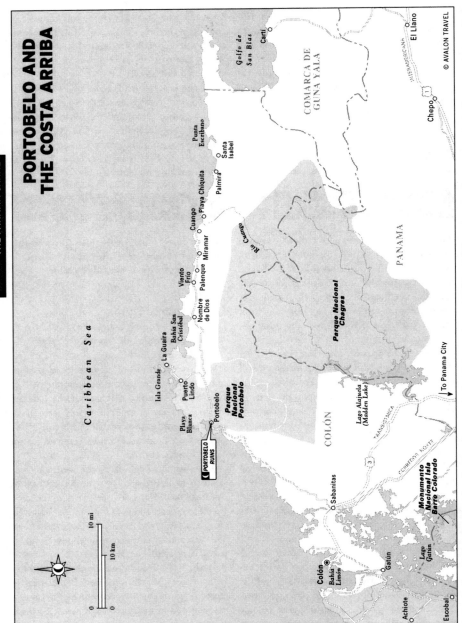

PORTOBELO AND THE COSTA ARRIBA

Caribbean Sea

Golfo de San Blas

Cartí

COMARCA DE GUNA YALA

INTERAMERICANA

El Llano

© AVALON TRAVEL

Chepo

Punta Escribano

Santa Isabel

Palmira

Playa Chiquita

Cuango

Miramar

Río Cuango

Viento Frío

Palenque

Nombre de Dios

PANAMA

Bahía San Cristóbal

Parque Nacional Chagres

Isla Grande

La Guaira

Puerto Lindo

To Panama City

Playa Blanca

Portobelo

Parque Nacional Portobelo

Lago Alajuela (Madden Lake)

TRANSISTMICA

◄ PORTOBELO RUINS

COLÓN

3

CORREDOR NORTE

Sabanitas

Monumento Nacional Isla Barro Colorado

Colón

Bahía Limón

Gatún

Lago Gatún

Achiote

Escobal

10 mi

10 km

0
0

building has recently been spiffed up with a few modern displays and a film on the history of the area. There's a small model of Portobelo's fortifications just outside the entrance. On the other side of the model is a second room where one can see a bit of the original foundation, but exhibits consist mainly of a few old tools, cannonballs, and mortars. There are also replicas of pre-Columbian tools and weapons mixed in with a few pieces of real pottery shards.

Admission to the **museum** (8 A.M.–4 P.M. Mon.–Fri., 8:30 A.M.–3 P.M. Sat.–Sun.) and to the neighboring Museo del Cristo Negro de Portobelo is US$1 for adults, US$0.25 for children. The price includes a guided tour of the displays, though the guides speak only Spanish.

Church and Museum of the Black Christ

The large white church nearby is the **Iglesia de San Felipe,** which is still in use. It dates from 1814, but its tower wasn't completed until 1945. It's famous as the home of the life-size effigy of the Nazarene of Portobelo, better known as the Black Christ. The effigy, depicting Christ carrying the cross, normally resides on a podium to the left of the altar, but it is brought out to the center of the church for the Black Christ Festival (Festival del Cristo Negro), by far Portobelo's biggest event. The handsome altar of the church is adorned with gold images depicting various emblems of the crucifixion, including nails, instruments of torture, and the dice the Roman soldiers cast for Christ's robe. Small wooden carvings ringing the walls depict the stages of the cross.

Behind this church is the recently renovated **Iglesia de San Juan de Dios,** home to the new **Museo del Cristo Negro de Portobelo,** which displays several of the robes donated by Panamanians for the festival, some of which are more than 100 years old. It's well worth a visit. Among the more famous robes is the one donated by the champion boxer Roberto "Manos de Piedra" (literally, hands of stone) Durán.

© WILLIAM FRIAR

THE PANAMA CANAL

Portobelo was one of the Spanish Empire's most important ports.

The Black Christ figurine's robes are changed twice a year, and each is used just once. The statue is adorned with a red wine–colored robe for the Black Christ Festival held each October 21. This is changed to a purple one for Holy Week. Many of the robes are donated anonymously. Some are simple and others are quite ornate, done up in gold trim and the like, and cost thousands of dollars to make.

If this museum is locked, walk over to the museum at the *aduana* and ask the attendant to open it for you.

Other Forts

If exploring these ruins and buildings doesn't satisfy your historical urges, hire a water taxi near Castillo Santiago de la Gloria for US$2 per person to take you across the bay to visit what's left of **Castillo San Fernando,** which was designed in the 1750s to replace Castillo San Felipe, demolished in 1739 by Edward

THE BLACK CHRIST FESTIVAL

© KAREN FRIAR

the Black Christ

Every October 21, Portobelo comes back to life at the Festival del Cristo Negro (Festival of the Black Christ). It's quite a spectacle. Thousands throng the Church of San Felipe, home to the life-size wooden effigy of the Nazarene of Portobelo, otherwise known as the Black Christ. Some come by foot from distant parts of Panama. Others come crawling on their hands and knees, their friends sweeping the ground in front of them free of debris or rocking a small shrine before their faces to keep the pilgrims' eyes on the prize. Still others let their companions pour candle wax on them as they crawl, as a further act of penance.

What's this all about? There are several legends of the origin of the statue and its festival. One has it that the statue arrived in Portobelo on a ship bound for Cartagena, Colombia. A storm arose each time the ship tried to continue on, and the crew members decided the effigy wanted to stay in Portobelo. Variations on the story have the ship either sinking in the storm and the statue washing up on shore or the crew members throwing the statue overboard in fright. Then, the story goes, on October 21, 1821, Portobelo residents prayed to the Black Christ to be spared from a cholera epidemic sweeping the isthmus; they were.

Each October 21 since, people from all over Panama who have prayed to the Black Christ for help with an illness or other problem give thanks by making a pilgrimage to Portobelo, often performing some act of devotion or penance along the way. Most find just walking here from Sabanitas in the heat and humidity to be

sacrifice enough. That's a walk of nearly 40 kilometers; health stations are set up along the way for those who need them. There are no portable toilets anywhere, so you can imagine what Portobelo is like by the end of the night.

Devotees often wear purple robes in emulation of the Christ statue. Those who have asked for a major favor make the pilgrimage for several years. Each year they cut a bit of cloth off the hem of their robes. Some of the robes end up awfully short, presenting the interesting paradox that the most pious also have the most scandalous attire.

The festival is a blend of the sacred and profane in other ways as well. For many, it's an excuse to get very drunk and dance all night. It's not unusual to see a pilgrim in resplendent purple robes making his way to town carrying a beer. The whole vibe is sort of spring-break-with-self-flagellation.

Once in Portobelo, pilgrims crowd into the church to worship before the Black Christ. Many offer necklaces, which are draped around the effigy. Mass is held, and devotees burn hundreds of votive candles and sing songs about the festival and the effigy. Late at night the statue is carried out of the church and paraded through the streets on a litter. The procession takes a long time, as the statue is carried with a peculiar rocking, back-and-forth gait: three steps forward, two steps back.

Those in Panama on October 21 should make an effort to attend the festival. It's a fascinating spectacle. But be forewarned it's also a major mob scene. Be prepared for epic traffic jams and stay alert for pickpockets. Traffic is generally stopped several kilometers outside of Portobelo, forcing even non-pilgrims to walk in. It's best to drive or come with a tour operator. Trying to get a return bus is a nightmare; many pilgrims go back home right after they arrive, so the line for the bus is hours long even in the morning. One strategy is to hire a boat near Portobelo and motor into town, skirting the traffic. Suggest this to your tour guide ahead of time, or call a hotel, restaurant, or dive operator to arrange it.

Pilgrims walk to the Black Christ Festival from all over Panama.

Vernon, a British admiral. Unfortunately, American builders used rock from the fort in the construction of the canal, further damaging what little that time, war, and pirates had spared. Also, a short, steep hike above town leads to some fortifications with a good view of the bay; if you're heading east, it'll be on the hill to the right just before town. Drivers can park by the side of the road.

SPORTS AND RECREATION

Portobelo has long been a popular spot for scuba divers and yachters. There are also appealing spots for beach lounging. It's possible to hike in the forests of Parque Nacional Portobelo, but this should be attempted only with an experienced guide.

In 1996, John Collins, the creator of the original Ironman triathlon in Hawaii, visited the Portobelo area on a yacht and decided it would be a perfect place for a triathlon. The

first **Portobelo Triathlon** (www.triathlon.org.pa) was held in 1997, and it has become an annual event. It is slated for March or April and increasingly attracts world-class athletes. The event includes a 1,800-meter swim from La Guaira to Isla Grande and back, a 35-kilometer bike ride to Portobelo, and a 10-kilometer off-road run in the Portobelo area.

Playa Blanca

Playa Blanca is a pretty little beach, by far the nicest in the area, situated on a remote cove at the tip of a forested peninsula 20 minutes by boat from Portobelo. There are no roads leading to it, and it is accessible only by sea, which gives it the feel of an island. Day-trippers can hire a water taxi to the beach from the ruins of Castillo Santiago de la Gloria in Portobelo for about US$30 per couple.

Diving and Snorkeling

There are 16 dive spots around the Portobelo area, with attractions that vary from coral reefs and 40-meter-deep walls to a small airplane and a cargo ship. The best diving in the area is off the rocky Farallones Islands, a fair boat ride away. There's a chance of seeing nurse sharks, spotted eagle rays, and schools of barracudas there. But any honest dive operator will be the first to admit the diving around Portobelo is for the most part just average: Expect no more than 10 meters of visibility on a typical day. And visibility is quite volatile: up to 30 meters on a great day, and down to 3 when it rains (several rivers empty into the ocean here; the diving is better in the dry season). As always when you dive, bring evidence of certification and ask to see the dive master's credentials.

Scubaportobelo (tel. 448-2147 in Portobelo or 261-4064 and 261-3841 at the main office in Panama City, www.scubapanama.com) is five kilometers west of Portobelo. The spot is pleasant, with a wooden mirador built on rocks over the ocean. This is the Portobelo division of Scubapanama, Panama's largest dive operation. Divers pay for everything separately here. Complete equipment rental is US$20, including one full tank. The second tank costs US$6, and additional tanks US$4.50. Boat transport is about US$7–20, depending on the destination. Dive tours that include transportation from Panama City are also available.

Other Activities

Selvaventuras (tel. 442-1042, cell 6680-7309) is a shoestring operation started in 2001 by four eager guys from Colón. They no longer have an office, but they still offer excursions. These include jungle hikes to waterfalls, overnight camping in the forest, horseback riding, fishing trips, and boat transport to nearby beaches. Prices vary depending on the destination and length of trip. For instance, a tour of the closest forts (which you can really do yourself) costs US$2 per person; a half-day hike is around US$20 per person. The guides speak a little English.

There's a **zipline ride** west of Portobelo in an area called Río Piedra. It's operated by a group called **Panama Outdoor Adventures** (cell 6605-8171, http://panamaoutdooradventures.com), west of Portobelo. It consists of nine cables strung between platforms that are up to 30 meters above the forest floor. The tour lasts about 2.5 hours, including a forest walk. On the way to Portobelo, the group has signs posted shortly after the turnoff to María Chiquita and before Río Piedra. Panama Outdoor Adventures offers other excursions, such as river tubing for US$25 and nature walks for US$10.

ACCOMMODATIONS

El Otro Lado (tel. 202-0111, info@elotrolado.com.pa, www.elotrolado.com.pa, US$539 s/d, including breakfast and round-trip boat transportation from Portobelo) translates to "the other side," which in this case refers to the fact that the property is across Drake's Bay from the

Portobelo ruins and accessible only by boat. It's only a five-minute boat ride, but this is enough to give this place a sense of seclusion. El Otro Lado describes itself as a "private retreat," and it consists of only four houses, one with two bedrooms and the others with one, each decorated differently. There's an infinity pool and a large gazebo that houses the restaurant, bar, and common areas. The whole place looks like it has an appealing retro-modern Caribbean vibe. The staff can take guests to a nearby beach and arrange tours. Food and service are good here.

Sunset Cabins are part of Scubaportobelo (tel. 448-2147, http://panamaportobelocabins.com, starts at US$52.80 s/d), which is the local branch of Scubapanama. The cabins are meant primarily for divers, but during the frequent slow periods landlubbers can get a room here too. The rooms are basic, small, with low ceilings and crammed with beds. But they have air-conditioning. Up to four people can be squeezed into each room, but you'd better really like each other. There's a basic restaurant on the premises.

Coco Plum Eco-Lodge (tel. 448-2102 or 448-2309, US$45 s, US$55 d) offers more attractive accommodations. It's just before Restaurante La Torre on the way to Portobelo. It's a cheerful place, with conch shells ringing the door frames of the rooms and murals of fish painted on the walls inside. Rooms are clean and pleasant, though a bit dark. There are a dozen rooms, most with air-conditioning. This place used to be quite friendly, but lately there have been some complaints of unfriendly service.

FOOD

Seafood is the attraction around here, particularly dishes done in a Caribbean style (usually spicier than Pacific-side food, often with coconut milk). Simple but cute, moderately priced places are dotted along the coast on the way to Portobelo.

◀ **Restaurante Los Cañones** (about six kilometers before Portobelo, tel. 448-2980,

11 A.M.–10 P.M. Mon.–Fri., 8 A.M.–10 P.M. Sat.–Sun.) is a charming little open-air place on a small bay. Looking out at the Caribbean, it's easy to imagine Sir Francis Drake's ships gliding past on the way to a sneak attack. Seafood is the specialty at this popular place. The food is good. Try the *pulpo en leche de coco* (octopus in coconut milk).

A little farther down the road is **Restaurante Las Anclas** (tel. 448-2102, 10 A.M.–8 P.M. daily), at the Coco Plum Eco-Lodge. It's a cute place entirely decorated with detritus recovered from the sea, including sewing machines, the wheel of a boat, wheelbarrow parts, gas containers, and so on. Seafood is again the specialty here. The chef is Colombian, so be sure to order the enormous, Colombian-style *patacones* (fried green plantains).

Restaurante La Torre (tel. 448-2039, 10 A.M.–7 P.M. Mon.–Fri., 7:30 A.M.–7 P.M. Sat.–Sun.) is a little open-air restaurant just beyond Restaurante Las Anclas. It's easy to spot because of the stone tower that gives the place its name. Again, seafood is its main thing. The service is friendly and courteous. There's an illustrated capsule history of Portobelo, in Spanish and English, along one of the wooden walls.

INFORMATION AND SERVICES

Just as you enter Portobelo there's a large, unmarked wooden building, one of the biggest structures in town, at a fork in the road. This is yet another CEFATI building (tel. 448-2200, 8:30 A.M.–4:30 P.M. Mon.–Fri.), a tourist center run by ATP, Panama's government tourism institute. It's usually rather barren, but the last time I was there it had a few devil masks used in the *congos* dances and entries in a competition to design a new bus stop.

The last gas station on this entire stretch of road is at María Chiquita, roughly halfway between Sabanitas and Portobelo.

GETTING THERE
By Bus
Portobelo is about 100 kilometers from Panama City. Those coming by Colón-bound bus from Panama City will have to change buses in Sabanitas. Do not go all the way to Colón, and make sure ahead of time that the bus stops in Sabanitas, which is on the Transístmica 60 kilometers from Panama City. Passengers are let off near the El Rey supermarket. Buses between Sabanitas and Portobelo run only during daylight hours. The fare is US$1.25.

The main bus stop in Portobelo is next to the Iglesia de San Felipe. Colón-bound buses leave Portobelo every half hour 4:30 A.M.–6 P.M. To get from Portobelo to Panama City, take a bus to Sabanitas (Colón-bound buses stop there). Get off at Sabanitas, cross the highway, and take any of the frequent long-distance buses running from Colón back to Panama City.

By Car
Take the Sabanitas exit off the Corredor Norte. The turnoff to Portobelo is at Sabanitas, on the right side of the Transístmica just past the El Rey supermarket as you head north, in the direction of Colón. Stay on this road to Portobelo, about 35 kilometers away.

GETTING AROUND
Portobelo is a small town and easily walkable, though be alert and try not to wander around alone.

A **water taxi** (tel. 448-2266; ask for Carlos) is on the edge of the bay next to Castillo Santiago de la Gloria, the first fort as you enter Portobelo from the west. It's next to the Restaurante Santiago de la Gloria. A trip across the bay to the ruins of Castillo San Fernando is US$2 per person. Prices to area beaches range from US$10 per couple to nearby Playa Huerta up to US$30 per couple for a trip to Playa Blanca. Prices are likely negotiable if business is slow.

NOMBRE DE DIOS AND VICINITY
Eight tiny towns—villages really—run along the coast east of Isla Grande. Five of these are linked by a road, which is in remarkably good condition.

All look pretty dismal and deserted, especially during the day, when their inhabitants are out working in the fields or fishing in the ocean.

The first five—**Nombre de Dios, Viento Frío, Palenque, Miramar,** and **Cuango**—are lined up one after another on a lonesome, 30-kilometer stretch of road that runs along the edge of the sea. The last three—**Playa Chiquita, Palmira,** and **Santa Isabel**—are even more isolated, separated from the others by the Río Cuango. This river is known for gold, and it still attracts wishful-thinking prospectors. The road ends at the river, and those final three towns are accessible only by boat. Santa Isabel is the last town before the Comarca de Guna Yala (the San Blas Islands). All these towns are so sleepy they're practically comatose.

There isn't much reason for tourists to come to this part of Panama, at least these days. The beaches aren't that great, the area is in the middle of the boonies, and the lovely tropical forest covering its rolling hills is being hacked and burned as quickly as possible to make way for cattle farms.

Historically, this is the home of so-called Afro-Colonials, the descendants of escaped African slaves from the Spanish era. These escaped slaves, known as *cimarrones,* slipped away and established hidden towns called *palenques.* They would emerge from the forest from time to time to raid Spanish mule trains along the Camino Real, more to harass their former captors than for treasure that was useless to them. It's fun to think that the anglers chatting with you about the tides may very well be descended from *cimarrones* who helped Drake in one of his famous exploits.

In modern times, Costa Arriba has attracted settlers from Los Santos province. They are famous or notorious, depending on your perspective, for their prowess at cutting down trees. Having mostly deforested their own province, they're diligently working on doing the same to this area, which borders a vitally important national park.

Sights

The first, largest, and most famous of the little towns is **Nombre de Dios** (pop. 1,053), about 25 kilometers east of Portobelo. It was the original Caribbean terminus for the Camino Real, the overland route used by the conquistadors to transport plunder from the destruction of the Incan Empire. The first European to lay eyes on the area was Rodrigo de Bastidas during his voyage of discovery of the isthmus of Panama in 1501. Columbus rode out a terrible storm here in 1502. Legend has it that Nombre de Dios (name of God) got its name when the unlucky Spanish explorer Diego de Nicuesa ordered his beleaguered and starving crew to take refuge in the harbor, shouting, "Let us stop here, in the name of God!"

Nombre de Dios was a poor, shallow harbor and proved nearly impossible to defend. Sir Francis Drake attacked it in 1572, though a wound forced him to retreat. He returned in 1595 and sacked it. The Spanish abandoned Nombre de Dios and moved the Caribbean end of the Camino Real to the far better and more defensible harbor of Portobelo in 1597. Nombre de Dios quickly faded away.

Today it is a poor, out-of-the-way, oceanside settlement of squat cinderblock buildings connected by dirt roads, as are the other towns along this road. There's nothing to recall its rich past except a modern-era sign that reminds you this humble place is one of the oldest surviving towns in the Americas. The left fork leads to the old part of town, inhabited mainly by anglers. The right fork leads to the new side, which is where most of the settlers from Los Santos province live. There's an artificial water channel that runs right through the middle of town; the builders of the Panama Canal scooped up sand from Nombre de Dios to build Gatún Locks after the Gunas turned them away from beaches in the San Blas Islands.

Festivals and Events

These sleepy towns live for festivals, especially Carnaval and their *fiestas patronales,* the saint's day corresponding to the anniversary of the town's founding. These dates are the best bet to catch the colorful, African-derived dances known as *congos*. Some *fiestas patronales* and other local celebrations in the region include April 27 (Nombre de Dios), June 8 (Santa Isabel), June 19 (Playa Chiquita), June 24 (Palmira), July 31 (Viento Frío), September 8 (Palenque), and September 24 (Río Indio). It's not worth making a trip all the way out here just for one of the celebrations, but those who plan to visit anyway should bear those dates in mind.

On October 12, Viento Frío celebrates a big **Día de la Raza festival,** the Latin American version of Columbus Day. In recent years, of course, attitudes toward that day have become ambivalent throughout the Americas, with some seeing it as a more appropriate time for mourning than celebration. It could be fascinating to attend such an unusual Columbus Day commemoration in an area Columbus actually visited.

Water Activities

Water sports are the main attraction. If you go for a swim, beware of the undertow and rip currents. There is also some scuba diving in the waters off the coast. Wrecks of Spanish ships are still being found out here, including a 500-year-old one discovered in 1998 just off Nombre de Dios that some believe is the *Vizcaina,* one of the four ships used by Columbus on his fourth and final voyage to the Americas. It's well documented that the *Vizcaina* was in fact abandoned in these waters, but studying this wreck and establishing its identity has been a slow process mired in controversy and red tape. However, the ship appears to date from the early 16th century, which makes it exceptionally rare whoever its captain was. Shipwrecks are off-limits to divers, and scavenging around them is a serious crime.

It's possible to hire local boatmen in these towns for trips to Guna Yala, but it's not recommended. The trip takes a minimum of 1–2

hours in small, open boats on a sea that can quickly turn rough. Bear in mind that some of the greatest navigators in history have lost ships in these waters.

Skilled, safety-conscious captains with well-maintained boats are in short supply in this area, and it may very well be risky to make the trip. At the very least, go with a captain who has life jackets, or bring your own.

Practicalities

There are few services of any kind in this remote, neglected part of the country. Most visitors arrange tours from Portobelo or Panama City. There's a pay telephone in each town, but that's about it. There are no banks or ATMs. The best chance of finding official help if one encounters trouble is in Palenque, the administrative headquarters of the district.

There are a few basic places to stay in this area, and as usual camping on the beach is free. This area doesn't get many foreigners, though, so people may wonder what you're up to. It's probably a good idea to let the police and townspeople know you come in peace.

As always, camp only in a tent. *Chitras* (sand flies) are likely to be the least of your troubles. This is cattle country, which means vampire bats, and it's poor and neglected, which means a risk of disease-carrying mosquitoes.

There is a small, open-air seaside restaurant in Miramar that offers heaps of fried seafood and other simple fare for a couple of dollars.

Getting There

To get to this area by car, first drive through Portobelo, making sure you have a full fuel tank. After about eight kilometers there'll be a crossroads known, logically enough, as El Cruce. Turn right here.

After about 13 kilometers there's a rickety suspension bridge. Grit your teeth and drive over it. The first sizable settlement is Nombre de Dios (15 kilometers from El Cruce, about

25 minutes). The paved road ends a little past Nombre de Dios, turning into a rocky dirt road that's passable in a regular car most of the way. The road continues through Viento Frío (8 kilometers past Nombre de Dios), and then through nearby Palenque, Miramar, and Cuango, which are bunched together within a few kilometers of each other toward the end of the road. The road gets rough beyond Miramar, requiring a four-wheel drive in the rainy season, before coming to a sudden end at the especially run-down Cuango, on the edge of the wide mouth of the Río Cuango.

A small gas station just east of Miramar is the only one in the entire region east of María Chiquita.

Getting to these remote areas by bus can be a hassle, as service is neither frequent nor speedy. Those coming from Panama City can take a Colón-bound bus to Sabanitas and get off at the El Rey supermarket. Look for buses with Costa Arriba or the name of the particular destination painted on the windshield. Buses also run between Nombre de Dios and the Colón bus terminal. It's also possible to hire a taxi in Sabanitas or Colón, but the fare will probably be rather steep, depending on the destination.

Isla Grande

This is the closest of the Caribbean islands to the mainland. It's mainly a place for locals who want a quick dose of natural Caribbean beauty and tranquility and don't mind that the hotels and restaurants are generally mediocre at best and the place a noisy party scene at times. Those planning to go to Bocas del Toro or the San Blas Islands can easily give Isla Grande a miss; those archipelagos have much more to offer. It's also quite a humid place; be prepared for some serious afternoon napping.

Isla Grande is not really all that grand—it's about five kilometers long and 1.5 kilometers wide and has around 1,000 inhabitants, most of whom live in the small town that runs along a single waterfront path facing the mainland. It consists mainly of a handful of simple hotels, some run-down houses, and a few tiny stores and open-air restaurants. The island is only a few hundred meters from the mainland.

Though Isla Grande has a couple of small beaches, this is not the place for vast expanses of sand. What the island mostly offers is the chance to laze about and enjoy some beautiful views of the forested mainland, clear blue ocean, and palm-covered nearby islands.

Isla Grande tends to be dead during the week, especially in the rainy season. At these times, there are few dining options, and some of the hotels may be closed. Those who visit during a dry-season weekend, however, will likely find plenty of people having a rowdy good time and blasting music late into the night. Bear that in mind when considering a hotel in town.

SIGHTS

The best, and most popular, stretch of beach on the island is in front of the Hotel Isla Grande. A better and less crowded beach is on Isla Mamey, a tiny, uninhabited private island with relatively calm, shallow waters. It's possible to snorkel or scuba dive here. This is a popular destination for boat tours. These tours usually include a trip near the mainland through a channel lined with beautiful mangroves. This channel has come to be known locally as the Tunnel of Love.

West of Isla Cabra is **Bahía Linton,** one of the safest anchorages between Colón and Cartagena, Colombia. (There's another anchorage at **José del Mar,** better known as José Pobre. It's in a cove next to the isolated village of Cacique, between Portobelo and Isla Grande.)

PRIVATE ISLANDS

On the boat ride over from the mainland to Isla Grande, there's a developed island that's largely deforested except for palm trees. This is **Isla Cabra,** a private island. It is not open to visitors, but those with binoculars should keep their eyes open for macaw nests.

At the entrance to **Bahía Linton** is **Isla Linton,** another private island one should not set foot on. However, boat tours of the waters near Isla Linton are popular because of the monkeys that have been introduced here, which can be summoned by clapping. Be careful: Tourists often feed the monkeys (something you should *not* do), which has made them bold around people. A monkey bit a woman in 2002.

The owners of Isla Linton, Allan and Rosalind Baitel, are conservationists working in conjunction with Florida State University to create a research facility on the island.

The Baitels also run an animal rescue and rehabilitation program behind their home on the mainland (again, this is not open to the public). Here they try to heal animals wounded by hunters or otherwise injured or interfered with, after which they return them to the forest. In some cases, all they can do is give the animals a safe home, as is the case with a couple of jaguars that some people kept as pets before the couple rescued them. These jaguars would no longer be able to survive in the wild. Unfortunately, Panama has no program for breeding jaguars in captivity, so the Baitels have been trying to find a way to export the big cats to a country that does have such a program. Ironically, the international CITES treaty, created to protect endangered species, prohibits the export of animals that were not actually bred in captivity, which has proved to be a major obstacle.

ACCOMMODATIONS AND FOOD

For such a small place, there's quite a range of places to stay, though no great bargains. Only the lucky or the easy-to-please will think they're getting their money's worth, at any budget. In the hoteliers' defense, it's not cheap to offer big-city amenities in such a remote area. And the cheaper places tend to cater not to foreign couples on a budget but rather to Panamanian weekend partiers who shoehorn as many people as possible into a room.

Most of the cheap hotels are clustered close together along the main strip overlooking the water. On dry season weekends, good luck getting a quiet night's sleep if you stay in any of these. Sister Moon is farther along still, on an isolated bluff accessible by a rocky path. Bananas Village Resort is clear on the other side of the island, secluded from everything.

At mealtimes, count yourself lucky just to find a place that's open, especially during a rainy-season weekday. The hotels are the best bet for food. Several of the ones along the main drag have simple, open-air restaurants right on the water's edge. What they may lack in quality they somewhat make up for in rustic island ambience.

◖ **Hotel Sister Moon** (cell 6948-1990 or 6789-4336, www.hotelsistermoon.com, US$25 pp in dorms, US$69 s/d) sits by itself on the hills of a palm-covered point overlooking a picture-postcard bay, rolling surf, and the emerald green mainland. The main accommodations consist of a series of thatched-roof cabins on stilts, dotted along the hillside. Each has a double bed. The cabins are rustic but pleasant. It's like staying in a tree house, and the breeze here is a welcome respite from the island's humidity. The bathrooms are cold water only, and the cabins are not air-conditioned and do not have screens on the windows. Dorm rooms with bunk beds go for US$25 a bed, including breakfast. Day guests can use the pool and other facilities for US$20 a day, including two drinks.

A small, rocky beach with a good surf break is close by. A sundeck juts out right over the surf break, and next to it is a little restaurant and a pub with a billiard table and dartboard. There's also a small, murky swimming pool that's more scenic than inviting. An odd thing about this place is that it seems to live a perpetual twilight existence. There's something perpetually unfinished about it. That can be great for those seeking seclusion, but those who make reservations far in advance should confirm before arrival that everything's up and running.

Bananas Village Resort (Panama City reservations tel. 263-9510, resort tel. 448-2252 or 448-2959, www.bananasresort.com, rates start at US$152.90 s/d, including breakfast) is the fanciest place on Isla Grande. It's on the north side of the island, tucked away in a lovely, isolated spot facing the ocean. It's accessible only by boat or forest trails. A variety of different, confusing packages are available. Rates go up on the weekends. Rates for day visitors are available.

The place, which opened in 1998, is nicely designed, cheerful, and small. The rooms are in eight A-frame cottages on stilts. Each cottage has three units: two large rooms below and one very large room above. They're the same price, but the upstairs ones are nicer. All have balconies, hammocks, and air-conditioners. There's a swimming pool, and guests have free access to sea kayaks, snorkeling equipment, beach chairs, and so on. Boat excursions to the surrounding area are extra. Though the resort is attractive, the service is bad, and the place is not well-maintained. Guests can't count on hot water, for example.

The open-air restaurant is the most expensive on the island, with entrées that reach the double figures. The food is okay, but tends to be deep-fried with heavy sauces.

INFORMATION AND SERVICES

There is no tourist office on the island. The island also lacks banks, ATMs, or much in the way of services at all. Bring cash. Tours and recreational activities are generally arranged through the hotels.

GETTING THERE AND AROUND

Access to Isla Grande is from the down-at-the-heels village of La Guaira, 120 kilometers from Panama City. La Guaira is 20 kilometers from Portobelo. Those with their own car just drive through town and continue along the same road. The trip from Panama City takes about two hours.

The road is often riddled with potholes. At the entrance to La Guaira look for a sign that reads Isla Grande. Take the left turn indicated. Park by the dock for free, or in the partially fenced-in area on the left, behind Doña Eme's kiosk, for US$3 a day. Obviously, don't leave anything valuable in the car. When you come back, one or more teenagers may hit you up for change for watching the car. It's up to you whether to give one of them anything, but they can be unpleasant if you don't.

Those coming by bus from Panama City should take a Colón-bound bus and make sure it stops in Sabanitas. Get off at the El Rey supermarket in Sabanitas, which is right on the highway, and switch to a bus bound for La Guaira. These don't come often, and the schedule changes frequently. Get an early start, as buses between Sabanitas and La Guaira run more often in the morning. Even then, be prepared to wait a long time, cough up the money for a cab, or ditch the whole idea and visit Portobelo instead.

Any of the boatmen hanging around the dock at La Guaira will take you to the island (don't expect life jackets). The ride takes about five minutes. The fee is US$3.50 per person (depending on fuel prices) to be dropped off in what passes for downtown Isla Grande. Expect to pay more at night, which you should avoid since few boats in these waters have lights. Boatmen may ask for more if they think you're a clueless gringo. Settle on a price ahead of time, and clarify whether the rate is per person or per group.

Nearly every place on Isla Grande is easily

© DANIEL HO/ISTOCKPHOTO.COM

Isla Grande

accessible by foot. Those who want to visit Sister Moon or Bananas and don't feel like hoofing it can hire a boatman down by the town waterfront for a couple of dollars. Your hotel can probably arrange for a boat back to the mainland at the end of your trip, but if not, it should be easy to find one along the waterfront.

www.moon.com

DESTINATIONS | ACTIVITIES | BLOGS | MAPS | BOOKS

MOON.COM is ready to help plan your next trip! Filled with fresh trip ideas and strategies, author interviews, informative travel blogs, a detailed map library, and descriptions of all the Moon guidebooks, Moon.com is all you need to get out and explore the world—or even places in your own backyard. While at Moon.com, sign up for our monthly e-newsletter for updates on new releases, travel tips, and expert advice from our on-the-go Moon authors. As always, when you travel with Moon, expect an experience that is uncommon and truly unique.

KEEP UP WITH MOON ON FACEBOOK AND TWITTER
JOIN THE MOON PHOTO GROUP ON FLICKR

MAP SYMBOLS

▒▒▒	Expressway	【	Highlight	✗	Airfield	⚲	Golf Course
▒▒▒	Primary Road	○	City/Town	✈	Airport	🄿	Parking Area
▒▒▒	Secondary Road	◉	State Capital	▲	Mountain	⬭	Archaeological Site
▒▒▒	Unpaved Road	✸	National Capital	✛	Unique Natural Feature	⛪	Church
-------	Trail	★	Point of Interest			
··········	Ferry	•	Accommodation	🗻	Waterfall	⛽	Gas Station
- - - -	Railroad	▼	Restaurant/Bar				Glacier
▒▒▒	Pedestrian Walkway	■	Other Location	♠	Park		Mangrove
▒▒▒	Stairs	⋀	Campground	🄑	Trailhead		Reef
				⛷	Skiing Area		Swamp

CONVERSION TABLES

°C = (°F – 32) / 1.8
°F = (°C x 1.8) + 32
1 inch = 2.54 centimeters (cm)
1 foot = 0.304 meters (m)
1 yard = 0.914 meters
1 mile = 1.6093 kilometers (km)
1 km = 0.6214 miles
1 fathom = 1.8288 m
1 chain = 20.1168 m
1 furlong = 201.168 m
1 acre = 0.4047 hectares
1 sq km = 100 hectares
1 sq mile = 2.59 square km
1 ounce = 28.35 grams
1 pound = 0.4536 kilograms
1 short ton = 0.90718 metric ton
1 short ton = 2,000 pounds
1 long ton = 1.016 metric tons
1 long ton = 2,240 pounds
1 metric ton = 1,000 kilograms
1 quart = 0.94635 liters
1 US gallon = 3.7854 liters
1 Imperial gallon = 4.5459 liters
1 nautical mile = 1.852 km

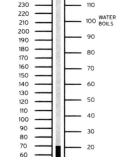

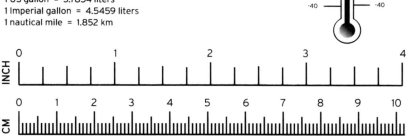

MOON SPOTLIGHT PANAMA CITY & THE PANAMA CANAL

Avalon Travel
a member of the Perseus Books Group
1700 Fourth Street
Berkeley, CA 94710, USA
www.moon.com

Editor: Leah Gordon
Series Manager: Kathryn Ettinger
Copy Editor: Ashley Benning
Graphics Coordinator: Tabitha Lahr
Production Coordinator: Tabitha Lahr
Cover Designer: Kathryn Osgood
Map Editor: Mike Morgenfeld
Cartographer: Chris Henrick

ISBN: 978-1-61238-298-2

Front cover photo: Red Door, French Quarter, Panama City © Adeliepenguin / dreamstime.com

Title page photo: colorful bus in Panama City © Morten Elm/www.123rf.com

ABOUT THE AUTHOR

William Friar

William Friar grew up near the banks of the Panama Canal. Though an American citizen, he has lived much of his life overseas. Besides Panama, he has called Denmark, India, and the United Kingdom home, and he spends as much time as possible traveling.

Bill has written several books on Panama including *Moon Panama*, *Adventures in Nature: Panama*, and a photo-essay book, *Portrait of the Panama Canal*. He has also written about the UK, San Francisco, and various bits of South America.

Bill began his writing career as a stringer for the metro desk of *The New York Times*, where he found that covering stabbings, shootings, blizzards, and hockey parades was surprisingly good training for travel writing. He has also worked as a rock music critic, technology journalist, human biology instructor, writing coach, fundraiser, and reporter for three daily newspapers in the San Francisco Bay Area. Bill's work has appeared in the *Los Angeles Times*, *Miami Herald*, *Arizona Republic*, *Neuen Zürcher Zeitung*, *San Jose Mercury News*, *Orange County Register*, and *Houston Chronicle*, among other publications.

Bill holds undergraduate and graduate degrees from Stanford University and a master's degree in journalism from Columbia University. He is now head of development at the London School of Hygiene and Tropical Medicine, an international research institution at the University of London. He lives in London with his wife, Karen. Contact Bill and get updated information through his website, www.panamaguidebooks.com, or follow him on Twitter @PanamaGuide.

CPSIA information can be obtained at www.ICGtesting.com
Printed in the USA
LVOW10s0500190416

484107LV00008B/17/P